OLIVER MTUKUDZI

AFRICAN EXPRESSIVE CULTURES

Patrick McNaughton, editor

Associate editors

Catherine M. Cole
Barbara G. Hoffman
Eileen Julien
Kassim Koné
D. A. Masolo
Elisha Renne
Zoë Strother

OLIVER MTUKUDZI

Living Tuku Music in Zimbabwe

JENNIFER W. KYKER

INDIANA UNIVERSITY PRESS   *Bloomington and Indianapolis*

This book is a publication of

INDIANA UNIVERSITY PRESS
Office of Scholarly Publishing
Herman B Wells Library 350
1320 East 10th Street
Bloomington, Indiana 47405 USA

iupress.indiana.edu

The paper used in this publication meets the minimum
requirements of the American National Standard for
Information Sciences—Permanence of Paper for Printed
Library Materials, ANSI Z39.48-1992.

Manufactured in the United States of America

Library of Congress Cataloging-in-Publication Data

Names: Kyker, Jennifer, 1979- author.
Title: Oliver Mtukudzi : living Tuku music in Zimbabwe / Jennifer W. Kyker.
Other titles: African expressive cultures.
Description: Bloomington ; Indianapolis : Indiana University Press, 2016. |
  ?2016 | Series: African expressive cultures | Includes bibliographical
  references and index.
Identifiers: LCCN 2016013096 (print) | LCCN 2016014578 (ebook) | ISBN
  9780253022233 (cloth : alkaline paper) | ISBN 9780253022318 (paperback :
  alkaline paper) | ISBN 9780253022387 (ebook)
Subjects: LCSH: Mtukudzi, Oliver. | Musicians—Zimbabwe—Biography. | Popular
  music—Zimbabwe—History and criticism.
Classification: LCC ML420.M72 K95 2016 (print) | LCC ML420.M72 (ebook) | DDC
  781.63092—dc23
LC record available at http://lccn.loc.gov/2016013096

1 2 3 4 5 21 20 19 18 17 16

We are caught up in an inescapable network of mutuality. . . . Strangely enough I can never be what I ought to be until you are what you ought to be, and you can never be what you ought to be until I am what I ought to be. This is the way the world is made.

Martin Luther King

Pasina rudo, hapana hunhu – Without love, there is no *hunhu*.

Sekuru Musanyange

CONTENTS

ACKNOWLEDGMENTS

This book began to take shape on a warm April day in 2004 as Oliver Mtukudzi and I talked on a fire escape at Mount Holyoke College, where I had studied as an undergraduate and had now returned to see Mtukudzi and the Black Spirits perform. By no coincidence, this genesis points toward the people to whom I owe the deepest gratitude in enabling this project to take shape. The first is Mtukudzi himself, who was unfailingly enthusiastic and supportive from our initial discussion at Mount Holyoke to the final stages of manuscript preparation. Mtukudzi generously accommodated me backstage at shows, on the band's bus from one gig to another, and at the Pakare Paye Arts Centre in Norton, Zimbabwe. His willingness to engage in discussions about the complex and sometimes controversial elements of Tuku music—both musical and social—is yet another example of his commitment to singing hunhu. The second person present that day at Mount Holyoke was my undergraduate advisor Holly Hanson, who was responsible for inviting Mtukudzi to perform. An inspiring scholar, teacher, and mentor, Holly may not have expected when supervising my undergraduate thesis that some fifteen years later, I would still be seeking out her incredibly sound advice.

In Zimbabwe, Oliver Mtukudzi's wife Daisy, his late son Samson, and his daughter Selmor were especially warm, welcoming, and helpful. Debbie Metcalfe was also immensely supportive, offering me a place to stay in Harare, patiently sitting through hours of conversation about Tuku music, and granting me access to her personal archives. I owe especially deep thanks to my mbira teachers Musekiwa Chingodza, Sekuru Tute Wincil Chigamba, Patience Chaitezvi Munjeri, and Sekuru Cosmas Magaya. Hilda and Winfilda Magaya and their daughters, Lillian Gomera and Daphine Sikalela, also housed me during the first few months of my research stay. Many other Zimbabwean musicians, artists, and scholars have likewise contributed to this project, both directly and indirectly. Foremost among them is my incredibly talented dance teacher Daniel Inasiyo, who has shared his love of Zimbabwe ngoma not only with me, but also with generations of young Zimbabweans both at Chembira Primary School, and through his work with the nonprofit organization Tariro (www.tariro.org).

Among the many other Zimbabweans who have contributed to this book are Tendai Muparutsa of Williams College; Sheasby Matiure of the University of Zimbabwe; renowned poet and musician Chirikure Chirikure; mbira players Chaka Chawasarira, Wiriranai Chigon'a, Irene Chigamba, Ambuya Judith "Nyati" Juma, Ambuya Rhoda "Tembo" Dzomba, and Benita Tarupiwa; dancers Julia Chigamba and Rujeko Dumbutshena; Marie-Laure Soukaina Edom and Blessed Rukweza of the Dance Trust of Zimbabwe; Rebecca "Mai Mano" Zeigler Mano, Gladys Tutisani and Dorothy Garwe at the United States Embassy; Maylene Chenjerai, Mathias Julius, Gilbert Douglas, and Anna Morris of Tumbuka Dance Company; Doreen Sibanda at the National Gallery of Zimbabwe; Christopher Timbe, Rumbidzai Chipendo, and Clayton Ndlovu of the Zimbabwe College of Music; Isabelle Nkawu, Taurai Moyo, Lillian Mabika, and Reuben Pembedza of Hloseni Arts; John Mambira, Mpho Mambira, and Trymore Jombo of Bongo Love; actress Chipo Chikara; mbira player Chartwell Dutiro; and Ed Banda, Tendai Ngirandi, and Farai Moyo of Capoeira Folha Seca. My fieldwork with these and many other individuals in Zimbabwe was made possible by a Fulbright-Hays Fellowship.

A number of Zimbabweans in Rochester, New York, have enthusiastically answered Shona language questions, sung "Chemutengure," and shared wonderful Zimbabwean meals with me; foremost among them are Lloyd Munjanja, Tonde Mufudzi, Gillian Nyereyegona, and Simbarashe Kamuriwo. Also in the United States, Esau Mavindidze participated in many hours of conversation about the lyrics to Mtukudzi's songs, while Emmanuel Sigauke graciously allowed me to include his poem "Hurry! Tuku in Concert." At Afropop Worldwide, Banning Eyre generously granted me permission to use several of his unpublished interviews with Oliver Mtukudzi. Thanks to Debby Chen, Mary Cairns, Mike Wesson, and Esa Salminen for permission to reproduce their wonderful photographs, and to Rob Cowling at Sheer Sound/Gallo Record Company for his work on securing permission to reproduce Mtukudzi's lyrics. Thanks also to Mai Shumba, for everything.

Among the many supportive colleagues I am privileged to work with at the Eastman School of Music and the College of Arts, Science, and Engineering at the University of Rochester, Ellen Koskoff has been a particularly wonderful mentor, colleague, and friend. At the University of Pennsylvania, I owe great thanks to Carol Muller for her support throughout the years; to Timothy Rommen for reading over early drafts of key chapters in the book; to Tsitsi Jaji for being a model of what is possible; and to Steven Feierman. At Wesleyan University, Eric Charry was instrumental in helping bring this project to completion; Mark Slobin, Su Zheng, and the many participants at the 2011 Summer Institute in Ethnomusicology, sponsored by the National Endowment for the Humanities and the Society for Ethnomusicology, also read and commented on early chapter drafts. Thanks also to Paul Berliner, Darien Lamen, Peter Hoesing, Tony Perman, Thomas Turino, and David Coplan for commenting on drafts at various stages of completion. Finally, thanks to editor Dee Mortensen for her sound advice, her patience, and her unfailing faith in this book.

Lyrics reproduced by kind permission of Tuku Music, which holds the copyright. All songs were composed by Oliver Mtukudzi and published by Tuku Music (Sheer Publishing), except for "Ngoromera," "Dzoka Uyamwe," "Wasakara," and "Todii," which were composed by Oliver Mtukudzi and Stephen Leslie Dyer and published by Tuku Music (Sheer Publishing) and Ikwezi Music. Images are used courtesy of Tuku Music, Sheer Sound/Gallo Record Company (www.tuku musik.com).

OLIVER MTUKUDZI

"Ngoromera"
(A fighting charm)

Ngoromera ingoromera	Fighting medicine is nothing but a charm
Harina zvarinoshanda, haringabatsire	It doesn't work, it cannot help
Ngoromera ingoromera ona	Fighting medicine is nothing but a charm
Harina zvarinoshanda, haringabatsire	It doesn't work, it cannot help
Ingoromera, ingoromera wani	It is only a charm, only a charm
Harina zvarinoshanda, haringabatsire	It doesn't work, it cannot help
Zuva nezuva haritonge matare ngoromera	Day after day, it cannot solve disputes
Harina zvarinoshanda, haringabatsire	It doesn't work, it cannot help
Zuva nezuva hachitonge matare chibhakera	The closed fist never resolves disputes
Hachina zvachinoshanda, hachingabatsire	It doesn't work, it cannot help
Zuva nezuva haritonge matare gonan'ombe	Day upon day, a horn cannot solve disputes
Harina zvarinoshanda, haringabatsire	It doesn't work, it cannot help
Hatidi hondo	We don't want war
Hondo hatiidi	War, we do not want it
Hatidi mhirizhonga	We don't want chaos
Ngatiwirirane, tiwirirane	Let's get along, come to an agreement
Hatidi hondo	We don't want fighting
Mhirizhonga hatiidi	Senseless violence, we don't want it
Hatidi mhirizhonga	We don't want senseless violence
Zuva nezuva haritonge matare ngoromera	Day after day, it cannot solve disputes
Harina zvarinoshanda, haringabatsire	It doesn't work, it cannot help
Zuva nezuva hachitonge matare chibhakera	The closed fist never resolves disputes
Hachina zvachinoshanda, hachingabatsire	It doesn't work, it cannot help
Zuva nezuva haritonge matare gonan'ombe	Day upon day, a horn cannot solve disputes
Harina zvarinoshanda, haringabatsire	It doesn't work, it cannot help
Kuwirirana kuwirirana ona	Agreeing with each other, getting along
Hatidi hondo	We don't want war
Hondo hatiidi	War, we do not want it
Hatidi mhirizhonga	We don't want senseless violence

Introduction
The Art of Determination

In 2008, Zimbabweans confronted a political crisis unprecedented since the days of the nation's liberation war in the 1970s. On March 29, voters around the country went to the polls, casting their ballots in synchronized presidential and parliamentary votes widely referred to as "harmonized" elections. Any impression of electoral harmony could not have been further off the mark, however, for the entire electoral process was marred by violence between the nation's long-time ruling party, the Zimbabwe African National Union–Patriotic Front, or ZANU-PF, and the recently formed Movement for Democratic Change, or MDC. Widespread reports of intimidation and torture emerged as ZANU-PF and the MDC jockeyed for position during the campaign season, with each party claiming to be victimized by the other. The situation became even more serious when the Zimbabwean Electoral Commission refused to release the results of the presidential race for several weeks after the vote. Finally breaking its silence, the electoral body declared a draw, scheduling a runoff election for late June. After this announcement, Zimbabweans witnessed an escalation in political violence, followed by the MDC's withdrawal from the electoral process, multiple attempts at international mediation, and the ultimate formation of a troubled Government of National Unity.

In this uncertain political climate, Harare residents were granted a brief reprieve in the form of the 2008 Harare International Festival of the Arts, which began less than a month after the harmonized elections. Since its inception in 1999, this annual festival, commonly known as HIFA, has offered Zimbabweans a collective experience of personal and social renewal. By far the biggest event of the year on Harare's social calendar, HIFA brings together music, dance, theater, and the visual arts; in 2008, its offerings ranged from a Japanese floral exhibition organized by the Zimbabwe Ikebana Society to a night featuring the London Festival Opera performing under the stars in the lush foliage of the Harare Gardens. Embodying a distinctively cosmopolitan Zimbabwean identity, the festival also featured Norwegian acrobatic group Cirkus KhaOom, Italian string quartet Trio Broz, multiracial South African pop group Freshly Ground, Harare's award-winning *mbira dzavadzimu* ensemble Mbira DzeNharira, and a poetry café organized by local author Chirikure Chirikure.

On the last night of the festival, Oliver Mtukudzi and the Black Spirits played a sold-out show for thousands of fans. One of Zimbabwe's most beloved popular singers, Mtukudzi's resonant voice cleaved the night, alternating between passages of bell-like clarity and gravelly lines tinged with a hint of mourning. To the far left of the stage, percussionist Kenny Neshamba pulled a flurry of angular, staccato notes out of his congas, while bassist Never Mpofu delivered the type of sparse, yet powerful lines so characteristic of the Black Spirits' sound. Standing next to Mtukudzi, Charles Chipanga's mallets flew across the wooden keys of a marimba, reflecting the Black Spirits' recent integration of the warm acoustics of neotraditional music. Behind them, Onai Mutizwa traced interlocking lines on the metal keys the *nyunga nyunga mbira*, yet another neotraditional instrument.[1] To the rear of the stage, kit drummer Sam Mataure anchored the band with his unshakable presence, bringing the distinctive triplet patterns of indigenous Zimbabwean music together with inflections from Koffi Olomide's Congolese rhumba, Cuban salsa, Kunle Ayo's Nigerian fusion jazz, and American R&B.

Flanking Mtukudzi onstage, two special guests heightened the intensity of the Black Spirits' performance. On one side was Zimbabwean guitar legend Louis Mhlanga, now a South African resident, who enlivened the show with his irrepressible, improvisatory guitar lines and technical perfection. On the other side was jazz saxophonist Steve Dyer, a South African who first met Mtukudzi while living in self-imposed exile in Harare during apartheid. In addition to collaborating extensively with Mtukudzi, Dyer had proved influential in mentoring Mtukudzi's youngest child, Samson, who began studying saxophone in secondary school. Onstage together at HIFA, father, son, and musical mentor unleashed a torrent of notes, with the pealing lines of two saxophones punctuated by the gentle sound of Mtukudzi's nylon-stringed acoustic guitar.

Performing in the Aftermath of Elections

Yet the atmosphere in the Harare Gardens hung heavy with an undercurrent of subdued malaise, as if resisting the Black Spirits' buoyantly animated sound. In the tense and uncertain postelection atmosphere, festivalgoers at HIFA encountered signs of increasing militarization. With aging president Robert Mugabe still at the helm, ZANU-PF orchestrated daily displays of power, with fighter jets making regular passes over Harare and riot police patrolling the streets. Within the walled grounds of HIFA's sculpture garden, ordinary citizens mingled with international journalists illegally covering the elections, uniformed officers of the Zimbabwe Republic Police, and undercover agents from the government's Central Intelligence Organization, their presence palpable yet invisible among the large crowds. Embodying a particularly postcolonial sensibility, these ambi-

On the 2008 HIFA Motto, "The Art of Determination"

You wouldn't restrict people in terms of their interpretation of the theme. People would interpret it at varied levels, actually. It could be the physical, and then the spiritual, then the psychological dimension. We take repression—freedom of expression, for example—then you take proper political freedom as well. Then you realize a lot of debate goes on in Zimbabwe as regards censorship—self-censorship and formal state censorship.

Then there's also the mere idea of determination in a society where the basics are a big challenge. I mean, you don't have water, you don't have power, it's hard to get food, but you still have to make ends meet as an artist. And you are torn in between queuing for food and sitting down and scribbling your song. So that determination to be able to operate under those difficult circumstances was a challenge as well. In a lot of ways I think we were also celebrating the local artist's ability to survive—like every other Zimbabwean—under extremely difficult circumstances.

— *Chirikure Chirikure*

guities and disjunctures were reflected in the festival's 2008 motto, "The Art of Determination," which clearly encouraged multiple readings in the context of an electoral process literally intended to determine national governance.

In the aftermath of the harmonized elections, HIFA offered participants a rare opportunity to voice popular dissent, collectively articulating political sentiments that might ordinarily be deemed far too risky. With a sold-out audience of several thousand people, for example, the festival's opening-night performance, called "Dreamland," offered particularly blunt commentary on the political turmoil engulfing the nation.[2] As one person later reflected, "It wasn't even abstract—it was politics, point blank." Taking song as its central metaphor, the performance depicted a dreamscape ruled by a dictatorial king, clad in a white suit jacket decorated with military medals, and clutching a vermillion cello. Seeking to acquire all the music of his realm, the king methodically went about bewitching his subjects and stealing their songs. Aided by military henchmen sporting safari helmets and drab olive fatigues, whose loping gait transformed them into spectral, hyena-like figures, he forcibly wrested their notes away in mid-verse, leaving them silently mouthing stolen melodies. In a symbolic

The 2008 HIFA program cover. *Courtesy HIFA.*

invocation of recent political violence, his brutish agents then beat these dispossessed vassals into submission, stuffing their songs into burlap sacks. In a deliberate reference to ZANU-PF's politically motivated—and economically disastrous—efforts at land reform, they also bribed the king's subjects with cardboard
cutouts of tractors.

Initially despondent after losing their music, the citizens of this dreamscape
realized that certain songs, harbored deep within their hearts, could never be
captured or suppressed. Resurrecting their political agency, they began to sing
again, beginning with the indigenous drumming, dance, and song genre known
as *mhande*, and moving through renditions of several popular songs that included
Bob Marley's famous anthem of African self-determination, "Zimbabwe," as well
as the Cranberries' "Zombie." Enacting a decidedly musical revolution, the children of this imaginary realm finally arose. Singing "Somewhere over the Rainbow," they overthrew the king's animalistic henchmen and carried them offstage. Led by mbira player Chiwoniso Maraire, the performance culminated
in a rendition of John Lennon's "Imagine," with a chorus of children cupping
glowing candles in their hands on the darkened stage. Ringing out through the
night air, Lennon's utopian reverie breached the void between the pajama-clad
performers and the thousands of audience members spilling across the grass
in front of them. In the aftermath of the nation's recent elections, Harare resi-

dents quickly understood this musical portrayal of dispossession and resistance as profoundly political. Many of those present responded immediately to its depiction of a collectively felt loss of political agency. As one local artist would later recall, "From where we were standing, people kept looking at each other and saying, 'Oh, what is this? It's political. It's heavy.' There were very few moments that people could celebrate." Offering a more optimistic perspective, a local blogger observed that the performance also served as a reminder of the audience's collective "dreams and aspirations as Zimbabweans," concluding, "The beauty of art though, is that it can be interpreted in so many ways."[3] Taken together, these comments remind us that political significance is not inherent in particular songs, performances, or texts. Instead, as Mamadou Diawara has observed, music and other forms of popular culture are often "launched into unpredictable, infinite spaces."[4] In the process, music's social meaning is jointly negotiated by artists and audiences alike.

We Don't Want Senseless Violence

Questions of interpretation continued to loom large during Mtukudzi's performance on the final night of HIFA. Clad entirely in white, the Black Spirits appeared luminous against long columns of hanging yellow cloth, printed with a repeated motif of blue crosses reminiscent of the marks made on election ballots. Yet Mtukudzi considered the blunt political commentary of the festival's opening performance divisive. As he told me, "There were videos of *Murambatsvina*, houses being bulldozed, there were videos of police hitting people.[5] It was centered on the bad that happened to the people. . . . in other words, it's encouraging revenge, that's how I felt. And I didn't go along with that. . . . the message didn't get through, the determination message didn't get through to me. 'Cause I was the audience!" In contrast, Mtukudzi sought to project a politically neutral stance by emphasizing the importance of national unity: "My theme, in my set, was actually to encourage people to love each other even more now than ever before. 'Cause we are all standing on an edge—we don't know what to do anymore, we don't know what to support and what not to support. So we need to hold each others' hands and balance. . . . What we need more now is love and unity. If we are to come up with something constructive, we have to be on the same side, in peace." Emphasizing this view, Mtukudzi began his set with a Shona language rendition of the Lord's Prayer titled "Baba Vedu," or "Our Father" (*Pfugama Unamate*, 1997). He followed this with "Kuipedza" (*Tsimba Itsoka*, 2007), which he described to me as a song emphasizing that "we are all a creation of God and it's a waste of time to hate the next person. There's no profit out of that."

After "Kuipedza," the Black Spirits were joined onstage by professional MC Emmanuel Manyika, whom Mtukudzi had invited to address the audience.

Emmanuel Manyika's Address during Mtukudzi's 2008 HIFA Performance

Ladies and gentlemen
Tonight is a night of peace
Tonight is a night of unity
Hatidi hondo [We don't want war]
Hatidi mhirizhonga [We don't want fighting]
We want peace and togetherness
For as HIFA is drawing down to a close
The message under the Tuku Music label is that of peace
  and unity
As we come together, let's join in, in this peace and love
The word of togetherness
And let's drive it together and move Zimbabwe forward in
  peace and one love
Ladies and gentlemen, with thousands in attendance
And thousands wishing they were here
Ladies and gentlemen, introducing Oliver "Tuku" Mtukudzi
It's show time
Hatidi hondo [We don't want war]

Oliver Mtukudzi!

Reiterating Mtukudzi's message of peace, Manyika quoted frequently from what would be the band's next song, "Ngoromera" (*Bvuma-Tolerance*, 2000). Originally written to commemorate the fiftieth anniversary of the United Nations in 1995, Mtukudzi named "Ngoromera" after a medicinal charm that conveys strength and fearlessness, rendering its practitioners invincible in a fight.[6] In Zimbabwe, archival evidence suggests that the history of the *ngoromera* charm extends at least as far back as the early 1900s, when it was apparently imported from Sena province, in neighboring Mozambique.[7] At this time, ngoromera involved a compound made up of burned and powdered pieces of lions, crocodiles, hippos, and other predatory animals, which was rubbed into incisions in the wrists and other joints and could only be administered by another initiated practitioner.[8]

In his song, Mtukudzi rejects the practice of ngoromera, which seeks to produce power through violence. As he observed, "The inspiration came when people argue over something, and they end up trying to fight. From an argument, to a fight. And for me, it's not sensible. 'Cause when they fight, it doesn't mean they have rectified their dispute. They've just fought. But the dispute is still there, you see? That's how that song came to be." In place of conflict and violence, "Ngoromera" advocates for dialogue, tolerance, and understanding.[9] In this way, it embodies a vision of moral social relations grounded in the Shona concept known as *hunhu*, which acknowledges that both individual and collective identities are formed through the ongoing negotiation of interpersonal relations between the self and others.[10] As Mtukudzi continued, "It's a matter of making me understand what you think, and me making you understand what I think. And come to a solution somehow, to an agreement: 'Okay, okay, you think it's this way, but I think it's this way.' So you go somewhere in between, and come up with one thing. That's all it is. But if you disagree to the point that you want to clap me, then you're not solving anything. You're not making me understand you. You're making me hate you."

Hearing Politics in Hunhu

Despite Mtukudzi's professed desire to remain above the fray of national politics, audiences at HIFA quickly interpreted "Ngoromera" as profoundly critical of ZANU-PF's tenacious hold on power. Once lauded as the party that won Zimbabwe's independence, ZANU-PF had more recently been described as mobilizing traces of political violence in order to legitimate itself, to which President Robert Mugabe responded by claiming that he held "degrees in violence."[11] In this climate, "Ngoromera" acquired powerful political innuendo, with many people interpreting it as what Murenga Chikowero has called "a metaphor for the vast machinery at the disposal of the one who itches for unjustified and excessive violence. Having failed to present a winning argument in the political processes, he goes around spoiling for a fight."[12]

Political readings of "Ngoromera" were heightened by one particular line in the song's first verse, in which Mtukudzi invokes the image of a clenched fist, or *chibhakera*, in order to condemn the violent exercise of power.[13] One of ZANU-PF's most distinctive signs, the closed fist was initially adopted as a revolutionary symbol of black empowerment during Zimbabwe's liberation war. Throughout the harmonized elections of 2008, it remained a prominent image in ZANU-PF's parliamentary and presidential campaign materials. In the wake of widespread reports of political violence, however, this revolutionary gesture increasingly struck people not as a symbol of black empowerment, but rather as a sign of ZANU-PF's iron grip on power. Playing upon these associations, Zimbabwe's main opposition party, the MDC, adopted the image of an open palm as its own party emblem, a postrevolutionary gesture meant to symbolize neoliberal ideals such as transparency and political accountability.

"A true child of Zimbabwe": ZANU-PF 2008 campaign advertisement.
Courtesy of the Zimbabwe Independent.

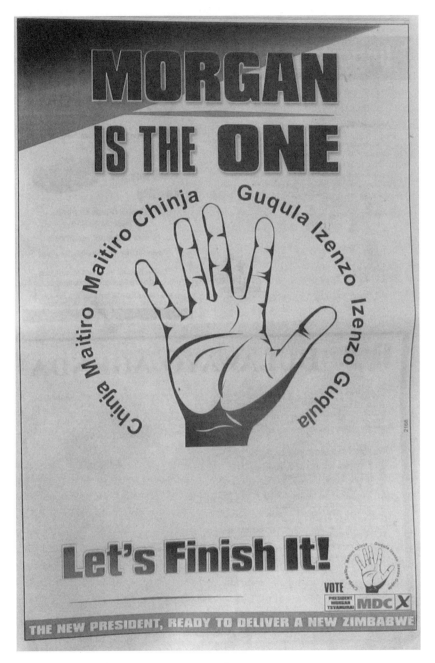

"Change your ways": MDC 2008 campaign advertisement.
Courtesy of the Zimbabwe Independent.

At HIFA, Mtukudzi's audience immediately responded to the clenched fist portrayed in "Ngoromera" by raising their own hands in a massive demonstration of support for the MDC. From their position onstage, the Black Spirits looked out across a sea of waving, open palms. The feeling in the crowd was one of solidarity, courage, and determination, demonstrating music's power to create what anthropologist Johannes Fabian has referred to as collective "moments of freedom" in precisely those situations where individual rights are severely circumscribed.[14] As one listener later observed, "People had just gone through a traumatic experience, you know, with the elections. And he sang peace . . . it's a song that he released years ago, but it's a song which will always have a meaning." As another commented, "Mtukudzi, and others, and HIFA itself, is putting a mirror to what is happening." Yet a third simply cried out, "Ah, he has made history, *sha* [friend], he has made history."

Written over a decade before Mtukudzi's 2008 performance at HIFA, "Ngoromera" acquired striking new political meaning in the context of the harmonized elections. Offering audiences a vibrant musical imaginary of moral social relations, the song invited listeners to reflect upon failures of domestic governance, which had risen to the fore during recent election-related violence. Exemplifying postcolonial struggles over musical meaning, this performance of "Ngoromera" illustrates how Mtukudzi's unique style of urban, popular music is closely intertwined with contemporary Zimbabwean experiences, offering particularly fertile ground for musical ethnography.

Moral Personhood as Politics in Tuku Music

A prolific songwriter, Mtukudzi belongs to a generation of musicians who pioneered a new approach to popular music in the 1970s, adapting indigenous sounds for electric instruments such as the guitar and writing original lyrics in local languages. His distinctive musical sound, called simply "Tuku music" after his personal nickname of "Tuku," integrates a variety of wide-ranging influences and sounds, from the *katekwe* drumming of his family's place of origin in northeastern Zimbabwe to the American soul music of artists such as Otis Redding, and from South African popular genres such as *mbaqanga* to the distinctive timbral qualities of Zimbabwean mbira-based guitar. Featuring acoustic and electric guitars, keyboard, and bass alongside indigenous instruments such as the *hosho* shakers, and more recently the neotraditional Zimbabwean marimba and nyunga nyunga mbira, the unique sound of Tuku music has appealed to audiences throughout the world. By the late 1990s, Mtukudzi had risen to superstar status in the "world music" scene, playing to packed houses at festivals and jazz clubs in Europe and North America. Back home, he maintained an extraordinary ability to draw in successive generations of listeners, playing for audiences

Mtukudzi performs at the Triple Door in Seattle, Washington, in 2007.
Courtesy of Mary Cairns.

who saw his music as "essential, like food," and described themselves as "born listening" to his songs.[15]

A fascinating figure, Mtukudzi's life is studded with the type of compelling events that make for good musical biography, from his encounters with Rhodesian soldiers during Zimbabwe's liberation war to his friendship with American blues artist Bonnie Raitt. Yet his story is more than simply a gripping account of one local artist's rise to global fame, for Mtukudzi's distinctive style of popular music is also grounded in the indigenous Shona concept of personhood known as hunhu, which articulates a vision of human identity predicated upon moral relationships between the self and others. In song after song, Mtukudzi has invoked hunhu in order to encourage listeners to reflect upon what it means to live well with others, and to embody principles of mutuality, reciprocity, and dialogue in the context of their own lives. So important is hunhu within Mtukudzi's music that he refers to it as "the main umbrella, which covers whatever I talk about, in every song of mine."

The story does not end there, however, for Mtukudzi's listeners have frequently interpreted his musical imaginaries of hunhu as metaphorical commentaries on national governance, or *matongerwo enyika* (literally "the ruling of the nation"), imbuing his songs with powerful political meaning. As we shall see, they have heard Mtukudzi's renditions of indigenous drumming, dance, and song genres as a form of resistance to colonial rule, and his original lyrics about domestic violence and aging as blunt criticisms of Zimbabwean President Robert Mugabe. They have interpreted his warning about the dangers of tracking a wild beast as a cautionary tale for political leaders bent on forging blindly ahead on a dubious path, his praise for farmers as an indictment of ZANU-PF's controversial land reform program, and his songs about migration and diaspora as a lament for worsening political, economic, and social conditions back home. In the process, Tuku music illustrates how Southern African conceptions of song as a privileged form of social criticism continue to resonate not only in the domain of rural, acoustic music making, but also in the sphere of mediated, commercial popular culture.

The way Zimbabwean audiences have interpreted Mtukudzi's songs about moral personhood as critiques of immoral social relations, extending from the domestic sphere to the nation-state, is the subject of this book. Throughout, I engage with an already rich body of literature on African expressive culture, as well as a growing scholarly interest in musical listening, long an undertheorized subject in ethnomusicology and related disciplines.[16] As I illustrate, musical subjectivities are not only shaped through live performance, but are also produced, articulated, and negotiated through listening, a domain that has only recently begun to attract scholarly attention.[17] In the words of Veit Erlmann, "a new thinking seems to be taking hold, one that is increasingly drawing attention away from readings—of scores or meanings that are the result of acts of inscription—and focusing it on the materiality of musical communication, issues of sensuality, and the like."[18] Joining this emerging body of scholarship, I view questions of listening and reception as critical in understanding the social meanings of Mtukudzi's songs. Through an ethnographic approach to Tuku music, I suggest that these questions are critical not only in understanding participatory musical practices, but also in grasping the social significance of presentational performances and mediated commercial recordings, which have increasingly come to represent a dominant mode of contemporary musical exchange.[19]

Listening, like performing, assumes specific contours in different local contexts.[20] Among Shona speakers, for example, the very word for hearing, or *kunzwa*, can also mean tasting, smelling, feeling, and understanding.[21] As such, kunzwa is a multisensory domain that integrates diverse semiotic elements, producing complex fields of meaning. Among Zimbabwe's Ndau speakers, for example, ethnomusicologist Tony Perman has argued that the integration of music, dance, beer, and snuff in the context of *zvipunha* spirit possession ceremonies serves to "satisfy sight, smell, hearing, taste, touch, and the demands of intersubjectivity."[22] Involving what Robert Kauffman has called "a unity of the senses and cognition," this distinctive local conception of hearing establishes a framework within which audiences naturally incline toward interpreting performances contextually, vesting expressive practices such as proverbs, praise poems, and songs with immense power as forms of social criticism.[23]

At the same time, kunzwa is profoundly intersubjective in nature, placing the self inescapably in relation to others.[24] The social dimensions of listening, for example, take on heightened importance in words closely related to kunzwa, including *kunzwana*, which refers to mutual respect, agreement, or peace, and *kunzwanana*, which denotes mutual understanding.[25] Both terms, which translate respectively as "listening to each other," and "listening to one another," crystalize listening's relationship to the moral ethos of hunhu, with its emphasis on mutual obligation and social reciprocity.[26] Throughout this book, I suggest that the fundamentally intersubjective nature of listening, with its close ties to the moral imperatives of hunhu, has informed the way Shona-speaking audiences have evaluated and interpreted Oliver Mtukudzi's songs. As such, my account of Tuku music is part of what scholars have called an "aural reflexive turn," linking socially and culturally positioned experiences of listening to questions of politics and power.[27]

A Note on Methodology

My account of Tuku music is based in eighteen months of fieldwork with Mtukudzi and his audiences, both in Zimbabwe and in the United States. It is also grounded in my own extended history of involvement with Shona music. In 1990, I began studying Zimbabwean marimba music with Maggie Donahue, an American student of the late Zimbabwean ethnomusicologist Dumisani Maraire. I also took Shona singing lessons with Maraire's wife, Mai Chi Nemarundwe.[28] Through my early exposure to the marimba, I developed an interest in learning to play the mbira dzavadzimu, with its historic ties to Zimbabwean ritual life and practice.[29] With few mbira teachers available in the United States, I traveled to Zimbabwe in order to study the mbira in 1995. There, I lived with Mai Donnie Chauruka, an independent female landlord, spirit medium, and active member of the Catholic Church in Mtukudzi's home neighborhood of Highfield, a high-density township located on the periphery of the nation's capital city of Harare. For six months, I learned Shona and took mbira lessons on a daily basis with master mbira player, or *gwenyambira*, Musekiwa Chingodza. I was also regularly invited to join Chingodza and members of the Chauruka family as they performed at spirit possession ceremonies called *mapira* (sg. *bira*). Finally, weekends offered the opportunity to see live shows at the nearby Mushandira Pamwe hotel, a venue graced by popular musicians such as Mtukudzi and Mapfumo since the days of the liberation struggle.

After several subsequent visits, I returned to Zimbabwe in 2008–2009 in order to conduct the fieldwork that informs this book. Arriving in Harare less than two weeks after the harmonized elections, I became one of the last researchers to enter the country before the US government suspended the research program that had brought me there.[30] Shortly after my arrival, Mtukudzi's HIFA performance provided an excellent point of entry, amply illustrating entanglements between music and politics in postcolonial Zimbabwean society. While political tensions restricted my fieldwork in many ways—such as preventing me from traveling to certain parts of the country—being present during this pivotal moment in Zimbabwean history also enabled me to witness music's role in the political process that unfolded during the weeks leading up the troubled presidential runoff held in June, followed by the eventual formation of a Government of National Unity.

During my yearlong stay in Zimbabwe, I conducted over sixty interviews, including multiple interviews with Mtukudzi and his band members. I also spoke with individuals who had collaborated with Mtukudzi on a variety of artistic and social projects, including feature films, theatrical productions, live recording projects, public health campaigns, development projects, and more. Complementing these formal interviews, I participated in informal conversations about Mtukudzi's music with diverse figures, including pastors, minibus drivers, students at the Zimbabwe College of Music, the traditional musicians with whom I studied mbira, and many others. I also spent several days in the National Archives of Zimbabwe poring over articles published in the popular press. Dating back to the beginning of Mtukudzi's career in the 1970s, these sources furnished many details about the emergence and evolution of his distinctive musical style. I attended several of Mtukudzi's live performances in Zimbabwe and regularly spent time at his newly constructed cultural center, Pakare Paye, where I sat in on classes, rehearsals, and recording sessions, among other events. Reflecting the growing importance of multisite ethnography, I spent an additional month following the Black Spirits on a tour of the United States, where I interviewed audience members about their experiences listening to Mtukudzi's music in a growing Zimbabwean diaspora.[31]

Hearing Hunhu in Song

Laying the groundwork for the rest of the book, the remaining section of this introduction both explains hunhu in greater detail, and illustrates how this concept of moral personhood is woven throughout Mtukudzi's songs, from the narrative text of his lyrics to the dialogic nature of his musical arrangements. The kind of term anthropologists call emic, or emanating within a particular social group, *hunhu* expresses a concept of moral personhood unique to Shona-speaking communities, rendering it difficult to translate into English. As a result, different authors have variously described it as "a philosophy that sets a premium on human relations," a simultaneously ontological and epistemological approach to "being human," or in one case, simply "personhood."[32] In Zimbabwe, Shona speakers likewise explained hunhu to me in different ways. Placing an emphasis on the domain of *tsika nemagariro*, or customs and ways of life, female mbira player and ritual specialist Patience Chaitezvi Munjeri told me, "When we say hunhu, we are talking of good behavior, which is accepted in our culture. And there are certain behaviors expected from girls, boys, men, and women . . . it touches so many things." Invoking the concept of *kuzvibata*, or self-restraint, young urban musician John Mambira said, "Hunhu is self-restraint, by a person among others. To be a person among others, with others. Someone who is humble, who respects others, although he may not know them." Echoing Mambira's comments, Oliver Mtukudzi sees the English term *self-discipline* as synonymous with hunhu, which he described to me as "the inner self of a human being." As he elaborated:

> It tells us, this is good, this is bad. And that is what is called a human being. That is the soul of a person. We don't need qualifications to attain self-discipline. And self-discipline simply translates to respecting the next person. To love the next person. It all comes from self-discipline. It's not something that we acquire academically; you are born with it. You know what's good and what's bad. And, the more you talk about that, the more you remind people how we should live. So it's way above what we think. It's what we're supposed to be.

Each of these definitions shares the common understanding that our human selves are constituted only through our interactions with others, a belief reflected in the Shona aphorism *Munhu munhu nevanhu*, or "A person is a person through others."[33] As such, hunhu constitutes a philosophy of mutual social obligation. As Mtukudzi told me, "You respect the next person, you put value to the next person. . . . It's not only about *I* live, and you don't care about living with others." As a result, Shona speakers frequently describe hunhu simply as "being a person among others," or *kuva munhu pane vanhu*. As Mtukudzi declared, "*Kuva munhu pane vanhu*. There's no other, better way. *Kuva munhu pane vanhu* is self-discipline." In its purest form, we might thus understand hunhu simply as an expression of love shared with others.[34] In the words of the great *gombwe* spirit Sekuru Musanyange, founding ancestor of the *Mhofu Nyakudirwa* lineage, "Without love, there is no hunhu."[35]

Singing the Social Imaginary

Among Zimbabwe's popular musicians, Mtukudzi is not alone in singing about social relations. Indeed, themes of kinship, reciprocity, and moral obligation surface in many artists' songs, from the Four Brothers' emphasis on filial obedience in "Mashoko Ababa Namai" (*Makorokoto*, 1988) to acoustic guitarist Kireni Zulu's dramatization of a married woman's discontent in "Zveimba" (*Marabi Music*, 2005).[36] Yet few other artists have demonstrated Mtukudzi's sustained commitment to singing hunhu, which has remained a prominent theme in Tuku music over the duration of his long musical career. Over the decades, his songs have offered listeners exceptionally vivid musical imaginaries of moral personhood, with a focus on kinship relations forged in the crucible of the domestic household.[37] Mtukudzi has been widely praised by listeners as a "story telling genius," and his lyrics have portrayed nostalgic parents longing for distant children, new brides humbling themselves before their husbands' parents, aspiring sons-in-law struggling to pay bridewealth, brothers consoling widowed sisters, children admonished to respect their parents, and elderly people exhorted to acknowledge their limitations.[38]

Through these vibrant stories, Mtukudzi's songs encourage listeners to situate themselves within an imagined world of kinship. This is particularly apparent in his early hit "Madzongonyedze," or "Turmoil" (*Africa*, 1979), in which he intones a litany of kinship terms in quick succession:

Watora amai	Mother has been taken
Apo ndisekuru	And now, grandfather
Vana vanochema	Their children are crying
Mhuri yongopunyaira	The family is grieving
Vanochemeiko ava?	Why do they mourn?
Ndimadzongonyedze chete baba	It is turmoil, father
Rufu ndimadzongonyedze	Death is turmoil
Pane vakayanana	For those who were at peace together

The type of kinship terms woven throughout the lyrics to "Madzongonyedze" are widely used by Shona speakers even in the absence of actual blood ties in order to signify relative status, establish social distance or proximity, enhance the efficacy of a request or command, or create fictional bonds between two previously unrelated individuals.[39] Through his creative use of kinship terms, Mtukudzi thus creates a sense of musical belonging, drawing his listeners into an imagined world of social relations. As one person exclaimed after hearing his song "Dzoka Uyamwe" (*Tuku Music*, 1997), which describes a mother yearning for her lastborn child to return after a period of extended absence, "I am the person he's singing about."

Music as Dialogue

Drawing listeners further into these musical imaginaries of kinship, Mtukudzi has placed special emphasis on facilitating dialogue, one of the central pillars of hunhu. As Stephen Chifunyise, Zimbabwe's former permanent secretary for Education, Sports, and Culture, told me, "He believes in people who dialogue . . . using language, and using talking and dialogue as a means of educating people: extending wisdom; correcting the younger ones; promoting dialogue across the age groups; using dialogue as a means of promoting understanding of critical aspects in his culture, which he wants maintained. . . . So his mission has been to talk, and to allow that talk to then cover the various socio-economic and political issues without fear of reprisal, as long as dialogue is allowed." This emphasis has permeated the lyrics of many of Mtukudzi's songs, such as "Kuropodza," or "Empty talk" (*Wonai*, 2006):

Ipa mukana wekuteerera	Take time to listen
Zvinotaurawo vamwe	To what others say
Worega kuropodza	Stop doing all the talking
Kuropodza zvisina maturo	Talking too much without reason
Chinonzi hurokuro	It is called discussion
Kutaura tichinzwanana	Speaking, listening to each other
Vanokurukura	They discuss together
Vanotaura pachinzwanana	They speak, listening to each other
Iwe wotaura ivo vachiteerera	You talk, as they listen
Wotaurawo ini ndichiteerera	You speak, as I listen
Chinonzi kukurukura	What we call dialogue
Kutaura tichinzwanana	Is speaking and listening to each other
Ivo votaura iwe uchiteerera	They speak, as you listen
Ndotaurawo iwe uchiteerera	I speak, as you listen

Anthropologist Karin Barber has observed that the way songs such as "Kuropodza" refer directly to aurality and communication both "dramatizes, and represents in heightened form, dialogue as such."[40] Yet Mtukudzi's efforts to create dialogue extend beyond his lyrics alone, encompassing other aspects of his songwriting. As marimba player Charles Chipanga explained, for example, Mtukudzi has deliberately sought to create dialogue between the various musicians in his ensemble: "The way he arranges the lyrics is that he sings, *vakomana vanodaira* [then the boys respond]. Then *vasikana vanodaira* [the girls respond]. Then everyone, *vozopindira, vakomana navasikana, endi iye* [finally joins in, boys and girls, and him]. You know, you find four or five things in one. It's so unique. *Istyle yandakaona* [It's a style I've observed]. . . . He wants it to be like a conversation, and it's great." As in many other Zimbabwean performance styles, the interaction of various instruments and voices within Mtukudzi's songs produces a musical and social groove that both endorses and embodies a vision of human relations grounded in principles of tolerance, dialogue, and mutual respect: the very foundation of being "a person among others."

Listening to Listeners

From the liberation struggle of the 1970s to the increasingly fraught political climate of the late 1990s and beyond, Mtukudzi's commitment to singing hunhu has been central to his relationship to listeners. Not only have his audiences symbolically read themselves into Mtukudzi's musical imaginaries of hunhu; they have also turned to his music in order to navigate their own social worlds, often in ways that are as creative as they are unexpected. In order to illustrate their passionate investment in Mtukudzi's musical discourse of moral social relations, I offer the following listener narratives. The first two are drawn from my interviews with listeners, and the third is my translation of a radio request letter sent to the Zimbabwe Broadcasting Corporation headquarters, located in Harare's Mbare township.

Singing for School Fees

While following Mtukudzi on tour in United States in October of 2007, I met graduate student Lewis Madhlangobe at a performance in Austin, Texas. The day after the show, Madhlangobe drove for an hour to meet me for an interview, which focused largely on his experiences as a diasporic listener, a subject discussed in greater detail in the last chapter of this book. As a parting question, I asked whether Madhlangobe had any favorite songs. I was startled when he replied by describing an incident from his childhood, in which Mtukudzi's music enabled him to negotiate divisions within his own family. As a result, he successfully obtained money for school fees from his father, who had separated from his mother. Madhlangobe's story revolves around "Shanje," or "Jealousy" (*Pfambi/ Shanje*, 1981), a song that cautions listeners against the divisive effects of envy among members of the same family:

> There's a song that my mother used to sing, especially when she was abandoned by my dad, when she had her eleventh child. He came back only like four times to make her pregnant, but he was already living out. So my mother used to sing that song, just to express. There's a song called "Shanje." Have you heard that song? My mother used to sing that song.
>
> So one day when I wanted to have tuition fees, I went to my dad. And then, because he was living with a certain woman, the moment I go there—you know the structures of the buildings—I could hear them arguing. He was inside, and he was saying, "No, he's my son, I have to give

From *Pfambi* to *Shanje*

"Pfambi" really means a prostitute. And in the song I'm saying, "Don't blame the prostitute. It's those who approach prostitutes who are doing wrong. It's you who is losing your respect by going after prostitutes. And a prostitute doesn't approach you. You are the one who goes after her. So, let's look at ourselves. Who is wrong, really? Is it the prostitute? Or is it me, the man, who is going after them?"

I had released it. Yeah, that's when the minister noticed it in shops, and all over. They were taken out of the shops. Yeah, they just ordered the record company to take it off, they don't want that name. 'Cause we had a censor's board that could go through your song and find out whether you have the right lyrics, there's no vulgar lyrics.

They didn't have a problem with the song. It's just the displaying of the word, "Pfambi, Pfambi," all over. The minister said, when he spoke to me, he couldn't have the word displayed all over town. 'Cause I mean, the album was likely to be popular, and the word "Pfambi," having it displayed all over, culturally, it's not really—I understood, really. Yeah. So I just changed the name.

—*Oliver Mtukudzi*

him tuition." And she was saying, "No, tell him not to come here because then. . ."

Suddenly that song, because my mother used to sing it, it really fitted that context, when you say, "Don't do things from jealousy." So I started singing that song. And when I sang that song, my father got—it touched him. Right? And, well, when they woke up and it was time to drink tea—you know, we drink tea around five—and so he said, "Just why were you singing that song?"

Can you see the impact of the song? They were in the house. And I was singing, "*Shanje hadzivake musha. Hadzivake.* [Jealousy does not build a household. It does not build.]" And then he was—they were—listening. And the moment when they were arguing, and she was saying, "Don't give him money." And then she was complaining that, "Their mother should not be sending you here."

Pfambi. Courtesy of Tuku Music and Sheer Sound/Gallo Record Company.

She is fighting against my mother, for her husband. But my mother is not coming to harass her. And so that's when I sang that song. And it impacted my father. That's why I'm telling you, Mtukudzi's songs—really, you know, they've got meaning.

Tuku Music as Moral Scripture

On another occasion, I interviewed Harare resident Tafadzwa Muzhandu, who had recently returned to Zimbabwe from graduate study in the United Kingdom, and whom I had known for many years as a long-time Mtukudzi fan. As we spoke, Muzhandu described attending a "kitchen party," or Zimbabwean version of a bachelorette party. Much to her dismay, the usually rowdy atmosphere associated with kitchen parties was nowhere in evidence at this event, which instead featured an hour-long sermon, followed by a call for everyone present to offer moral guidance to the bride-to-be. As a self-described "non-practicing Christian,"

Muzhandu found herself at a loss when everyone around her began invoking biblical scripture. By quoting lyrics from two of Mtukudzi's songs, "Mwana Wamambo," or "The king's child" (*Ndega Zvangu*, 1997) and "Ninipa," or "Lowly" (*Nhava*, 2005), however, she found a creative way to offer advice grounded in the moral ethos of hunhu. As she told me:

> There were two songs from Tuku's music that came to my mind when I was sitting there. *"Mwana wamambo muranda kumwe* [The child of a chief is a slave elsewhere]" was one, and then the other one was *"Kuzvininipisa kune pundutso* [Humbling yourself is to your advantage]." Everyone was talking about a good wife, and quoting from Genesis, or whatever. And I was thinking, "Who do I really know, that would have said something to a *muroora* [daughter-in-law]?" And I was like, "Oh yeah, Tuku."
>
> So I said, *"Kuzvininipisa kune pundutso. Ukasadaro, chimoto.* [Humbling yourself is to your advantage. If you fail to do so, watch out.]" What's *kuzvininipisa* in English? Being humble, I suppose. I guess you have to *zvipeta* [literally, fold yourself in half], like being humble as a *muroora*. So, I didn't come out as, like, the crazy friend who quotes Tuku. 'Cause it's a good song, and it speaks to what everyone else was talking about, so that made a difference.
>
> I didn't want everyone to sort of look at me like, "Ah, the non-churchgoer friend," you know? So I was like, "You know what? I have a favorite artist, and I think he speaks a lot about culture, and how we live, and I think his messages are just as important as what everyone else has been saying, even though they're not from a book of holy scriptures. And so I'm just going to quote a few things from Tuku's songs and music."
>
> So, that's how I started it. And it went well, 'cause no one threw stones at me, or tomatoes. They were quite impressed actually, 'cause it's hard to find appropriate things to say that are not from the Bible, or from a preacher's wife, or whatever. So a lot of the people who were speaking were speaking from the church point of view, and I was speaking from the world point of view. But it still was the same message. Except, you know, it's something that I love, and that I want to share with other people.

"It Doesn't Mean I Don't Have Love, My Children"

Several months into my fieldwork, I came across another example of how Mtukudzi's audiences have used his songs to negotiate kinship at the Mbare headquarters of the Zimbabwean Broadcasting Corporation (ZBC), where I had gone to interview radio DJ Richmond Siyakurima. At the end of our interview, Siyakurima escorted me to the ZBC archive, where staff members granted me permission to browse through their catalogue of old Mtukudzi albums and to read through hundreds of radio request letters mailed in by listeners. A creative response to extreme economic hardship, fan mail written to the ZBC during the late 2000s exemplified the nation's improvisatory response to multiple political and social challenges. Written on small scraps of cardboard salvaged from boxes of Cerelac breakfast porridge, Five Roses tea, and Red Seal oats, many letters had no postage, suggesting that they had been hand-delivered to the ZBC headquarters. These unconventional pieces of post had poured in from far-flung regions of the country, including Checheche, Birchenough Bridge, St. Matthew's Mission in the rural district of Wasomba, Musizi Farm 96, and Khami Maximum Security Prison in Bulawayo.

The most interesting letters were those addressed to programs such as *Kwaziso*, or "Greetings," in which salutations written to distant kin are read aloud on air, followed by a musical request.[41] A mediatized domain of kinship, *Kwaziso* brings music, technology, and family together, allowing individuals to perform private, domestic relationships on the public stage of national radio.[42] As in Mtukudzi's songs, the letters written to *Kwaziso* frequently portrayed people struggling to negotiate the complexities of kinship. On occasion, letter writers even used Mtukudzi's lyrics in order to narrate their own personal stories. In one such letter, a man named Steve T. addressed his estranged children by quoting the words *"Rudo ndinarwo vana vangu,"* or "Love, I have it, my children," from the chorus to Mtukudzi's song "Hazvireve," or "It doesn't mean" (*Nhava*, 2005).[43] Yet even as he sought to reconnect with his children, he simultaneously exculpated himself from any blame, pinning all responsibility for their estrangement squarely on his former wife:

> One year, with one lover, I met one young girl, and we fell in love and then had a baby. After we had lived together for a while the girl's relatives started fighting like leopards wrestling for a piece of meat, fighting like baboons, getting involved in our domestic affairs. I persevered until my heart was swollen like the gizzard of a bird and I said to myself, "Maybe things will get better."
>
> To make matters worse, my wife took advantage, acting spoiled, and whenever she ran into one of her relatives, she acted like someone who has seen gold. I said to myself, "Maybe this is a traditional matter (*chivanhu*)." I tried going to a traditional healer (*n'anga*) but nothing changed, so I then said, "Maybe we need a faith healer." These were all the impassioned efforts I took to stabilize my home because of my love for my family. Sorry my children, I do love you, it is your mother's fault as she failed to correct her behavior. It is painful but there's no use crying over spilled milk. Now these are but memories. I realized what a grudge they have against me. Love I have it, my children.

Songs: Oliver Mtukudzi, "Hazvireve Rudo Handina"; Maxwell Masherenge, "Daka Neni"; Simon Chidaza, "Ndangariro Dzinondibaya Moyo"; and Calista Nyamwede, "My Children I Love You"[44]

Through the mediated space of radio broadcasts, listeners such as Steve T. seek to create, articulate, and navigate bonds of kinship across distance.[45] As with Madhlangobe and Muzhandu, they often draw upon popular songs in order to do so, not only by requesting that certain songs be played on air to accompany their letters, but also by creatively redeploying song lyrics in order to publicly narrate their own lives and to communicate with distant kin.

Listening as Politics

Muzhandu, Madhlangobe, and Steve T. are among the many thousands of listeners who have so thoroughly internalized Mtukudzi's musical imaginaries of *hunhu* that his songs have become an important part of the expressive resources they use to navigate their own lived experiences of sociality and kinship. Yet Mtukudzi's songs have simultaneously encouraged audiences to reflect upon much larger political realities. Throughout this book, I illustrate how the dialogic aesthetics inherent in Mtukudzi's music have prompted audiences to actively respond to his songs. In the process, they engage in a range of participatory behaviors that are seldom recognized in relation to commercially mediated, popular genres.[46] I suggest that political interpretations of Mtukudzi's music are directly related to this type of participatory engagement, which leads listeners to personalize their readings of his songs in relation to their own lived experiences. As a result, songs that ostensibly address social issues—such as gender relations, HIV/AIDS, or transnational migration—may assume metaphorical significance as forms of political commentary.

Despite these readings, Mtukudzi has repeatedly rejected characterizations of his songs as critiques of national governance, stating flatly that his intentions as a songwriter are "not political."[47] At a public discussion prior to a performance in the United States at the height of Zimbabwe's political crisis, for example, Mtukudzi responded as follows when one listener asked whether political messages in his music had brought him into conflict with either the Zimbabwean government or its people: "I truly believe I'm way above governments. I'm way above politics, because I am an artist. I'm not a politician in art. You see where's the difference between a politician in art and an artist? An artist represents everybody. A politician in art represents a certain class of people. It's partisan. . . . If you're an artist, you are way above that. You are a culture they all fall into." In the following chapters, I suggest that the dialogic nature of Mtukudzi's approach to singing about human relations is critical in making sense of how his avowed political neutrality can coexist alongside listeners' highly politicized interpretations of his songs. Exceeding conventional boundaries of the political, Mtukudzi's approach to singing hunhu speaks to the formation, negotiation, and maintenance of human relations at multiple levels, exemplifying an ongoing field of social struggle.

Questions of listening and reception are critical to this process, in which Mtukudzi and his audiences have been jointly involved in articulating, negotiating, and reimagining an evolving social order. Invoking Mtukudzi's song "Chiro Chakanaka," or "Something good" (*Rudaviro*, 2011) as an example, one listener perceptively observed:

> He leaves people to interpret, to put his lyrics into a context. For example, in a context where people might be angry at a political establishment, and then he's talking about *humambo* [kingship] as being a nice thing, and then interpreting that if he was a leader, he would always be smiling—then people can make opposites, can look at the opposite, and can interpret it the way they want to. I think to be political is not just to be singing slogans and to be naming names. I think it is also to be provocative, and to make people think without you interpreting the language for them. You give them the opportunity to fill the gap, and then you empower them actually, if you let them fill the gap. And they will put it in the context that applies to them.

Capable of accommodating multiple, often radically divergent interpretations, Mtukudzi's musical imaginaries of hunhu signify at the level of the nation-state even as they remain outside of conventional political discourse, giving them special valence as a way of thinking about relations of power. Uniting moral personhood, popular culture, and politics, Tuku music offers a musical perspective on a uniquely Zimbabwean way of being in the world; one in which humanity is possible only when it is shared with others. In turn, the audience reception of Mtukudzi's popular songs illustrates how postcolonial and postmodern subjects are actively engaged in producing a social and cultural life in excess of mere survival, enabling them to navigate the world with dignity and grace; the very essence of the shared humanity of hunhu.[48]

Charting Tuku Music

Joining hunhu, two other emic concepts—the ritualized friendship of *husahwira* and the drumming, dance, and song genres collectively known as *ngoma*—have proved particularly important in shaping Tuku music. In chapter 1, "Hwaro/ Foundations," I turn to these terms, illustrating how Mtukudzi has positioned himself as a ritual friend to the nation, and how his songs have mobilized the sounds and participatory aesthetics of ngoma. Together, husahwira and ngoma participate in bringing Mtukudzi's musical imaginaries of hunhu to life, with important implications for questions of listening and reception.

In chapter 2, "Performing the Nation's History," I chart Mtukudzi's rise to fame during the conflict-ridden years of Zimbabwe's liberation struggle in the 1970s. As a young singer and guitarist born in the township of Highfield, a neighborhood often referred to as the cradle of Zimbabwean nationalism, Mtukudzi was soon caught up in a wave of musical innovation as popular artists increasingly turned to the emerging genre of "trad music," which incorporated local languages, sounds, and influences. For Mtukudzi, this meant writing songs such as "Mutavara," based in a ngoma piece from Dande, his family's place of origin in the nation's rural northeast. Playing upon ngoma's privileged position as a form of social critique, these songs proved effective in responding to an increasingly repressive white settler regime, establishing an important precedent for later readings of his music. I close this chapter with a brief section on the contested reception of trad music, in order to illustrate how Mtukudzi's music has been caught up in ongoing debates over musical meaning from the early days of his career, turning listening and reception into a site of struggle over the social significance of musical sound, as well as national politics.

In chapter 3, "Singing Hunhu after Independence," I document how contests over musical meaning intensified in the decades after Zimbabwe attained independence in 1980. As the concept of trad music broke down, Mtukudzi found himself at the margins of the various musical genres that emerged in its wake, provoking debate between the singer and his listeners over what his music would be called. Throughout this period, I illustrate how Mtukudzi's relentlessly innovative spirit propelled him both to refine his approach to singing hunhu and to break free of many of the strictures of the Zimbabwean music industry. At his best, Mtukudzi's tightly knit musical arrangements during this time consolidated the type of performance style that music scholars such as Samuel Floyd and Ingrid Monson have described as dialogic, enabling him to pull listeners into a unique musical and social groove.

In chapter 4, "Neria: Singing the Politics of Inheritance," I take up the story of one of Mtukudzi's most compelling songs, released as the theme song to a film that sought to educate audiences about women's inheritance rights. With exceptional clarity, "Neria" illustrates how Mtukudzi's music has enabled ordinary Zimbabweans to reflect upon, articulate, and respond to their own experiences of moral kinship and sociality. Yet Mtukudzi's soundtrack departed in subtle but important ways from the carefully crafted message of the film's script, which approached inheritance from a modernizing, rights-based framework that privileged individuals over kinship groups. In contrast, Mtukudzi's songs conveyed his belief that moral kinship continued to play an important role in enabling families to navigate struggles over inheritance. Soon after the success of "Neria," however, Mtukudzi's drive to experiment led him to branch out even further, trying his hand at both musical theater and gospel music. In the closing pages of this chapter, I illustrate how these forays distanced Mtukudzi from the vibrant musical imaginaries of hunhu listeners had come to expect in his songs. As a result, they met with decidedly negative audience reception.

The release of *Tuku Music* (1998) heralded Mtukudzi's return to his roots, once more placing hunhu, husahwira, and ngoma at the heart of his musical project. As I illustrate in chapter 5, "Return to Dande," this album placed special emphasis on Mtukudzi's origins as a Korekore-speaking member of Dande's royal lineage of *Nzou Samanyanga*, or "Elephant, Keeper of Tusks." By invoking his origins in Dande, Mtukudzi positioned himself as a Zimbabwean "son of the soil," or *mwana wevhu*, a phrase often invoked as a claim to indigenous identity. In songs such as "Dzoka Uyamwe," or "Return and be suckled," I illustrate how audiences have read symbolic meaning into Mtukudzi's lyrics, which they have heard as a poignant social commentary on questions of kinship, place, and belonging in a changing world.

Yet *Tuku Music* was released just as a wave of political turmoil began sweeping the Zimbabwean nation. In chapter 6, "Listening as Politics," I offer the reception history of Mtukudzi's most politically controversial song, "Wasakara," or "You are worn out" (*Bvuma-Tolerance*, 2000). Mirroring the reception of his music under white settler rule, "Wasakara" exemplifies how postcolonial audiences have interpreted Mtukudzi's musical imaginaries of hunhu as decidedly political, expressing trenchant metaphorical critiques of state governance. Yet even as songs such as "Wasakara" have been read as powerful forms of political commentary, they have resisted being reduced to a single, politicized reading. Exceeding conventional boundaries of the political, I conclude that Mtukudzi's musical imaginaries of hunhu exemplify postcolonial struggles in which "the political cannot be meaningfully studied apart from the moral," in the words of anthropologist Richard Werbner.[49]

In chapter 7, "What Shall We Do: Music, Dialogue, and HIV/AIDS," I address Mtukudzi's long history of engagement with HIV/AIDS. Rending the nation's social fabric, HIV/AIDS has destroyed bonds of kinship, robbing the nation of a generation of parents, teachers, and workers. Through idiomatic language, Mtukudzi's songs about HIV/AIDS have described how the epidemic has devastated Zimbabwean society, primarily by narrating the disease's effects within the lives of individuals and families. In the context of an epidemic long characterized by silence, stigma, and erasure, I suggest that Mtukudzi's music has offered audiences the possibility of singing HIV/AIDS out loud, provoking listeners to reflect upon and respond to the epidemic. Finally, I observe that Mtukudzi has participated in shaping the public culture of HIV/AIDS in Zimbabwe through his involvement in public health campaigns, as well as at his own cultural center, Pakare Paye.

The final chapter, "Listening in the Wilderness," extends my arguments about the political significance of Mtukudzi's musical imaginaries of hunhu to the realm of Zimbabwe's growing diaspora. Foregrounding intersections between moral obligation, kinship, and diaspora, I suggest that Mtukudzi's musical imaginaries of hunhu have enabled diasporic audiences to symbolically reposition themselves within the social relations of a remembered home. In the process, audiences have routinely interpreted his songs about migration and diaspora, ostensibly directed beyond Zimbabwe's borders, as reflecting back within the nation, conveying a powerful yet subtle critique of postcolonial domestic politics.

"Baba"
(Father)

Imi baba manyanya	Father, you are excessive
Imi baba manyanya	Father, you are excessive
Imi baba manyanya kurova mai	Father, you beat mother too much
Imi baba manyanya kutuka mai	Father, you insult mother too much
Munoti isu vana tofara seiko?	How can we, children, be happy?
Isu vana tofara seiko?	How shall we children be happy?
Kana mai vachichema pameso pedu?	While mother is crying in our sight?
Kana mai vachingochema pamberi pedu ava?	While mother just keeps on crying in front of us?
Vati ponda ako ndifire pavana vangu	Saying, "Kill me in front of my children"
Ponda ako ndifire pavana vangu ava	"Kill me, let me die in front of my children"
Tozeza baba	We fear father
Vauya vadhakiwa	He has arrived intoxicated
Tozeza baba	We fear father
Baba chidhakwa	Father is a drunkard
Tozeza baba	We fear father
Vauya vakoriwa	He has arrived drunk
Tozeza baba	We fear father
Hoyi hoyi hoyi hoyi manyanya	Hoyi hoyi hoyi hoyi you are excessive
Chavanotadza chiiko?	What is her offense?
Chinomirira madhakiwa?	That he awaits her drunk?
Idoro here rinoti mai ngavatukwe?	Is it alcohol that says to insult mother?
Idoro here rinoti mai ngavarohwe?	Is it alcohol that says to beat mother?

ONE   *Hwaro*/Foundations

During the height of the dry season, in September 2002, I was invited to attend a postfunerary ceremony at my host family's home in the Chiweshe rural areas, located along the way from Harare to Oliver Mtukudzi's rural home, or *musha*, in the village of Madziva. Long relieved of their harvest, fields crackled with the parched stubble of maize stalks waiting to be plowed into the soil. Cows grazed at leisure, ambling together in small herds peppered by the brilliant white flecks of cattle egrets. Against a backdrop of bare boughs, a few trees clung to a last scrim of leaves. Low on the horizon, the morning sun was already hot as we awoke the morning after the ceremony. Just out of its reach, small groups of women rested in the shade. Seated on handwoven reed mats, or *rukukwe*, they gazed out at the modest structures of a rural homestead—a round kitchen with its thatched roof, a few square, brick bedrooms topped by sheets of corrugated asbestos, a crumbling, roofless toilet block, and a grass enclosure for bathing.

Mostly *madzisahwira* (sg. *sahwira*), or ritual best friends, these women had spent three days assisting the residents of this compound with the ritual of *kurova guva*, held roughly a year after the death of a family member to reincorporate his or her spirit into the family's ancestral lineage. After staying awake all night, most people had stolen away for some much-needed repose. Yet these female madzisahwira spontaneously rose again, forming a circle in the middle of the dusty yard. Their long skirts swung out behind them as they began the weaving, counterclockwise movements of *mafuwe*, a ceremonial genre associated with rainmaking.[1] Clapping their hands to keep time, the women launched into song, their voices settling into a high-pitched, narrow range as the lead singer called out:

Zvemusha uno / What is happening in this home

The others immediately answered her with a unison refrain:

A hiye wohiye rava dembetembe / Reflects a state of disorder[2]

Pausing momentarily, several of the singers interjected exclamations—*Hokoyo* / Watch out!—as well as frequent ululation, or *mhururu*, a ritualized expressive form reserved for women.

Soon, a group of men emerged from the house, carrying two drums, or ngoma. Throughout Southern Africa, several different varieties of ngoma share roughly the same construction technique. With cylindrical wooden bodies carved from whole tree trunks, their cow-skin heads, held firmly in place by a series of wooden pegs, can be struck with sticks or hands. From tall, slender instruments played while standing to wide, short drums capable of producing an incredible resonant bass sound, ngoma come in various sizes and can be played singly or in pairs. Depending on region, size, and genre, ngoma are known by an astonishing variety of names, even within Zimbabwe: *mhito, dandi, mutumba, mhiningo, usindi,* and *mbete-mbete* are but a few.

The staccato timbre of wooden sticks on hide shattered the early morning as the drummers launched into the powerful, syncopated rhythms of mafuwe. Joining them, a hosho player performed a simple pattern on a pair of shakers made of dried gourds filled with canna lily seeds. While he did little more than mark each triplet grouping, the hosho's rich spectrum of frequencies immediately added sonic density and thickness, filling out the musical texture of the performance.

Celebrating the successful completion of kurova guva, the women whiled away the time with this recreational performance of mafuwe. Their position in the yard, a secular space that contrasts with the sacred realm inside the thatched kitchen of the family home, symbolically separated them from the deep work of ritual, now already completed. Yet the women remained preoccupied by themes of kinship, sociality, and moral relations, situated at the very heart of kurova guva. Invoking the moral personhood of hunhu, the lead singer intoned:

Zvemusha uno / What is happening in this home
VekuChihota we / Those from Chihota
Vanga vachiti hakuna hunhu amai / They have been saying, "It lacks
  hunhu, mother"

In the performance of these madzisahwira, we see with particular clarity how ngoma enables contemporary Shona speakers to articulate, negotiate, and critique evolving social relationships, transforming experiences of disorder, loss, and disjuncture into the moral relations of hunhu. We also see the madzisahwira's special license to perform social criticism, which is linked to a long-standing Shona institution of ritualized friendship known as husahwira. Together, hunhu, husahwira, and ngoma represent the type of local forms of social organization that anthropologist Claire Ignatowski has described as "rooted in, though not unchanged from, the precolonial past," and which continue to shape the experiences of millions of people throughout Southern Africa.[3]

Women dancing mafuwe at a kurova guva ceremony in Chiweshe. *Photo by Jennifer W. Kyker.*

The Zvido Zvevanhu ngoma ensemble performing in Harare. *Photo by Jennifer W. Kyker.*

Hunhu, Husahwira, and Ngoma in Tuku Music

While Oliver Mtukudzi's urban, popular music seems far removed from this rural, ritual setting, the very elements so foundational to this performance of mafuwe—the social ethos of hunhu, the ritualized friendship of husahwira, and the participatory aesthetics of ngoma—are precisely those at the heart of Tuku music. In this chapter, I illustrate how husahwira and ngoma are enmeshed with Mtukudzi's approach to singing hunhu, forming an essential frame of reference in understanding how Zimbabwean audiences have imbued his songs with larger social and political implications. Throughout the chapter, I return frequently to the song "Baba," or "Father" (*Shoko*, 1993), which offers a representative example of how Mtukudzi has invoked the concepts of husahwira and ngoma in order to craft particularly vivid musical imaginaries of hunhu, enabling him to communicate more effectively with his audiences.

Houses of Stone

Before delving into these themes, I offer a brief overview of the political developments leading to Zimbabwe's emergence as a modern nation-state, in order to situate my discussion of Mtukudzi's music within a larger historical arc. Bounded by the Zambezi River to the north and the Limpopo to the south, the territory now known as Zimbabwe became a British Protectorate in 1891. After a series of uprisings known as the First Chimurenga failed to quash British ambitions, the colony was rechristened Southern Rhodesia in 1898.[4] With a substantial settler population and the sort of extractive economic policies typical of colonialism, Southern Rhodesia was ruled by the British for the next sixty-five years, including a brief period of federation with the neighboring colonies of Nyasaland (Malawi) and Northern Rhodesia (Zambia), from 1960 to 1963. Shortly after the federation's collapse, Southern Rhodesian Prime Minister Ian Smith unilaterally proclaimed the colony's independence from Britain in 1965, largely in an attempt to circumvent the British Crown's demand for a transition to majority rule.

Yet Smith's Unilateral Declaration of Independence merely hardened the determination of emerging African nationalist movements. Foremost among them was the Zimbabwe African People's Union (ZAPU), a predominantly Ndebele organization, and ZANU, a predominantly Shona group. Soon, the struggle for self-governance evolved into a brutal and protracted armed war, which became known as the Second Chimurenga. In a desperate attempt to quell the rising tide of nationalist power, Ian Smith formed a coalition with yet another nationalist movement, the United African National Council, in 1979. The nation was renamed Zimbabwe-Rhodesia, and United African National Council leader Bishop Abel Muzorewa was inaugurated as titular prime minister. As nationalist parties were still banned, however, this compromise quickly disintegrated. Finally, a negotiated settlement facilitated by the British government paved the way for majority rule. With ZANU stalwart Robert Mugabe as its newly elected prime minister, Zimbabwe was born on April 18, 1980, making it the last African state to achieve independence with the exception of apartheid South Africa.

Emerging from the ashes of European imperialism, the nation of Zimbabwe, or "Houses of Stone," took its name from the ruins of one of Africa's most impressive precolonial empires, governed by a succession of rulers from the twelfth to the fifteenth centuries. Surrounded by the rolling grasslands and acacia forests of the Southern African savannah, the dynasty's ruined complex of stone buildings, now a national park, lies a few miles southeast of the mid-sized town of Masvingo. Reaching toward the sky, its undulating walls of carefully stacked granite slabs are decorated with chevron and dentate crocodile patterns, as well as low doorways with worn wooden lintels. Set at intervals, stone cairns and monoliths point skyward, the visual embodiment of a vanished power.[5] A tangible manifestation of history, these cool, rough stones have survived the turbulence of centuries. As an emblem of shared political identity, these houses of stone, or *dzimba dzemabwe*, offered Zimbabwe's new leaders a rich trove of symbolism, and the ruins' iconic conical tower and soapstone birds were quickly incorporated into the nation's new flag, currency, and coat of arms.[6]

Zimbabwe's storied past was accompanied by tangible progress in the decades after independence, with the nation's relatively developed infrastructure and comparatively democratic political structure contributing to gains in food security, education, health, and gender equality.[7] Beginning in the mid-1990s, however, Zimbabwe entered a period of growing political, economic, and social turbulence as it faced the effects of a growing HIV/AIDS epidemic, a World Bank Economic Structural Adjustment Program, a war in the Democratic Republic of Congo, massive payouts to veterans of the Second Chimurenga, a disastrous land reform program, and the emergence of the Movement for Democratic Change as a formidable opposition party.[8] As a result, Zimbabwe seemed to be edging ever closer to paradigmatic conditions of postcolonial disorder, challenging both residents and outsiders alike to make sense of emerging social, political, and economic realities.

Husahwira

Throughout the trials of the liberation war, the jubilance of independence, and the confusion of the late postcolonial era, Mtukudzi has consistently positioned himself as a counselor and advisor to his listeners, drawing upon the

long-standing Shona social institution of ritualized friendship known as husahwira. Calling himself a *"sahwira* to the nation," Mtukudzi has described the
sahwira, or ritual friend, as indispensable in negotiating the moral relations of
hunhu: "If I can translate what sahwira is, it's a family friend. A friend that kind
of oversees how you are living in your home, and doesn't overtake the family,
but is always giving advice. . . . he helps us, or coordinates us to discuss." Mtukudzi places special emphasis on the sahwira's social importance in several of his
songs, including "Mutorwa" (*Mutorwa*, 1991), "Kurerutsa Ndima" (*Rombe*, 1992),
and "Jeri," (*Gona*, 1986).

One of the most important aspects of the sahwira's role is his or her license to
speak out in ways that may not otherwise be acceptable. This includes permission to indulge in jokes, insults, and vulgar forms of speech. At one kurova guva
ceremony I attended in Mhondoro, for example, a group of female madzisahwira
entered a room where several women were resting. Lightheartedly accusing the
ceremony's hosts of leaving all the hard labor of cooking and washing dishes to
them, the madzisahwira threatened to drag these women outside by their gen-
itals and set them to work. More frequently, the sahwira exercises his or her
special dispensation to speak out through relatively open criticism of unethical
conduct, particularly on the part of someone in a position of authority. Commenting on the sahwira's ability to mediate domestic disputes by directly confronting a household head, for example, Mtukudzi told me, "He's open, he goes
there and says, 'Eh, ah, what? You think you're good?' . . . He'll be just shouting at you. But, it's up to you to listen. And you get to know where you're going
wrong."

With the liminal position of someone who is not kin, yet is integral to the
functioning of kinship networks, the sahwira plays a particularly visible role
in rituals of transition, including burials and postfunerary rites such as kurova
guva. Almost inevitably, the sahwira's participation at these events includes some
form of musical performance, which is intended to enable bereaved family members to carry out the work of repairing a kinship network fractured by death.[9]
As Mtukudzi told me:

> Mtukudzi: In our culture, in our traditions, that is the purpose
> of song. You're trying to pass a message. Even at the burial,
> madzisahwira, they come singing, and acting happy. Because
> they're trying to neutralize the tension which is there, and
> the pain which is there. That want that pain to diminish. You,
> Jennifer, if you lose someone today, if someone passes away,
> and if I come to you and say, "Oh boo-hoo, you are suffering,"
> what am I doing?

Kyker: I'll cry even harder.

Mtukudzi: Worse! You will be in even worse pain. So, that is not what song was meant for. Song was meant for when you are suffering; song must loosen your pain, so you can be a better person and have a better perspective. To enlighten your mind, because even though you are suffering, it doesn't mean your life is over. You see?

Much like Mtukudzi himself, the sahwira is thus a consummate performer who delivers both emotional support and critical moral guidance through song.

Further extending the performative dimensions of husahwira, the late mbira player Ambuya Beauler Dyoko emphasized that other forms of expressive culture are likewise part of the sahwira's domain. During a funeral, for example, the sahwira may act out short theatrical skits dramatizing the life of the deceased, which often focus on outlandish, comical, or even disgraceful personality traits of the departed family member: "Everyone will be crying. No one will be feeling alright. . . . That is when the sahwira comes. Maybe the person was a driver, maybe he drove a taxi, maybe he was even a thief, one of those thieves. They come and act, there inside the house, surrounded by people. The sahwira comes right there, saying, 'You, you, you.' Pretending like he is a pick-pocket! At that moment, he is performing." An excellent example of how joking relationships serve to dissolve social tension, the sahwira's performance offers clarity, perspective, and hope during a time of great distress. As Mtukudzi explained:

Instead of me concentrating on the effects of the funeral, the sahwira comes in. Either he's talking something different, or he's disturbing me from thinking too much of the funeral. He eases up my brains; I refresh from what this sahwira is doing. Maybe he portrays what this dead person has been doing when he was alive. Goes there, gets his clothes, puts on the clothes of the deceased. He makes funny out of it, makes a joke out of it, for the main reason to ease up the situation. And you concentrate more, and you find things are a lot easier because of this sahwira.

Singing as a Sahwira

In contemporary settings, the ritual friendship of husahwira has acquired symbolic new dimensions, offering Shona speakers a familiar way of engaging a changing social landscape. In the city, for example, two strangers might address each other as sahwira in order to create an immediate bond, symbolically linking themselves together through the mutual rights and responsibilities

inherent in this form of ritualized friendship.[10] The invocation of husahwira between strangers is a way of intimating that the reciprocal moral obligations of
hunhu are possible not only among kin, but also among more extended social
contacts, a necessity in the context of urbanization and proletarianization. By
positioning himself as a "sahwira to the nation," Mtukudzi has similarly sought
to establish this type of bond with his audiences, thereby drawing listeners more
firmly into the social imaginaries of his songs.

Much as the family sahwira is called upon in times of conflict or distress,
Mtukudzi sees particular value in singing about difficult topics. As he told me,
"That's the role of an artist. . . . To talk about where we are going wrong, what
we can't say, what we have to do, what we can't do. It's about reminders—what
the nation, or the family, is neglecting, or don't realize they are doing. It's up to
the artist to identify that thing and talk about it. Just like a sahwira." As a song
that speaks out against domestic violence, "Baba" illustrates precisely the type
of situation where the sahwira, as a trusted family advisor, is well-positioned to
intervene. As Mtukudzi explained:

> The father is supposed to be the head of the family, and he could be going
> wrong somewhere. And the wife and the children can't really confront
> him . . . you can't just go direct and say, "Hey dad, no, I can't do that." Or
> as a wife, you can't say, "Hey, I can't do that." It needs a sahwira now to
> come in. 'Cause probably the sahwira is a friend to your dad. . . . So he'll
> go there and say, "Ah, *ishe*, [king, or Lord], can't you see what you're doing
> to your wife is bad, man! You!"

By critiquing a father's abusive treatment of his wife and children, "Baba" seeks
to redress a situation in which hunhu is clearly lacking, moving away from conflict and violence and toward a moral order in which family members live well
with others.

With their powerful depictions of disordered moral relations, songs such as
"Baba" have moved Mtukudzi's audiences to sing, dance, and even cry. As one
long-time fan told me after seeing Mtukudzi perform "Baba" at a live show: "I
could tell from a lot of the people who were singing and dancing that this song
maybe has a much bigger meaning to their lives, because domestic abuse is something which is very common . . . people are dancing, but also really singing every
word. And you can see from their faces that they're really into the song. And you
cannot be into that kind of song without really knowing the content and the context." At the Zimbabwe Broadcasting Corporation headquarters, radio DJ Richmond Siyakurima similarly observed, "If you go to some public place—some
beerhall, some stadium where he's performing—it's not surprising to see some
people sobbing to the music. You know, it's touching . . . that emotion alone tells

a story. The fact that someone is listening to Oliver Mtukudzi's music and he's sobbing, he's crying, he's dancing to it—it's impact. I measure that as impact. It is emotional, and it has done something to that particular individual."

Joining this emotional impact, listeners also hear songs such as "Baba" as performing the important didactic function of communicating moral values, even when their own personal situations do not exactly mirror those depicted in Mtukudzi's lyrics. As kombi driver John Muchena, who played Mtukudzi's music for his riders every day at rush hour, told me: "'Tozeza Baba' helps me, in a way. Even though I myself don't drink alcohol, it still helps me in my relations with my family, in that I should not act threatening toward my children. . . . You should be someone who is free with your family, who gets along with your family. Don't be someone who is frightening for your family, and when they see you coming they all run away, saying, 'There he comes again,' or whatever. So those are the messages I find helpful, among his messages." Recounting his interactions with radio audiences, DJ Siyakurima further described how listeners sought to mobilize the moral imaginaries of Mtukudzi's songs in order to reshape their own relations of kinship:

> You know, if you play things like "Tozeza Baba," children can phone in and say, "*Hiii*, my father is hell. Thank you for playing this song. Would you like to play it around five, when he's home?" Even women, some married women . . . would phone and say, "*Sha* [friend], would you play that around five for me? Please?" You ask why, they say, "*Hiii, shamwari* [friend], I've got problems with my husband, he is quite something. I mean, he is hell. When he comes home, *hiii*, everything changes" . . . So people phone in when you play this type of music and say, "Please, could we have some more of it? Or can you play it such and such a time?" The purpose is so that it has the impact, it does what she expects it to do, for the other person.

Offering yet another example of this tendency to use Mtukudzi's songs in order to communicate moral values, artist Lazarus Mahoso described creating an original drawing bringing the lyrics of "Baba" to life in the form of a visual image:

> I saw that it was good for his words not to be contained only as they are heard in the ear; I wanted people to also see them in an image. So that is what impassioned me. Because Oliver Mtukudzi's words are stories that are found among the people. It is a song in which I see him singing about four things, telling people that they are bad. Truly, they cause families to suffer. Drinking too much beer, as he sings about in "Tozeza Baba," I see that it is drug abuse. He sings, "Father, you beat mother excessively." That is domestic violence, which is also in the song. I also see him saying, "We,

"We fear father." *Drawing by Chimanimani artist Lazarus Mahoso*

children, how can we be happy when mother is crying in front of us?" And I see that as child abuse in the mix. And then in our customs, it is despicable for a father to beat his wife in front of their child. So I see that there are four things being sung about in the same song. So it moved me, and then I thought that I should make a picture that would be seen by the people. Because its words are deep; they are able to teach people how to live well with their families, in their homes.

Mahoso's extended comments both emphasize how Mtukudzi's music teaches listeners what it means to live well with others and offer an excellent example of how audiences have made his musical imaginaries their own, launching them into new social orbits through creative acts of listening.

Kuridza Kurunga: Music as "Flavoring"

As a sahwira to the nation, Mtukudzi views music primarily as "a way of communication. It's a way of talking to people. Now if people don't get your message of your song, then we have lost the purpose of song. You see?" While Mtukudzi acknowledges the communicative potential of purely instrumental music, he places special emphasis on the importance of his song texts, describing his lyrics as one of the primary factors underpinning his longevity as a musician.[11] In contrast, he sees musical settings primarily as attractions, or *hwezvo*, which function to draw listeners further in to his imaginaries of hunhu. Using the word *kurunga*, which literally means adding salt to food, Mtukudzi describes playing music, or *kuridza*, as a way of "flavoring" his songs. As he explained to me, "*Kuridza kurunga* [To play is to flavor]. It's just a flavor. What you are talking about is the song. What ends up being played, you're just flavoring the song. So myself, I start by coming up with my lyrics, then come up with the song. Because what the words I'm saying mean will give me the right expression, of what kind of expression I need. So, the tune must follow along with what the song means." Further elaborating on his compositional process, Mtukudzi emphasized the importance of creating musical settings that flow effortlessly with the messages of his lyrics: "When I write my songs, I write the lyrics first. That will give me the harmony, and the tune. 'Cause if I have my lyrics, the meaning of my lyrics will give me, what kind of a tune do I need on those lyrics? If the words are sorrowful, then the tune automatically must be sorrowful. For example, say I'm talking about my mother who died. I can't have a happy beat there. In other words, I can't smile while I'm crying. You see, I can't be laughing when my mother is dead."[12]

Even as Mtukudzi elucidates these relationships between music and text, he firmly rejects any notion that his songs are "compositions," which he perceives as laden with artifice. Using the code-switching typical of contemporary urban speech, Mtukudzi told me:

> I hate comments like, "Eh, that's a beautiful composition." How does he come to know it was composed? Meaning that there's something wrong with that song, which makes him think that it was created for him. [*Anembenge amboziva sei kuti icomposition? Kureva kuti there's something wrong nerwiyo urworwo. Chamupa kuti afunge kuti, it was created for him.*] I would rather have a comment like, "Hey, listen to what this guy is saying." Yes. That's a good song. "Listen to what this guy is saying, boys! Do you hear what is being said in this song?" He has no thought that it was composed. [*"Inzwai zvaari kutaura munhu uyu vakomana, hey! Muri kunzwa zviri kutaurwa nerwiyo?" Haana pfungwa yekuti it was composed.*] It means your message is getting through to him, you know? But if it's composed, it's like, "Okay, yeah, he created this song, he wanted to mean that. He doesn't mean what he's saying."

In these comments, the different ways Mtukudzi invokes the Shona word *rwiyo*, or song, and the English word *composition* are particularly interesting. On the one hand, he ascribes a particular type of musical authenticity to the Shona concept of song, based in the singer's genuine identification with the message of his or her performance; this theme emerges with particular clarity in the lyrics to his song "Mean What You Say" (*Grandpa Story*, 1989). On the other hand, he views the term *composition*, which has no easy Shona language equivalent, as an imported concept antithetical to indigenous aesthetics of music as social dialogue.

Ngoma

Throughout Zimbabwe's history, music has played a prominent role in the social, political, and religious life of its communities. The nation's most iconic instrument, for example, the mbira dzavadzimu, has long-standing ties to political and religious authorities.[13] By the 1960s, the mbira had begun migrating into new performance contexts, with local innovations ranging from Thomas Mapfumo's mbira-based guitar music to Simon Mashoko's use of the mbira in Catholic worship services.[14] The instrument likewise began circulating in global space, moving into concert halls and modern recording studios, and into the hands of a growing number of foreign students, concentrated primarily in the United States.[15] In a nod to the mbira dzavadzimu's prominence, one collection of field recordings made by Hugh Tracey between 1948 and 1963, which featured lesser-known Zimbabwean mbiras such as the *njari*, *matepe*, and *mbira*

"Mean What You Say"

Oh grandpa told me he said, "Grandson, you have a lot to know"
My grandpa told me he said, "Grandson, you have a long way to go"
I said, "Grandpa, won't you let me know, tell me all you know"
"Well Grandpa won't you let me know, teach me all you know"

He said, "Grandson I have a lot to tell, how old do you think I am?"
"Well grandson I have a lot to teach, how old do you think I am?"
I said, "Grandpa, you are about very old, almost very old"
"Hahaha!" He laughed, "Ah, clever boy, clever boy"

He said, "If you have a word, say it loud, say it from your heart"
"If you have a word, just say it loud, say it from your heart"
"Cause you've got to mean what you say, say what you mean"
"And you've got to sing what you mean, mean what you sing"

That's why if I have a word, I say it loud
If I have a song, I sing it loud
If I have a word, I say it loud
Have a song, I sing it like,
"Rove ngoma Mutavara"
"Amai ndiri bofu ini mune rino pasi, wohuwo baba"
"Gunguwo!"
"Hwema handirase"
"Nyarara mwanawe, mwanawe nherera"
"Murombo haarove chinenguwo, zvinogumbura kwazvo"
"Please ndapota"
"Kunoda amai, kwemwana kunodzima moto"

"Zvangu zvazara jecha"
"Rufu ndimadzongonyedze"
"Chimusoro, wanyanya!"
"Pamusoroi, pamusoroiwo varume"
"Muroyi ndianiko, muroyi wapedza hama"
"Chokwadi chichabuda pachena"

That's why if I have a word, I say it loud
If I have a song, I sing it loud
If I have a word, I say it loud
Have a song, I sing it like

"Rove ngoma Mutavara"

dzaVaNdau, single-string musical bows such as the *chipendani* and *chitende*, and aerophones such as the *ngororombe* panpipes, was titled simply *Other Musics from Zimbabwe* (2000).

By far the most common indigenous musical styles performed in Zimbabwe today, however, are the nation's legion ngoma genres. Just as hunhu has cognates in numerous Bantu languages, the term *ngoma* is widespread throughout Bantu-speaking communities, including large swathes of Southern, Eastern, and Central Africa. At a basic level, *ngoma* simply means "drum," although it can also refer to specific musical styles—such as mafuwe—that combine drumming, dance, and song, accompanied by participatory practices such as handclapping, ululation, and whistling.[16] Further extending its meaning, ngoma can also be used to designate the very concept of music itself. Reflecting this type of extended usage, one listener described Mtukudzi's approach to singing hunhu by saying, "The ngoma that he sings has so much teaching within it [*Ngoma dzaanoimba dzinenge dzine dzidzo yakanyanya*]."[17] Finally, there is often a ritual, therapeutic dimension to ngoma, which is widely considered efficacious in strengthening performers' bodies, leading some musicians and dancers to describe it as "better than medicine."[18]

One among many Southern African styles of what ethnomusicologist David Coplan has called "auriture," or forms of performance in which verbal, musical, visual, and kinesthetic elements are inseparable, ngoma is both discursive and dialogic in that it is intended to provoke performers and audiences to jointly consider its multiple potential meanings.[19] Ngoma is thus intimately connected to ideas of listening, dialogue, and mutual agreement. As Zimbabwean scholar Jerry Rutsate has observed, for example, performers of the ngoma genre known as mhande use kunzwanana, or "listening to one another," to refer to successful coordination between members of an ensemble.[20] Conversely, Tony Perman has reported that the word *kupesana*, which refers to disagreement, division, and social discord, is used by performers of another ngoma genre, *muchongoyo*, to refer to a lack of coordination between group members.[21]

Hearing Ngoma in Tuku Music

Oliver Mtukudzi has frequently been described as a particularly eclectic songwriter, who has gathered an incredibly diverse range of influences together under the rubric of Tuku music.[22] Among them are forms of proverbial and allusive speech, or *tsumo nemadimikira*, songs from the Methodist and Presbyterian hymnals, the interlocking melodies of the mbira dzavadzimu, lines from speeches given by Robert Mugabe, quotes from the dramatic skits of entertainer Safirio Madzikatire, rhymes taken from Shona school textbooks, a poem written by contemporary author Chirikure Chirikure, a Shona version

"Marutsi"
(Vomit)

Kanyanisa!	Mix it!
Kanyanisa zvose	Mix everything
mbovha, mabori,	drivel, rheum,
madzihwa, misodzi,	mucus, tears,
dikita, urwa,	sweat, pus,
ndove, marutsi!	dung, vomit!
Kanyanisa!	Mix it!
Kanyanisa ndizvidye;	Mix it, I shall eat it;
ndichoka chido chako:	that is your wish:
chawatema hachikanukwi,	what you appoint shall not be challenged
chawarota chinotoitwa.	what you dream of shall be done
Saka kanyanisa!	So mix it!
Kanyanisa undipe,	Mix it and give it to me,
asi ndangodya, hokoyo:	but once I have eaten it, watch out:
ndichakurutsira iwe	I will vomit back at you
mumuromo	in your mouth
mumhino	in your nostrils
mumaziso	in your eyes
uchabitirwa!	you will suffocate!

It was one of those poems that just hit you. The inspiration comes and sinks in your mind, and it becomes part of you. You can wake me up any time of the night and I can jump out of the bed and perform that poem without thinking twice.

The poem can be interpreted at a political level, and a lot of people take it to be a political commentary. It basically says, "OK, give me—let's say vomit, that's my part, which Mtukudzi left out—mucus, vomit." My original version is, "Throw it at me, I shall eat it."

He wanted to narrow it down specifically to personal relationships. But it's the socio-political experience, basically. It's so far back, actually, the late '80s, early '90s. You could see then the trend in which the country was going, and you would immediately want to throw in a word of caution, hoping that people would listen and get to do things in a more organized, sincere, constructive manner, instead of the bullshitting which was already going on then, which has now reached the highest level one would have ever imagined. But the signs were already there in the '80s.

—*Chirikure Chirikure*

of the Lord's Prayer, and the Southern African political anthem "Nkosi Sikelel'
iAfrica."

Yet even with these decidedly wide-ranging tendencies, Mtukudzi has been
particularly influenced by Zimbabwe's many ngoma genres, raising questions
about how ngoma intersects with commercially mediated popular culture. Just
as the mbira has often been associated with Thomas Mapfumo's innovative
style of *chimurenga* music, the sounds and aesthetics of ngoma permeate much of
Mtukudzi's extensive repertory.[23] In the words of Christopher Timbe, the Zimbabwe College of Music's former director, "It is amazing how much of our dances
he knows, and our styles he knows. You can only listen to those—or get an idea
of what styles he's using, which are quite traditional Zimbabwean—when you
analyze his songs, when you listen to the beat. It is clear, like I have said, that
he's using *jiti*, he's using *mbakumba*, he's using mhande; that it is so deeply rooted
in that, so deeply rooted." Among the various ngoma genres that Mtukudzi has
acknowledged as particularly influential in Tuku music are the harvest dance
of mbakumba, the fast-paced recreational music of *tsavatsava* and jiti, and the
therapeutic ritual genre of *dandanda*. He has also claimed a particular musical
affinity for katekwe, a ngoma style played in the far reaches of Zimbabwe's rural
northeast, whose residents speak a Shona subdialect called Korekore. As I explain in greater detail in chapter 5, this area is Mtukudzi's place of origin, giving
his claims to katekwe strategic meaning as a means of authenticating his unique
musical identity. Yet ngoma's influence on Tuku music has gone largely unrecog-
nized, with written accounts alternately describing his sound as based primarily
in South African mbaqanga music, or as a fusion in which "indigenous genres
supply elements, not overriding structures."[24]

I suggest that this oversight is largely a result of the continued marginalization of ngoma itself, for while dozens of drumming, dance, and song genres
flourish in contemporary Zimbabwe, ngoma is decidedly neglected as a field
of musical and social practice. Even after certain genres—including dandanda,
dinhe, jerusarema, mbakumba, muchongoyo, and *shangara*—became canonized
as what ethnomusicologist Thomas Turino has called "the paramount national
music-dance traditions of Zimbabwe," they remain difficult to find either in recorded collections or in written accounts of Zimbabwean music.[25] Yet other
genres—*chidzimba, chinyambera, chinyamusasura, chokoto, humbekumbe, jekunje*,
katekwe, mafuwe, *mangwingwindo, madanhi, ngondo*, and *pfonda* among them—
languish in even greater obscurity. This is particularly true in the case of performance practices such as katekwe, which originate in regions far from the
capital.[26] Not only has this marginalization impoverished our understanding
of ngoma itself, it has also detracted from ngoma's influence on Zimbabwean
popular music, obscuring for example how the recreational drumming, dance,

Members of a ngoma ensemble led by Douglas Vambe perform jerusarema at the 2010 HIFA. *Photo by Jennifer W. Kyker.*

and song genre of jiti relates to the electric, urban *jit* of artists such as the Four Brothers or the Bhundu Boys.[27]

Ngoma in Historical Perspective

While we know little about ngoma performance in the precolonial era, archival records suggest that much like the mbira, it has long been associated with political authority. Drawing upon the sixteenth-century writings of the Portuguese explorer João Dos Santos, for example, historian Stan Mudenge has suggested that the rulers of the Mutapa state had professional musicians in their employ, including singers, drummers, dancers, and mbira players.[28] Joining this archival evidence, oral histories depict ngoma as evolving in response to changing social conditions during the precolonial era. The Zezuru genre of *mbende* (a species of mouse known for its quick, darting movement), for example, reportedly emerged during the nineteenth-century wars, or Mfecane, that broke out around the Limpopo River as a result of Boer expansion within South Africa.[29]

During the early colonial period, ngoma performance was increasingly restricted. Missionaries in particular sought to transform Zimbabwean musical practice by replacing indigenous styles with European ones.[30] Instruments associated with ritual, such as the mbira, were subject to particular scrutiny. Yet even predominantly recreational ngoma styles were widely discouraged, partly because of their associations with dancing African bodies.[31] Soon, dances such as mbende, with its emphasis on quick, twisting movements of the waist, were officially outlawed.[32]

As Shona and Ndebele communities responded to the dual pressures of colonization and missionization, ngoma practice was further transformed. In one particularly interesting instance, mbende was renamed *jerusarema*, the vernacular Shona term for the holy Christian city of Jerusalem. As dance scholar Kariamu Welsh-Asante has explained, this was apparently a direct response to the European prohibition on its performance:

> The chief was sent to the missionary who had proposed the ban with an explanation for the dance as a sacred celebration. Accordingly, when the chief arrived at the home of the missionary, he told him that he had dreamed of the "baby Jesus" of whom the missionary had frequently spoken. In the dream, the baby Jesus was being born and all of the chiefs were coming to Jerusalem bearing gifts and singing praises to the newborn child. In his dream, the chief said, he had also seen the Zezuru dancing and celebrating the birth of Jesus. This dance was a sacred dance that pleased all of the holy men. The chief then explained to the missionary that he wanted his people to be allowed to perform the dance that he had dreamed of because it was a "divine" dance and should be officially permitted. . . . Despite the Chief's inaccuracy regarding the birthplace of Jesus, the missionary was impressed with his story and agreed that the dance should be performed.[33]

By sacrificing the name mbende, Zezuru communities were able to maintain this form of ngoma practice.

Yet even those genres that survived missionization were subject to sweeping change both during colonization and in the postcolonial era. As their original performance contexts disappeared, for example, many ngoma styles moved into new settings, such as the urban beerhalls built for a largely male colonial labor force.[34] In this environment, music previously associated with ritual became recoded as recreational, a secular form of social entertainment.[35] The materials used in ngoma performance were likewise modified, with cloth skirts replac-

"Sara Regina"
(Stay behind Regina)

Ndakuti sara ehe	I say, "Stay behind, yes"
Ndakuti sara kumagobo	I say, "Stay behind, at magobo"
Sara Regina	Stay behind, Regina
Sara kumagobo	Stay behind, at magobo
Sara unoroyiwa	Stay behind, lest you be bewitched
Sara kumagobo	Stay behind, at magobo

ing costumes made of skins, and durable plastic toilet floats substituting for leg shakers, or *magavhu*, previously constructed of the fragile shells of wild *matamba* fruits.[36]

Even as ngoma was being reshaped by the social transformations inherent in colonization, its performers used it to reflect upon this very process of social change. As historians Leroy Vail and Landeg White have observed, a "convention of poetic license that privileges poetry and song above all other forms of oral discourse" is widely dispersed throughout Southern Africa, imbuing song with the freedom to violate normal social conventions, and granting it the moral authority to comment upon ever-changing relations of power.[37] Mobilizing this long-standing Southern African poetic aesthetic, ngoma performers took advantage of song's special license as a form of social criticism to craft new lyrics protesting various aspects of colonial rule. As mbira player Chartwell Dutiro told me, for example, the jerusarema song "Sara Regina" was a response to villagers' experiences of being forced to dig contour ridges, a much-hated colonial agricultural practice: "*Magobo* means cutting down trees, not only cutting down, but uprooting, so that you are creating the land. . . . So the people started singing songs. You know, '*Magobo, ndakuti sara*' [Magobo, I say, 'Stay behind']. Mbende—jerusarema—now they're saying, 'Regina, stay behind. You don't go to magobo.' They are complaining about contour ridges." Sometimes, these protest songs were banned by colonial officials.[38] More often, they entered the public domain as musical "maps" of colonial experience, both reflecting and transcending the historical contexts in which they were originally created.[39]

After independence, new social and political developments continued to reshape ngoma practice. As jerusarema and other ngoma genres were integrated into the repertory of the newly formed National Dance Company, for example, they became subject to processes of modernist reform, with its concomitant forces of folklorization and canonization.[40] In more recent years, the hegemonic political ideology of "Mugabeism," with its impulse toward appropriating indigenous cultural resources in the name of Shona nationalism, has likewise reshaped ngoma performance, cannibalizing local practices such as the Ndau genre of muchongoyo and placing them in the service of the nation-state.[41] With this long history of ritual, political, and social significance, ngoma continues to represent a dynamic and evolving cultural practice, placing it at the center of postcolonial contests over musical meaning.

"Baba"

As we seek to grasp these relationships, "Baba" offers a particularly compelling example of Mtukudzi's affinity for ngoma. As the Black Spirits' former lead guitarist Clive "Mono" Mukundu observes, "Baba" is based in the rhythmic patterns of a ngoma genre known as mhande.[42] With origins in the province of Masvingo, contemporary mhande performances typically highlight a signature pattern played in partial unison by two drums, or ngoma, accompanied by *makwa* hand-clapping patterns, hosho shakers made of dried gourds, and complex, shifting footwork patterns executed by dancers wearing magavhu leg rattles.[43] Responding to a solo vocalist, who performs improvisatory lead, or *kushaura*, singing lines, other participants contribute a common, largely unchanging refrain, known as *mabvumira* or *kudaira*. Above this densely heterophonic musical texture, the distinctive sounds of ululation, or mhururu, rhythmic whistling, or *muridzo*, and the *hwamanda* aerophone, made from a spiral antelope horn, may be heard at intervals, punctuating the performance. Reflecting its close associations with ritual performance, the texts of mhande songs frequently speak to spiritual concerns, naming ancestors such as the powerful regional *mhondoro* spirits and calling upon them to send rain, thus ensuring both agricultural fertility and social harmony.[44]

In order to demonstrate mhande's influence in "Baba," I offer a musical transcription of one contemporary rendition of mhande, as performed by students at Chembira Primary School in Glen Norah.[45] Here, mhande's signature rhythmic pattern is immediately apparent in the sound of the dancers' leg rattles, which divide the $\frac{12}{8}$ cycle into successive groupings of two, four, and three notes, with each grouping separated by a rest. This pattern is often verbalized by performers and teachers using mnemonic syllables such as "te ngi/te-ngi te-ngi/te ngi te," or simply by counting in English, "one two, one two three four, one two three."[46] This pattern is reiterated in slightly modified fashion by the second drum part and is also evident in the syllabic articulation of the vocal response, or mabvu-

Mhande Song: "Tovera"

Kwaziwai Tovera mudzimu dzoka	Greetings Tovera, ancestral spirit, return
A-ha hiye mudzimu dzoka kwaziwai Tovera	Ancestral spirit, return, greetings Tovera
Tovera vana vanorwara	Tovera, your children are ill
A-ha hiye mudzimu dzoka kwaziwai Tovera	Ancestral spirit, return, greetings Tovera
Tovera vana vanochema	Tovera, your children are crying
A-ha hiye mudzimu dzoka kwaziwai Tovera	Ancestral spirit, return, greetings Tovera
Tovera Tovera	Tovera, Tovera
A-ha hiye mudzimu dzoka kwaziwai Tovera	Ancestral spirit, return, greetings Tovera
Tovera weMasvingo	Tovera, from Masvingo
A-ha hiye mudzimu dzoka kwaziwai Tovera	Ancestral spirit, return, greetings Tovera

mira. Together, these parts illustrate how performers in a ngoma ensemble bring elements of drumming, dance, and song together in a coherent musical whole.

In "Baba," Mtukudzi invokes several elements of mhande performance.[47] These range from mhande's distinctive signature rhythmic pattern to characteristics common both in mhande and in other Zimbabwean musical genres, such as call-and-response vocal lines and hosho. As in his other ngoma-based songs, however, Mtukudzi significantly modifies the rhythmic relationships of mhande, reinterpreting its constituent rhythms and redistributing them across a range of contemporary instruments, including acoustic and electric guitars, keyboard, bass, and drum set.[48] As Mukundu observes, metric ambiguity is one of the most distinctive features of mhande, which can be felt in either $\frac{12}{8}$ or $\frac{3}{4}$ time. In "Baba," this metric ambiguity is preserved in the way different, syncopated rhythms are carried by various instruments in the ensemble. The first guitar, for example, divides the bar into four triplet groupings that mirror the first drum part of mhande, while the bass drum conveys a decidedly duple feel. Particularly for audiences familiar with mhande, the resulting metric ambiguity of "Baba" is

Chembira Primary School's traditional dance ensemble performing mhande.
Courtesy of Deborah Chen.

both exciting and eminently danceable. As one person told me, "'Baba,' that one, it has this mhande thing in it, this cool flavor." As another said, "His mhande-based music is danceable, you see? You just jive to it."

Participatory Aesthetics and Interpretive Moves in Ngoma

Inherent in this last comment is the suggestion that Mtukudzi's relationship to mhande and other ngoma genres extends beyond their surface features, and to the participatory aesthetics at the very heart of ngoma performance. Indeed, whether listening to Tuku music on the radio in the thatched huts of Zimbabwe's rural areas or gathered at a live show in London, Mtukudzi's Zimbabwean listeners frequently engage in precisely the type of participatory behaviors associated with indigenous ngoma genres such as mhande, including responsorial singing, makwa handclapping, rhythmic dancing, mhururu ululation, and muridzo whistling.[49]

Partial transcription of Chembira Primary School's mhande performance.

As Mtukudzi performed "Baba" at Harare's Andy Miller Hall in 2008, for example, traditional dancers Isabel Nkawu and Lillian Mabika, of Bulawayo's Hloseni Arts, executed dance steps drawn from mhande, as well as the Ndebele ngoma genre of *amabhiza*, or "horses." At another performance in the rural town of Chimanimani, actress Chipo Chikara and neotraditional musician Godfrey Mambira enacted the song's condemnation of domestic violence. As Chikara cowered from Mambira's imaginary blows, their dramatic performance moved one man standing near them to cry out, "*Unokuvara iwe! Nengoma!*" This interjection—which translates to "You shall be injured! By the ngoma!"—neatly summed up the affective power not only of Mtukudzi's song

Partial transcription of Mtukudzi's song "Baba."

and of Chikara and Mambira's performance, but also of ngoma as a form of social critique.

   Alongside the relatively skilled participation of these trained musicians and
artists, ordinary audience members likewise engage in a wide variety of participatory behaviors. Like Chikara and Mambira, for example, they frequently greet
his songs with creative gestures. As Mtukudzi sings the lyrics to songs such as
"Ziva Nguva," or "Know the time" (*Vhunze Moto*, 2002), they tap their wrists,
as if gesturing to imaginary watches. As he performs "Kumbira," or "Request"
(*Mutorwa*, 1991), they engage in the ritualized clapping, known as *kuombera* or
kuuchira, that typically accompanies verbal requests among Shona speakers. As

he utters the well-known proverb *"Kukwira gomo / kupoterera,"* or "To climb a mountain / Is to circle around" in the lyrics to "Mutserendende," or "Sliding" (*Paivepo*, 1999), they raise their hands gradually in the air and circle them around.

Joining these mimetic gestures, listeners also engage with Mtukudzi's songs through specifically musical behaviors. Particularly when he plays pieces with the $\frac{12}{8}$ metric feel that is common to many ngoma genres, listeners often execute the same type of makwa handclapping patterns heard in ngoma genres such as mhande, and in other participatory musical practices such as mbira. Above these clapping patterns, men frequently interject the piercing, syncopated whistling known as muridzo, and women contribute the corresponding female expressive form of ululation, or mhururu. Finally, both genders engage in improvisatory, percussive footwork similar to the formal dance steps executed by skilled professionals such as Nkawu and Mabika.

The way audiences sing along to Tuku music, whether in live performances or while listening to recordings, further illustrates how listeners are engaged in making Mtukudzi's music their own. As might be expected, audiences often simply sing along with Mtukudzi and his backing vocalists. Yet almost as frequently, they depart from the script, taking advantage of music's social license to freely express things that may be prohibited in everyday speech. At a graduation ceremony for orphaned teenaged girls enrolled in a clinical trial in Harare's satellite city of Chitungwiza, for example, I observed a large group of girls formulate a decidedly insouciant response to "Baba." Using language that would be deemed utterly unacceptable in almost any other context, they replaced the song's portrayal of an abusive father with their own image of a husband overzealous in bedding his wife. Commenting on this phenomenon, one of their group leaders, Barbara Ncube, lamented the girls' response, even as she described it as a product of much larger social and economic pressures: "This has just started happening here. I don't know why. . . . Once they start, that's it [*ndiyo yacho*]! And you've got to face Zimbabwe's a stressed nation. And, things like that are, 'Oh, it's embarrassing [*zvinonyadzisira*]!' People laugh and before you know it, it becomes normal."

Shaping Music's Social Meaning through Participatory Listening

Taken as a whole, these creative forms of engagement with Tuku music reflect an aesthetics of listening that is profoundly participatory in nature, mirroring the dialogic nature of Mtukudzi's songs. No matter what form they take, these participatory behaviors serve to draw Mtukudzi's audiences further into his vivid musical imaginaries of hunhu. In the words of listener Lewis Madhlangobe, "If you listen, if you look at somebody, say, taking a small phrase and repeating it with Mtukudzi . . . go back and ask him. He will tell you, maybe it reminds him of his late mother, or it reminds him of a day when he was enjoying with some friends—that very moment, he will visit the old moments." In the wide range of participatory behaviors associated with Tuku music, we see with exceptional clarity how Mtukudzi's audiences seek to "project themselves into sounds."[50] In the process, they become involved both in shaping their relationship to Tuku music and in positioning themselves as listening subjects negotiating a series of dialogic musical encounters.

Critical in producing a sense of musical ownership, these participatory listening practices are an essential part of the way Mtukudzi's audiences have sought to redeploy his songs about hunhu in the context of their everyday lives. This is true whether listeners are quoting his music at a kitchen party or responding to crises of national governance. Turning back, for example, to Lewis Madhlangobe's account of singing "Shanje" for his school fees, we would do well to note that he was inspired to do so not simply by the song's lyrics, but rather by his memories of hearing his own mother sing it as a reflection of her personal situations. Reflecting on her experiences at live shows, Tafadzwa Muzhandu similarly connected participation to a sense of musical ownership, telling me, "You always find your songs and dance." As Mtukudzi's audiences symbolically inhabit his musical imaginaries of hunhu through participatory listening practices, they become actively engaged in shaping the social significance of his songs, enhancing their power as a collectively shared form of expressive culture.

"Mutavara"

Rova ngoma Mutavara we	Beat the drum, oh Mutavara
Ndonofire musango amai	Mother, I shall go die in the forest
Rova ngoma Mutavara	Beat the drum, Mutavara
Sango rinopa waneta chete	The forest gives once you are exhausted
Sara zvako Marunjeya we	Stay behind, oh Marunjeya
Ndonofire musango inini	I shall go die in the forest
Sara zvako Marunjata kani	Stay behind, oh Marunjata
Ndonofire musango inini	I shall go die in the forest
Ndonovhima ndonovhima	I will go and hunt, go and hunt
Ndonovhima musango dema	I will hunt in the dark forest

TWO

Performing the Nation's History

On a Saturday night in May 2008, shortly after the Harare International Festival of the Arts, the rich strains of Mtukudzi's tenor voice rang out in the cavernous hall of the Chitungwiza Aquatic Complex. A hulking cement structure built in 1995, the complex sits in the sprawling, high-density municipality of Chitungwiza, where over a million people reside just within commuting distance of Harare. One of Africa's premier swimming facilities, it once hosted world-class athletes, including Olympic gold-winner Kirsty Coventry. Yet it quickly underwent a startling decline, reflecting a more widespread collapse of the nation's infrastructure, from streetlights and roads to schools and hospitals. Filled with algae and litter, its Olympic-sized swimming pool now lay empty, ringed by tendrils of thorny vegetation.

In a nation where improvisation had increasingly become key to survival, however, the Aquatic Complex was anything but abandoned. Instead, it had been transformed into one of the largest indoor entertainment venues in the country, playing host to crowds of thousands who gathered to immerse themselves in the soaring melodies, intricate guitar work, showy choreography, and tight vocal harmonies fashioned by artists such as Alec Macheso, Leonard Zhakata, and Nicholas Zacharia. These superstars of *sungura*, a genre with roots in the rhumba music of Central and Eastern Africa, had captured a lion's share of the domestic music market in recent years.[1]

Capitalizing on the genre's popularity, Mtukudzi shared the bill at the Chitungwiza Aquatic Center with two sungura singers, Sulumani Chimbetu and Tongai Moyo. In order to ensure maximum turnout, the show was scheduled for the last Friday of the month, when the dwindling number of Zimbabweans employed in the formal sector received their paychecks. Indeed, several thousand audience members had converged for this performance despite the tough economic times. Together, they participated in a familiar process of alchemy, transforming part of their earnings into shared sociality through the collective consumption of both musical and alcoholic libations.[2] For many listeners, the last weekend of the month represented a sort of standing date with Mtukudzi. As one young professional described somewhat cheekily telling her mother, "Friday night at the end of the month, when Tuku is playing, don't expect me home."

A rare joint billing between three of the nation's top artists, this performance was bracketed, like so many other moments in Zimbabwe's history, by the untimely loss of one after another of the nation's most beloved musicians. Sulumani Chimbetu's father, the late Simon Chimbetu, was a member of Mtukudzi's generation who had pioneered a version of sungura he called *dendera*, or Southern Ground Hornbill, in reference to the bird's booming, lion-like call. While Chimbetu's death in 2005 was a major blow to sungura, Sulumani's tight vocal harmonies and energetic dance routines demonstrated that he was well-poised to further his father's musical legacy. Singer Tongai Moyo, on the other hand, had first encountered Mtukudzi during the mid-1990s, when both musicians lived in the small town of Kwekwe. Sadly, Moyo passed away less than three years after this triple billing at the Chitungwiza Aquatic Center, reportedly of non-Hodgkin's lymphoma.

At the least, for that moment, music lessened the sting of so much *nhamo*—the Shona word for suffering, poverty, and death. Grabbing a microphone, the MC introduced Mtukudzi with a phrase as memorable as it was incongruous in this distinctly urban environment. *"Ngatitsigise musha!"* (Let us strengthen our home!), he called out across the crowd, invoking a ritual known as *kutsigisa musha*, in which clay pots are filled with medicinal substances and buried at various entry points to the swept, earthen yard surrounding a rural home.[3] Clearly symbolic in a concrete hall filled with strangers, the phrase nevertheless retained significance in a society whose members regularly move between rural and urban realms. Taking to the stage, Mtukudzi followed this reference to the indigenous ritual of kutsigisa musha with his original musical arrangement of the Lord's Prayer, making historical entanglements of colonialism and missionization immediately palpable.

Moving through a series of increasingly up-tempo dance songs, the Black Spirits alternated between recent releases such as "Unaye," or "You've got him" (*Rudaviro*, 2011), and old favorites like "Baba," or "Father" (*Shoko*, 1993). Midway through the set, the crowd's excitement reached a peak as Mtukudzi's band launched into the song "Wasakara," or "You are worn out," (*Bvuma-Tolerance*, 2000), which Zimbabwean audiences have widely interpreted as a critique of ZANU-PF's seemingly endless rule, as discussed at length in chapter 5. As Mtukudzi sang the particularly suggestive line, "Growing old is a sign of the passage of a long time," one especially enthusiastic listener clambered up on stage and began rhythmically showering the singer with money. With studied nonchalance, he timed each bill perfectly to the music, until Mtukudzi was surrounded by a cascade of colorful notes fanning out around his feet.

This practice of "spraying" musicians with money, common across wide swaths of Sub-Saharan Africa, took on particular irony in Zimbabwe's hyperinflationary economy, with inflation raging at well over a million percent at the time of Mtukudzi's Chitungwiza performance.[4] Once a highly visible show of prestige, spraying was now within the reach of listeners on successively lower rungs of the socioeconomic ladder. Thanks to increasingly worthless denominations such as Zimbabwe's ten-million dollar note, valued at less than two American cents at the time, what appeared to be an ostentatious display of wealth could in fact require less than a single American dollar.

Transporting listeners far from these economic woes, the Black Spirits launched into the opening bars of a song called "Mutavara" (KDZ 109, 1977). An original arrangement of a ngoma song from Zimbabwe's rural northeast, Mtukudzi had first released "Mutavara" over twenty years prior to this performance, during the height of the nation's liberation struggle, or Chimurenga.

"Rova ngoma Mutavara!" Mtukudzi intoned—"Play the drum Mutavara!" Upon hearing these words, the throngs of listeners gathered in the cavernous hall let out a collective cheer. Perched high in the bleachers, one enthusiastic listener began slapping the air energetically, pulling a series of soundless notes out of an invisible drum.

"Hande!" Mtukudzi called out—"Let's go!" While common in everyday speech, this term also has specific musical meaning in ngoma performance, where it is immediately apprehended as a signal for dancers to transition between steps, much as a djembe break functions in West Africa. Reverberating across the stage, Mtukudzi's directive was immediately answered by the Black Spirits, who launched into an intensely rhythmic instrumental section.

"Hoyo!" backing singer Namatai Mubariki cried out from the front of the stage, initiating a series of escalating call-and-response interactions with the audience. Trading vocables back and forth, Mubariki and the crowd engaged in a musical exchange reminiscent both of the communal settings of indigenous Zimbabwean music, and of the mediated, secular contexts typical of Jamaican dancehall, or US rap.

Lifting their knees chest high, the members of the Black Spirits began a choreographed dance routine. Their tense stances and sharply defined movements recalled the distinctive Southern African protest dance called *toyi-toyi*, which drew its aesthetics from the military marching drills of Zimbabwe's Chimurenga war.[5] Raising the energy in the vast hall to almost electric levels, the momentum of their movements prompted the audience to dance with renewed vigor.

Mobilizing Ngoma Aesthetics in Popular Song

In this chapter, I chart Mtukudzi's rise to fame during the conflict-ridden years of Zimbabwe's liberation struggle, when "Mutavara" was first released. As I illustrate, Mtukudzi's early musical trajectory was shaped by various influences, from the American soul music of Otis Redding, Arthur Conley, and Wilson Pickett to the choral music of the Presbyterian church his family attended, and from the emerging style of mbira-guitar played by musicians such as Jordan Chataika to the popular songs of pioneering entertainer Safirio Madzikatire. Yet the most influential sound Mtukudzi encountered during this time was the ngoma music from his family's place of origin in Dande, located in the far reaches of the nation's rural northeast. As I will illustrate, northeastern ngoma genres such as katekwe are immediately audible in several of Mtukudzi's early songs, infusing Tuku music with a distinctive sonic aesthetic. Beyond ngoma's musical surface, I suggest that Mtukudzi also began mobilizing the dialogic aesthetics associated with this indigenous performance practice from the very beginning of his career. In this way, he both invited listeners to become actively engaged in deciphering the political meaning of his musical imaginaries during the last years of the liberation war and established an important precedent for later readings of his music.

The Early Years: 1952–1979

In the dusty township of Highfield, the hot, dry winds of September quickly grow wearing, their monotony broken only by the vibrant, purple blossoms of jacaranda trees bursting into bloom. Established in the 1930s, Highfield is located a good five miles south of Harare's city center, just past the light industrial areas lining Willowvale Road. As the first residential neighborhood in the capital open to black families, however, it was immediately endowed with prestige, offering an emerging African middle class an appealing alternative to the barrack-like hostels built for single male workers in nearby Harari township, now known as Mbare.

With its concentration of educated black elites, Highfield was home to many of the nation's most prominent figures, from musicians to politicians. At its center, Robert Mugabe's old home still stands riddled by bullet holes and guarded by soldiers, reminding residents of the days when Highfield served as what Thomas Turino has called the "cradle of Zimbabwean nationalism."[6] Laying claim to the township's proud past, Mugabe would continue to vote at Highfield's Mhofu Primary School, the screeching sirens and bristling automatic weaponry of his motorcade piercing the quiet hum of the township streets every few years on election day. Just a few blocks away from the Mugabe house is the bustling shopping center of Machipisa, with its famous Mushandira Pamwe Hotel, a prominent venue for many of the nation's top musical acts during the 1970s. Just across Main Street, a stone's throw away from Mushandira Pamwe, the solid walls and fading bleachers of Gwanzura Stadium have played host to innumerable political rallies over the decades. Here, musicians have regularly appeared onstage alongside politicians of various stripes—including ZANU's Mugabe, ZAPU's Joshua Nkomo, and the MDC's Morgan Tsvangirai—turning song into a potent form of political expression.[7]

On September 22, 1952, Oliver Mtukudzi had the great fortune to be born into the life of this vibrant township. From the beginning, he seemed predestined to sing; as his mother would later recall, even his birth cry sounded musical. Although the Mtukudzi family did not own a radio until the late 1960s, Oliver and his six younger siblings were raised in a home full of music. His parents, Jesca and Samson, were active members of the Highfield Presbyterian Church, and initially met at a church choir competition. At home, they regularly staged informal domestic singing competitions, enlisting the young Oliver and his siblings as judges. With his lovely tenor voice, Samson also sang semiprofessionally at local venues such as Harari township's Mai Musodzi Hall. Occasionally, he performed further afield, traveling as far as Bulawayo to sing alongside prominent acts such as the Cool Fours, an all-male vocal group.

Taking Up the Guitar: Safirio Madzikatire's Influence

Among Samson Mtukudzi's closest musical friends was Safirio "Mukadota" Madzikatire, who rehearsed at Highfield's Cyril Jennings Hall. A pioneering artist, the multitalented Madzikatire is most famous for his Shona language drama series *Mhuri YaVaMukadota*, or "The Mukadota Family." Yet Madzikatire was also a guitarist, vocalist, and songwriter whose influence proved critical in Mtukudzi's decision to take up the guitar:

> Well, first and foremost, my father had a friend who could play guitar, Safirio Madzikatire, who used to come home, and they used to sing together at home. And I fell in love with the guitar because that was the first instrument exposed to me. And I just loved the way he played it, but I was [too] young to play guitar. But I remember him coming home some of the weekends. You know, they would have fun with my dad and their friends. It wasn't Safirio Madzikatire's band. It was more like a collaboration thing they used to do. Safirio didn't have a band then. He was just a solo guitarist . . . and my father was a tenor. So they used to write songs, and Safirio would play the guitar and they would do their choreography, and so on.

While Madzikatire has largely languished in obscurity, his groundbreaking approach to musical theater significantly influenced the world of Zimbabwean popular culture. In response to his underappreciated legacy, Mtukudzi would release the song "Andinzwi," or "I don't understand" (*Ndega Zvangu*, 1997), which lauded Madzikatire as a "national hero" for his contributions to the Zimbabwean arts.

"Andinzwi"
(I don't understand)

Can anybody give an answer to my question?
Here?

What is a hero?

What does it take to be a hero?
A national hero?

Do you have to die to be a hero?
Then what is a hero?

To me Safirio Madzikatire is a hero
Our national hero

Yes I remember some of his lyrics in his plays
"Andinzwi"

That's a hero
What a hero, Mukadota

Why I came to write a song specifically about him is because when he died he didn't get the recognition that a nation should give to him. I consider him a national hero. And I wrote that song so that people go back and try to think about it. And I think the nation was behind that.

I picked on one single word to remind people of how significant Safirio was. And the word is supposed to be, "Handinzwe" but it was like, "Andinzwi." It came from one of his pieces. Definitely, if you leave your country, you will never forget the language. It's already in you. You'll always speak the language. But some people go there, and they stay two, three years out there. They come back and they can't speak Shona. He portrayed us as we go out there, and when we come back, we sort of give a picture that we can't speak our language anymore, because we have stayed two, three years out of the country.

I think he's a hero because I consider him the best actor, the best comedian. As a musician, well, I don't think it was his strength. His strength was in the acting and storytelling, in portraying a Zimbabwean character. You could tell, "This is us, really, this is who we are. This is what we are." He got his stories from the people, the way we live every day. His songs were full of comedy, and his stories were full of comedy, but factual. You would laugh, but you would be educated.

—*Oliver Mtukudzi*

Born in the Makoni District of Rusape, Safirio Madzikatire grew up in Salisbury's first urban black township, Harari, located just north of Highfield along Simon Mazorodze Road.[8] Madzikatire learned the guitar as a teenager, developing a style of solo performance that paired narrative song texts with a relatively simple style of guitar playing.[9] After working a series of odd jobs—from carpenter to dental assistant—he formed his first musical group, the Ocean City Band, in the early 1960s. Soon, Madzikatire struck up a partnership with Lever Brothers, which paid him to perform around the country in order to promote its products. Strengthening his association with Lever Brothers' brands, Madzikatire even renamed his group the Surf Band, after the popular laundry detergent.[10] Enabling him to devote himself to music on a full-time basis, this corporate patronage placed Madzikatire among Zimbabwe's very earliest professional entertainers, and his were among the first African popular songs to be recorded in colonial Rhodesia.[11]

Theatrical from the start, Madzikatire's early songs were frequently accompanied by humorous banter. As Mtukudzi recalled, "His songs were full of comedy, and his stories were full of comedy, but factual. . . . You would laugh, but you would be educated. You would learn, 'Oh, so life can be sour, eh? You can have no one else to blame but yourself in life, if you go the wrong route.' And you could learn from him." Over time, Madzikatire would develop this theatrical element into the Shona drama series *Mhuri YaVaMukadota*. Also sponsored by Lever Brothers, the show was broadcast almost continuously from the late 1960s to the early 1980s, first on radio and later on television; throughout the 1970s, it would prove one of the Rhodesian Broadcasting Service's most popular radio programs.[12] In it, Madzikatire played the role of a deliberately stereotyped rural patriarch, both cunning and clumsy.[13] As Mtukudzi explained: "Mukadota means someone who's always getting things from—what do you call it? You know ashes, when you have a fire? *Rota*, that is to say ashes . . . it's somebody who is always—either he's burning a sweet potato, or he's roasting a piece of meat. Someone who's always close by, close to the fire." Established an archetype that has greatly influenced subsequent Shona drama, this typecasting was essential in enabling Madzikatire to stage the entanglements of modern Zimbabwean life.[14] As Mtukudzi observed,

> His strength was in the acting and storytelling, portraying a Zimbabwean national character. . . . Safirio Madzikatire was that kind of person who covered who we are, who covered what we should be, who was open about what wrong we do. He was that kind of person, and his art really played the role of an artist. And his shows were always packed up, despite what kind of political affiliation or religion you take. You would find everybody

in his shows. Why? Because he was a people's person. He represented who
we are. He talked about what we should be, what we are. And I learned a
lot out of that.

Returning us to the social relations of hunhu, Mtukudzi suggests that Madzikatire's primary value as an artist lay in his ability to convey stories rooted in
the textures of ordinary life, yet which listeners interpreted as having much
larger social significance. Through his humorous musical storytelling, Madzikatire would profoundly influence not only Mtukudzi's decision to take up the
guitar, but also his approach to singing about social relations.

Learning in Secret

Despite his ties to professional entertainers such as Madzikatire, Samson Mtukudzi harbored serious concerns about the young Oliver's desire to become a
musician. After moving to Harare from the rural area of Madziva, Samson had
worked as a gardener until his white employer, noting how capable he was, encouraged him to transfer to the busy auto garage he owned in town. As Mtukudzi related, "He started making tea in the garage, and three, four months later,
he was in the spares filing room, filing all the spares and so on. He specialized
in spares." Like rural to urban migrants throughout the world, Samson found
himself obliged to combine this salaried job with informal labor, working as a
shoemaker in his spare time.

Struggling to support his family through these multiple survival strategies,
Samson Mtukudzi was acutely aware how little income musical performance
brought in:

He had the inside information that music doesn't pay, 'cause he never got
paid. So he knew very well that if I'm going to go into music, then I'm not
gonna survive. That was his belief, 'cause he actually experienced it. So he
was even more against it, even though part of him would enjoy seeing me
doing something, but not to take it as a profession. So my situation was
even worse than those who had parents who had never been in music.
'Cause those ones, they were just using the assumption that you can't survive through this. But my father actually didn't survive from it. So he knew
what he was talking about. You see? So he was like, "No you can't."

So determined was Samson to distract his son from playing music that he created
a position for him at the auto garage. As Oliver's wages were deducted directly
from his father's salary, however, the job ultimately proved unsustainable, leading the young Mtukudzi to seek work elsewhere.[15]

Much to his father's satisfaction, Mtukudzi soon found temporary employment at Philport and Collins, a stationary shop in the city center. Ironically, this

was the very job that enabled him to pursue his musical ambitions. As Mtukudzi recounted:

> As I browsed around in the shop, I noticed this little book that was called
> "It's Easy to Play the Guitar." It was going for nine cents. And I bought
> that book. That inspired me to look for a guitar. It just talked about three
> chords, G, C, and D. And as I got paid for four or five weeks, I bought my
> guitar. . . . It had a crooked bar, but I could afford that. So I bought that
> one. And fortunately this little book taught me how to tune the guitar, and
> have my first key, second key. And by the time I learned the second key,
> which was C, I was already composing songs in those two keys [G and C].

Although the book enabled him to master these basics, Mtukudzi was unable to
read either staff notation or tablature. Instead, he taught himself to play largely
by ear, painstakingly seeking out the right notes on his guitar as he listened to
recordings of early Zimbabwean solo guitarists such as Jordan Chataika and
Ngwaru Mapundu: "At times I could listen to Jordan Chataika's song. I would
find the notes, but I wouldn't know whether they were C or G. I didn't know. But
as long as I brought [out] that sound, I was happy. So, I got to know other keys,
like E, B, and so on. But I didn't even know what they were called. . . . I played
by ear, just looking for the note somewhere." By copying the playing of Chataika and other acoustic guitarists, Mtukudzi assimilated a number of elements
common to an emerging Zimbabwean guitar style, which featured interlocking
melodies, prominent ostinato figures, and a tendency toward structures based
in repeating cycles of two or four phrases.[16]

   While Mtukudzi's skill as a guitarist was improving rapidly, however, his father's opposition remained unchanged. Seeking to hide his musical ambitions,
Mtukudzi stored his guitar at a sympathetic neighbor's house, where he practiced
in secret. Far from marking Mtukudzi as a self-taught musical outsider, however,
this type of secretive learning is a widely reported phenomenon among Zimbabwean musicians.[17] Well documented in the life histories of mbira dzavadzimu
players, this trope likewise extends to other popular guitarists, emphasizing how
self-directed learning is particularly valued as a method of Shona musical transmission. Indeed, Mtukudzi's late son Samson would himself describe learning
to play the guitar in a strikingly similar way.

Breaking through: The Wagon Wheels

Finally, the young Oliver Mtukudzi was discovered "sitting on a dust bin and
playing traditional melodies" by talent scout and radio personality Brighton
Matewere.[18] Thanks to Matewere, Mtukudzi recorded his first songs at the
headquarters of the Rhodesian Broadcasting Corporation, located in Harari

Sam Mtukudzi on Learning to Play Guitar

I think I was about ten, I was asked to play guitar at my primary school's Christmas carols concert night. I had been learning how to play this instrument for like five years, you know? And now I was ready to do performances. I had been performing in small chapel services back at the primary school. So, you know, my headmistress and the music people there knew that I could play guitar. So when this concert came up, they asked me, "Can you use your instrument?" I didn't officially have an instrument. You know, I just used to pinch my dad's guitar that he just used to always leave at home. So, I asked for transport from the school. So they actually gave me the school's minibus. We went off to the house, took that guitar and a little amplifier—just a little combo—loaded it up, went to school.

In about a week from then—you know, my dad had been out, so he had just come back. Well, I didn't know that the school had sent invites to the parents back at home for all the boarders! So, my parents got their invite. So . . . they came to the concert. We played. It was beautiful. When my time came to actually do my ultimate performance, I hadn't seen my parents or anything. So, I stand up there, and then I play. When I'm done with the performance, I'm taking a bow and I'm thinking, "That guy looks like my father. And oops, the woman who's sitting beside him looks like my mom!" You know, I walked backstage, and, I'm there and I'm thinking, "What if it is?" You know? "What if it is them?" And everyone is clapping, clapping, and it was the last song.

We get dismissed, we go outside, and you know, there I am, I'm carrying my stuff back to the dorm. And I'm bumping into my dad, thinking, "Hi dude." And he actually didn't react in any negative way. He was quite surprised. He was thinking, when did I start learning? How did I get there? I mean, I was playing and singing at the same time! How did it happen? You know? So he's like, "No, no, well done, well done, well done. Since you didn't have a guitar, that one's now yours." And I was like, "Whew! Thank you! Thank you!" I was really happy. That was my first instrument, and, you know, it was an honor to have.

—*Sam Mtukudzi*

Sam Mtukudzi. *Courtesy of Mary Cairns.*

township.[19] While these early radio recordings were never released commercially, they were broadcast to a wide audience throughout the country, paving the way for Mtukudzi's first commercial recording, a seven-inch single released in 1976. Featuring Mtukudzi and his sister Bybit performing "The Only Two" and "Pezuma" as vocal duets, the record proved a commercial failure. As Mtukudzi recalled many years later, "my duet seven singles didn't do well. And people thought, 'Ah, you should do it with a band. It's too shallow, you need it.'"

Indeed, Mtukudzi's musical fortunes dramatically improved when he joined an emerging group called the Wagon Wheels later that year. The Wagon Wheels featured a number of well-known artists, including Susan and Jane Chenjerai, who had previously worked with Safirio Madzikatire. The group's lead vocalist, Thomas Mapfumo, was also well on his way to becoming a legendary Zimbabwean singer. At a time when most local groups were still playing covers of American pop songs, referred to by Zimbabwean musicians as "copyrights," Mapfumo had begun writing his own songs based in contemporary orchestrations of traditional Shona music, making a definitive break from copyright playing. While Mapfumo left the Wagon Wheels less than a year later, his approach to arranging indigenous songs had a lasting influence on Mtukudzi, who likewise became determined to develop his own original musical style.

Shortly after Mapfumo's departure, Mtukudzi recorded his first single with the Wagon Wheels, titled "Dzandimomotera," or "Troubles have surrounded me" (POP 24, 1977).[20] With a driving, upbeat quality, "Dzandimomotera" shared a common hi-hat pattern with many other Shona popular songs, which emphasized the offbeat of each triplet grouping within a $\frac{12}{8}$ metric framework. Set off by this highly danceable groove, its lyrical appeals for deliverance reflected Mtukudzi's Presbyterian roots and earned him the moniker of "Protestant singer."[21] Released in 1977 by the Harari Special label, a subsidiary of the South African recording label Gallo, "Dzandimomotera" quickly went gold. Breaking all existing records, it stayed on the hit parade for eleven weeks. As Mtukudzi recalled, the royalties he received for "Dzandimomotera" finally changed his father's mind about his decision to become a professional musician:

> When I had my first royalties—I remember they were eight hundred dollars—I took the check to my father. And I said, "Dad, you hear the song you hear on the radio? This is my pay." And, that was a payment after three months. Eight hundred dollars. And he couldn't earn that much. You see? He couldn't believe me, to the extent that he took the check back to Gallo, to actually understand—"Has he not played anything, is this real?" Just to confirm. So, he did that. And I do understand that he did that because he was so concerned about me. So, he was told, "No, this is his own money.

It's got nothing to do with the band members. It's his money on his own. The band has been paid." Then he started understanding that, "OK, our time was different. Things have changed. He can actually make a living out of this."

Mtukudzi's smash hit also attracted the attention of legendary South African producer West Nkosi, one of the most influential figures in South African music history. Nkosi quickly began working with Mtukudzi, lending what one local journalist described as "a distinct South African touch to Mtukudzi's first recordings."[22] In his dealings with South African musicians such as Mahlathini and the Mahotella Queens, Nkosi was often highly interventionist, determining every aspect of the musical recording. At least in hindsight, however, Mtukudzi reported maintaining a significant degree of artistic freedom in his dealings with Nkosi: "He was good in quality recording. But directing us wherever we should go, no, he didn't do that. He was interested, he loved what we did. So, he never used to make us change what he would do. He would suggest a few things here and there, but the ultimate decision was ours." Occasionally, Nkosi would bring in instrumental tracks laid down by session musicians in South Africa, and ask Mtukudzi to lay down original vocal lines. Yet Mtukudzi's biggest early hits were a series of seven-inch singles inflected with the sounds of indigenous music, including songs such as "Ziwere" (KDZ 115, 1977), "Gunguwo" (KDZ 118, 1978), and "Mutavara" (KDZ 109, 1977).

"Bganyamakaka"

While Mtukudzi's career began in the dusty streets of the nation's urban townships, his family maintained close ties with their village in Madziva, located in one of several areas designated by the Rhodesian government for black occupation as "tribal trust lands." Reflecting a rural-urban interface typical of the Zimbabwean experience, Mtukudzi frequently spent school holidays in the rural areas with his grandparents.[23] Yet his father also sang songs from the village at home in Highfield. As Mtukudzi recalls: "I didn't even have to go out to the rural areas to listen to that. It was played in our home. My father, with his friends, they used to play that at home . . . ngoma, whatever, guitars. My father used to do that at home. So, that was the first inspiration. Over school holidays, when I went to the rural areas to get the real thing, it wasn't anything new. It's something that I always listened to at home." By the 1970s, Mtukudzi had begun incorporating this music in his own songs. These included several original pieces that invoked elements of indigenous drumming genres, including a driving, danceable $\frac{12}{8}$ metric framework, call-and-response vocal lines, and cyclical song forms. Others tracks, such as "Mutavara," were Mtukudzi's own creative interpretations of indigenous ngoma songs.

The Early Days with West Nkosi

I was here from the beginning, when all the local music was starting, including the South African music that was coming toward
Zimbabwe. I started working for Gallo Records in 1975. Earlier,
people were just doing copyrights and so forth, but artists were
now getting involved in their own compositions.

And Oliver, he was engaged by a producer from South Africa,
West Nkosi. We actually talent scouted for him, for the groups.
He would then come all the way from South Africa. We recorded
in the studios in Zimbabwe, and then he would take the mas-
ters, and go to South Africa to remix and do all the mastering.
We didn't have cutting lathes at that moment, so they would cut
it in South Africa and send us a copy, send us stampers. Then we
would press in Zimbabwe.

At that stage, it was only a four-track machine that we used.
Can you imagine a four-track machine with Oliver's vocals and
backing vocals, bass guitar, rhythm guitar, lead, and keyboards,
and drums?

—*Timon Mabaleka, Zimbabwe Music Company*

Among them was his arrangement of "Bganyamakaka" (KDZ 114, 1977).
As mbira player Sekuru Tute Wincil Chigamba explains, the lyrics to "Bganyamakaka" are widely sung throughout Zimbabwe's northern regions, where they
are accompanied by various related drumming styles. In the eastern region of
Chiweshe, for example, "Bganyamakaka" would be considered part of the ngoma
genre known as dandanda. Further west, in Guruve, it would be called mangwingwindo, while in Hurungwe, it would be considered dinhe. As Chigamba
says, "On the ngoma, some call it dandanda, others say mangwingwindo, and
others say dinhe, but it is the same ngoma. It depends on the area where people
live. . . . But it is the same ngoma. When they sing, they sing the same way, and
the ngoma is played the same way. There's no difference."

Drawing on music's privileged position as a form of social criticism, "Bganyamakaka" exemplifies how the moral authority of ngoma empowers performers
to comment upon human relations.[24] In the words of Sekuru Chigamba, songs
such as "Bganyamakaka" constitute socially sanctioned responses to abuses

of power, enabling ngoma performers to express criticism while adhering to the moral values of hunhu, such as tolerance, dialogue, and mutual respect: "It comes from the song, as it is being sung. . . . They won't want to come out into the open and tell you what you have done. Instead they sing you a song. 'You, elder, you are excessive, elder, you are a bwanyamakaka [*sic*].' So you will realize, 'Oh,' I've made a mistake here, haven't I?'. . . . So, our songs, they speak, they teach. For the most part they teach, and they reprimand." As we shall see in subsequent chapters, the implications of this approach extend well beyond the late colonial period and into independence, offering audiences a way to navigate changing social relations and emerging struggles for power.

Released in 1977 as a seven-inch single, Mtukudzi's rendition of "Bganyamakaka" articulates the traditional rhythmic sensibilities of related drumming styles such as dandanda, mangwingwindo, and dinhe through a fast triplet pattern played on the hi-hat.[25] As in other early recordings, Mtukudzi's voice is heavily foregrounded in the mix, weighting the song with his sonic presence. Creating syncopated rhythms that play off the song's $\frac{12}{8}$ metric framework, Mtukudzi alternates between extended sections of vocables and a single verse of text, which he sings in call-and-response fashion with his male backing vocalists:

Ndiwe mukuru	You are an elder
Honde	*Honde*
Mukuru	An elder
Bganyamakaka	A short-tempered, unresponsive individual

Soon after it begins, the song is momentarily disrupted by the sound of high-pitched, threatening laughter, a sonic index of the type of daunting authority figure described in its lyrics.

Performing in a Nation at War

At the time "Bganyamakaka" was released, the Rhodesian settler state was convulsed by the African nationalist struggle. In a desperate attempt to stay in power, the Rhodesian government, led by Prime Minister Ian Smith, had seceded from the British Empire in 1965, ratifying a Unilateral Declaration of Independence in order to thwart British intentions to enact a peaceful transition to majority rule. Yet there was no stopping the rising tide of black nationalism. By the late 1960s, both ZAPU and ZANU were fronting active military branches, training civilians of all stripes in guerilla tactics designed to destabilize the Rhodesian regime. ZAPU called its military wing the Zimbabwe People's Revolutionary Army (ZIPRA), while ZANU named its armed unit the Zimbabwe African National Liberation Army (ZANLA). Soon the nation was engulfed by a full-fledged guerilla war, waged largely in rural districts where ZIPRA and ZANLA forces could both exploit the dense bush for cover and depend on the support of local villagers, whether offered willingly or elicited under duress.

Wartime conditions in the late 1970s were dangerous for musicians, whose incomes came largely from touring the country, an enterprise made difficult by petrol shortages, landmines, travel restrictions, and the escalating violence of the Chimurenga struggle. Frequently, the Black Spirits' extended tours took them to the remote reaches of the nation, where encounters between the freedom fighters and the Rhodesian army were at their peak. When performing in especially hot conflict zones, Mtukudzi and his brother Rob would often hide the extent of their travels from their parents. On one occasion, when the brothers were scheduled to play in a series of small towns ringing the country's conflict-ridden eastern border with Mozambique, they told their parents only that they were going as far as the city of Mutare, which was considered relatively safe: "Okay, fine, Mutare is no problem. But passing from Mutare to Birchenough Bridge, to Chimanimani, to Chipinge, to Checheche, and those places, he! If we tell the parents, do you think we'll go? So we all never used to tell our parents where we are going. We will tell them some close-by places where they think, 'Ah, they can make it and come back,' you know?" Whenever their mother, Jesca, discovered their actual itinerary, she responded by hiding their amplifiers and instruments in an attempt to prevent her sons from leaving the safety of the capital, desperate to keep them from harm.[26]

On the road, the Black Spirits navigated encounters both with the Rhodesian army and with ZIPRA and ZANLA forces. Once, traveling on a dirt track through the bush between the small towns of Shurugwi and Zvishavane, Mtukudzi and his band stumbled upon an army roadblock. Taking them for potential guerillas, the suspicious Rhodesian soldiers manning the roadblock demanded that they perform several American popular songs in order to prove that they were really musicians. Mtukudzi described feeling incredibly "lucky that they picked on songs we knew." As he told me:

> They would ask songs from Western countries, songs that one might not even know even if you are a musician. . . . They said, "Right, if you're musicians, can you play 'Hey Joe?' Who played 'Hey Joe?'" And we said, "Oh, its Jimi Hendrix." They said, "Play the song." And our bass guitarist would take the bass and play, and they would listen. And they say, "Okay, alright. Can you sing a song by Otis Redding?" Picking on anyone in the band. And we would sing. And they finally let us go, because they had found that, oh, we are truly musicians. Cause every question they asked, we were able to answer.

On other occasions, the Black Spirits encountered groups of freedom fighters who demanded articles of clothing and shoes—essential items for blending in with the civilian population in order to evade security forces. At one rural performance, also in Zvishavane, a group of freedom fighters even surreptitiously entered the hall where Mtukudzi was performing in order to hear him sing. As outsiders in this small, rural community, the Black Spirits were unaware of the guerillas in their midst until, as Mtukudzi recalled, unnerved audiences members "just stood up, one by one, going out and going home. . . . We are busy jamming, and people who have paid their money to watch us are not complaining, but they are just going before the show had even reached its peak."

Reflecting his view of the musician as sahwira to the nation, Mtukudzi saw performing as a serious responsibility for popular artists, whose songs offered consolation to a civilian population struggling with the violence, trauma, and displacement of the liberation struggle:

> A lot of artists, a lot of musicians served their purpose during war. Even those who didn't go further out, like we did, they did well in the cities too. . . . I truly believed, if we don't go and de-stress those people, who's going to do it? Are these people just going to stay in war, war, war? We have to go there and perform for them. So it wasn't going there for pleasure—it was part of war. And I truly believe that's the way I fought war for liberation in Zimbabwe. I fought it by my microphone, and my guitar.

Mtukudzi's songs offered more than simply solace, however, for his musical imaginaries of hunhu could also be interpreted as conveying oblique messages of support for the guerillas. Released in 1977, Mtukudzi's second single with the Wagon Wheels, "Mutavara" (KDZ 109) would exemplify this marriage between popular music and political consciousness.

Beat the Drum, Mutavara

"Mutavara" is Mtukudzi's arrangement of a song from the ngoma genre known as katekwe, which is unique to his family's place of origin in Dande, located in Zimbabwe's rural northeast.[27] As in other ngoma-based songs such as "Baba" and "Bganyamakaka," certain elements of katekwe, such as its call-and-response form and heavy reliance on sung syllables, or vocables, remained audible in Mtukudzi's popular arrangement of "Mutavara." Yet he dramatically reinterpreted many of the song's original characteristics. Most significantly, Mtukudzi's rendition replaced the distinctive triplet groupings of katekwe with a duple feel, in what might be described in Western musical terminology as a move from $\frac{12}{8}$ to $\frac{4}{4}$ time. Describing this metric shift, Chaka Chawasarira, who plays the matepe mbira indigenous to Zimbabwe's rural northeast, observed that Mtukudzi's version of the song seems to unfold in "slow motion. Katekwe is fast, it's fast-moving . . . but he's singing it in a different way."

Borne aloft by the repeating ostinato of its guitar lines, the minimalist lyrics of "Mutavara" exemplify how Mtukudzi's musical imaginaries were freighted with symbolic meaning for wartime audiences.[28] Within the context of the liberation struggle, for example, the song's imagery of a solitary hunter entering the wilderness of the bush could easily be read as "a subtle call for the youth to go and fight against the minority government of Ian Smith," in the words of local journalist Percy Zvomuya.[29] As Mtukudzi told me, this interpretation was logical given the context in which "Mutavara" was first released:

> It was during war. It's a song that I wrote to inspire people to go out there and fight . . . from wherever they are. And if you translate it literally, it's a very shallow song, it's got nothing serious. But if you take the idea of what we were saying then, it made sense then. "*Rova ngoma Mutavara, sango rinopa waneta* [Beat the drum Mutavara, the forest gives once you are tired]," it's, "Go and fight. And if you are in a bush or in a forest, and you're hunting, it's not easy to just get your prey. You fight hard to get whatever you want to get there. So, fight on, fight on. The time you are tired is the right time to get something. That's the time to get something. So, if you're not yet tired, you haven't done anything. So fight on, fight on." Yeah. That was the sense of the song.

Owners of the Land

For listeners familiar with the geography and history of Zimbabwe's rural northeast, the song's title carried even more symbolic weight, for the word *Mutavara* refers to a member of the Tavara people, descended from a collection of dynasties that once ruled the Zambezi Valley. As the area's original inhabitants, or autochthons, the Tavara have maintained what anthropologist David Lan calls "special ritual intimacy with the territory they occupy."[30] This relationship is manifest particularly in the ability of the Tavara ancestral spirits to provide rain, the source of all fertility. The next group of people to settle in the Zambezi Valley, known as the Korekore, would continue to recognize the Tavara as the true owners of the land. This relationship was also reflected in the spirit world, where the Korekore senior guardian spirits, or mhondoro, deferred to the senior spirits of the Tavara.[31]

The armed struggle of Chimurenga came early to the Zambezi Valley, with ZANLA guerillas entering the area in 1971.[32] In the context of the liberation war, questions regarding who should be regarded as true owners of the land appeared especially urgent.[33] As a Korekore speaker, Mtukudzi was particularly well-positioned to draw upon the symbolic meanings of *Mutavara*, linking his song firmly to the struggle. As he explained: "I wouldn't say, 'Boys in the bush, please fight on.' You wouldn't say that. So, because the war was in the Matavara area . . . I decided to use the clan that's there, and it would translate to those people fighting from that area. Never mind you're not a Mutavara, but, 'Play the drum Mutavara,' they would understand that—'Oh, it's us, cause we are in the Tavara region.' You see?" A powerful assertion of indigenous sovereignty, Mtukudzi's invocation of the Tavara as the legitimate owners of the Zambezi Valley metonymically suggested that the nation as a whole should be wrested away from the settler regime of Ian Smith's Rhodesia and restored to its rightful inhabitants.

David Lan has observed that "ideas about political authority are expressed in terms of 'ownership of the land,'" making the rural northeast into a palimpsest of successive lineages of autochthons and conquerors, each wielding different degrees of power.[34] In the lyrics to "Mutavara," we see how popular music participated in turning this type of locally specific argument about political ownership into a collectively shared form of expressive culture in the context of the liberation war. Summoning an entire set of associations between land and people, Mtukudzi's invocation of the local geography of Zimbabwe's rural northeast foregrounded his own musical and social identity as a Korekore speaker. At the same time, "Mutavara" symbolically extended the social relations of Dande to an entire nation of listeners, creating space for audiences to perceive themselves as belonging to an imagined world of social relations where local and national identities, cosmologies, and histories intermingled in song.

Controversy over Authorship

Describing "Mutavara" as "a traditional song, which was communally owned by the Kore Kore [sic] people," Mtukudzi has observed that neither he, nor anyone else "can claim to have written the song."[35] Yet Thomas Mapfumo, his musical contemporary and oft-competitor, has sometimes claimed credit for arranging "Mutavara," pointing to the complex politics that arise when collectively owned oral repertoires are brought into a commercial sphere. Mtukudzi has readily acknowledged that listening to Mapfumo's early hits, such as "Ngoma Yarira," or "The drums have sounded" (AS 105, 1974), was a musical revelation that inspired him to write original songs of his own:

He did one of my favorite songs, "Yarira nehosho" . . . When I heard that on the radio—*Yarira nehosho, yarira vakomana we, yarira* [The hosho have sounded, they have sounded boys, they have has sounded]"—I said, "Ah, wow! I was right in the first place when I was doing my own music. I think this guy is in the right direction. Why am I concentrating on this copyright? No, I'm doing my own now." I admired him for that. . . . He was doing it in our own mother language, and . . . each time I listened to his song, I could feel, "This is us. This is what we are supposed to be."

While the two artists used to sing "Mutavara" together on stage during their joint tenure with the Wagon Wheels, Mtukudzi has denied that Mapfumo played a direct role in arranging the song. As he told the local press, "I did not write the song 'Mutavara,' but rather did the most popular rendition initially in 1977. . . . I wrote it to inspire our freedom fighters, to inspire them during the height of the liberation struggle."[36]

Claiming Indigenous Sounds: The Politics of Musical Borrowing and Commodification

Even more important than resolving questions over the song's ownership, however, is recognizing how these claims and counterclaims are emblematic of larger concerns about musical circulation during the late twentieth century, as global flows of capital, people, and ideas rapidly intensified.[37] As songs such as "Mutavara" became caught up with new recording technologies, their musical identities were projected into national and transnational space. In the process, long-standing conceptions of music as an inalienable, collectively shared form of cultural expression collided with capitalist notions of individual ownership and copyright law. Mtukudzi's arrangement of "Mutavara" is one of many examples of the complex politics of musical borrowing, appropriation, and reinvention under late capitalism, from Herbie Hancock's recreation of BaAka hindewhu music in "Watermelon Man" (*Takin' Off*, 1962) to Paul Simon's collaboration with South African musicians on his album *Graceland* (1986).[38]

Seeking to understand these interactions, music scholars have proposed various theoretical frameworks, ranging from celebratory views of globalization to anxious narratives of musical appropriation.[39] As we continue to evaluate the impact of these debates on current musical scholarship, I suggest that late twentieth century musical encounters might be most productively viewed through the lens of musical entanglement. As used by anthropologists such as Jean and John Comaroff, the concept of entanglement offers a way to think about prolonged encounters between different social groups, each of which holds varying degrees of power. Highlighting the complexity of these interactions, it calls our attention to the multiplicity, paradox, contradiction, tension, and ambiguity inherent even in seemingly stable or hegemonic systems, such as colonization or imperialism. As a result, it is able to accommodate both celebratory and anxious discourses, enabling us to better understand how the social and musical histories of songs such as "Mutavara" are carved out of what the Comaroffs have called "the dialectics of exchange, appropriation, accommodation, struggle."[40]

Listening to "Trad": Popular Music and Indigenous Sounds in the 1970s

In her work in South Africa, ethnomusicologist Carol Muller has argued that song composition can offer "a mechanism for archival deposit, care, and retrieval in contexts of immanent loss."[41] By invoking ngoma genres such as katekwe, songs such as "Mutavara" offered listeners what Muller calls "a contemporary space for repertorial renewal and public display," exploiting productive tensions between Zimbabwe's political and economic center and its peripheries, as well as between the present and the past.[42] Absorbing audiences within a palimpsest comprised of what postcolonial scholar Achille Mbembe has described as interlocking "presents, pasts, and futures, each age bearing, altering, and maintaining the previous ones," these songs emphasized the contemporaneity of indigenous and popular musical forms.[43] Offering listeners a musical experience of what Mbembe calls "time as lived," Tuku music challenges us to recognize that indigenous as well as popular performance practices constitute contemporary modes of expression located firmly in the present, rather than in a timeless past.[44]

During the final years of Rhodesian rule, local musicians increasingly joined Mtukudzi in turning away from performing English-language copyrights in order to experiment with commercially mediated arrangements of indigenous songs such as "Bganyamakaka" and "Mutavara." Known as "traditional music," or simply "trad," their approach foregrounded a range of ideas, themes, and expressions drawn from traditional idioms, customs, proverbs, and stories.[45] The new trad sound featured melodic and rhythmic motifs from indigenous song repertories, as well as lyrics in local languages such as Shona and Ndebele. Yet trad music also incorporated influences from further afield, such as electric guitars, European studio recording technologies, and elements of South African popular music such as *kwela* and mbaqanga. Deeply tied to emergent social identities, the syncretic nature of trad music challenged local audiences to make sense of its diverse strands of origin. In 1978, for example, one anonymous author would describe trad music as "the now popular African-cum-pop-jazz sound emanating from Rhodesia."[46] By the late 1970s, the nation's capital was alive with the vibrant sound of dozens of emerging trad groups.[47] Reviewing an "Afro Music Concert" held at the Skyline Motel in late 1977, for example, journalist Alf Muronda listed a number of groups with colorful names, including Jam-Jam, the Co-Axies, the Acid Band, and M'punzwana, as well as the Wagon Wheels.[48]

Indigenous Aesthetics and Popular Sounds

Reflecting the rise of trad's new musical aesthetic, even Mtukudzi's original songs clearly foregrounded indigenous musical influences and themes. Among them, Shona vocables—sung syllables with no strictly lexical meaning, which might be compared to scat singing in American jazz—featured prominently in many of his early songs, enabling Mtukudzi to craft virtuosic vocal improvisations laden with emotion. Vocable singing also facilitated complex rhythmic syncopation, transforming Mtukudzi's voice into an instrument that was simultaneously percussive and melodic.

Mtukudzi's early lyrics also exemplified his unique mastery of the Shona register known as *tsumo nemadimikira*, or "proverbs and allusive speech." The lyrics of his song "Kugarika" (KDZ 130, 1979), for example, revolved almost entirely around two proverbs, *"Raive dziva / Rave zambuko"* or "What were once deep pools are now crossing places," and *"Kugarika / Tange nhamo,"* or "Ease follows hardship," interspersed with passages of vocables sung by Mtukudzi's female backing vocalists. Similarly, the text of "Gudo Guru" (KDZ 132, 1979) was based on the proverb *"Gudo guru peta muswe / Vapwere vagokuremekedza,"* or "Big baboon, tuck your tail between your legs so that smaller ones will respect you."[49]

In addition to incorporating proverbs and vocables, Mtukudzi's early lyrics heavily emphasized indigenous lifeways, or *magariro*. Extending many of the themes present in "Mutavara," for example, he continued to sing about the nation's remote rural northeast in songs such as "Pamusoroi" (KDZ 118, 1978), which refers directly to his family's origins in Dande, as well as his ancestral lineage, the Nzou Samanyanga clan. Yet other songs, such as "Zivai Nemwoyo" (KDZ 114, 1977), approached questions of lineage, origins, and ancestors from a more universal perspective:

Midzimu yedu yaiziva Mwari vakomana	Our ancestors knew God
Midzimu yedu yaikudza amai aiwaiwaiwa	Our ancestors respected their mothers, oh
Madzitateguru yedu yaive nemitemo yakaoma	Our forefathers kept stringent laws
Isu nhasi tava kutyora mitemo yavo kani	Now, today, we are breaking their laws

Contesting Musical Fusion: Debating the New Trad Sound

By 1983, Mtukudzi had released enough hit singles to put together a compilation album called *Greatest Hits of Early Music (Traditional)*, the very title of which served to further reinforce his connection to trad music. Yet even as trad proved increasingly commercially successful, its rising prominence prompted impassioned debates about the relative merits of fusing indigenous and Western musical elements. In popular publications such as the monthly *Prize Magazine*, for example, letters to the editor remind us that readers were also listeners, who were often intensely invested in evaluating emerging musical styles such as trad.

Writing from Bulawayo's Makokoba township, for example, *Prize* reader Jazzmore Magirazi praised Mtukudzi as one of his favorite artists, and lauded trad's rediscovery of indigenous musical sounds: "May I extend my sincere thanks to all the great guys on the music scene who have done so much to keep us entertained over the past year. It is really pleasing to see our musicians taking pride in their identity as Black men, and going back to their musical roots, namely, traditional Shona music, for their inspiration."[50] In contrast, other readers were highly critical of trad music, perceiving its musical syncretism as a corruption of indigenous musical practices. As one letter writer argued, "Traditional music is beautiful if it is left pure and untainted by western rhythms—the latter are basically not traditional sounds, instead, that kind of music should be left to western oriented musicians."[51] Putting forth a similar claim, yet another reader invoked the moral authority of the spirit world, asserting, "Traditional music is far much better played on traditional instruments by traditional folks. If the present trend continues of using Western instruments, we shall be cursed by our ancestors for showing no respect to them."[52]

Ethnomusicologist Thomas Turino has suggested that during the 1970s, Zimbabwean popular musicians were motivated not only by an explicitly nationalist agenda, but by a constellation of professional, social, and musical concerns. Yet letters to *Prize* suggest that audiences clearly associated the emerging trad sound with the development of a distinctly African identity, one of the key components of cultural nationalism. Whether or not Mtukudzi or Mapfumo were operating out of deliberately nationalist artistic intentions, their music nonetheless played an important role in stirring nationalist structures of feeling for their listeners, as well as fervent debate over entanglements between "traditional" and "modern" musical practices. Shortly after the nation won independence in 1980, for example, one of the last letters on trad music to be published in *Prize Magazine*, written by Ezra Mafukidze in Bulawayo's Mzilikazi township, invoked the language of political nationalism in formulating support for emerging forms of syncretic popular music. Echoing the conscientizing slogans of the liberation war—"Forward with the struggle!" "Forward with ZANU-PF!" "Forward with the masses!"—Mafukidze concluded with his own creative slogan, "Forward with local traditional music!"[53]

The Moral Ambiguity of Singing the Struggle

The contributions trad artists such as Thomas Mapfumo, Zexie Manatsa, and Oliver Samhembere made to the liberation struggle took many forms, from carefully disguised messages conveyed through figurative song lyrics to the inherently nationalist dimensions of turning toward indigenous musical forms. Some singers, such as Comrade Chinx, were active members of ZIPRA and ZANLA military units. Others, such as Mtukudzi's childhood inspiration Safirio Madzikatire, were not directly engaged in the struggle for liberation, yet they too braved the perils of wartime by traveling throughout the country in order to perform.

Many accounts have emphasized music's role in Zimbabwe's liberation war.[54] Yet the political legacy of many of the popular artists active during the 1970s remains clouded by the ambiguities and entanglements of wartime. Initially perceived as a wartime hero for the defiant lyrics of songs such as "Tumirai Vana Kuhondo," or "Send your children to war" (AS 1074, 1978), for example, Thomas Mapfumo was later widely criticized for his association with the United African National Council's Bishop Abel Muzorewa, whose willingness to negotiate with Ian Smith resulted in the short-lived but widely despised political compromise of Zimbabwe-Rhodesia. Long celebrated for his role as one of the nation's first professional black entertainers, Safirio Madzikatire's legacy is likewise complicated by his corporate sponsorship from Lever Brothers, a company that offered both material and ideological support to the Rhodesian armed forces during the war.[55] The ambivalent positions of many of Zimbabwe's most popular singers serves as a powerful reminder of the moral ambiguities of war, reminding us that even musicians who were not explicitly political were nonetheless caught up in trying to make sense of the confusion, uncertainty, and chaos of the struggle for majority rule.

Hearing the Past in the Present

Among the many trad musicians who emerged during this era, only Mtukudzi and Mapfumo would manage to sustain vibrant careers for several decades after Zimbabwe's independence. Over the years, debate about the political implications of their songs has continued. Writing in the *Daily News* in 2000, for example, Leo Hatugari praised both Mapfumo and Mtukudzi for rerecording many of their wartime hits, stating, "the message in these songs is clear: politically, things are almost just as bad as during the traumatic years of the liberation war."[56] The following year, Maxwell Sibanda, also at the *Daily News*, quoted Mtukudzi describing "Dzandimomotera" as a "protest song about the problems young blacks faced at the time."[57] Whether an accurate reflection of his original intention in writing the song or a revisionist interpretation made with the benefit of historical hindsight, Mtukudzi's words neatly illustrated how the songs of the liberation years remained potent sonic reminders of the violence and confusion of the 1970s.

Many of Mtukudzi's early singles, including "Bganyamakaka," "Mutavara," "Dzandimomotera," "Ziwere" (KDZ 115, 1977), and "Ndipeiwo Zano" (KDZ 120, 1978), featured prominently in his live performances and recordings even after independence, immersing his listeners in a musical version both of his personal history, and of the nation's collective past. After attending a live show in 2004, for example, one journalist described how the auditorium "reverberated with song and dance" as the crowd sang "Mutavara" and other wartime hits along with Mtukudzi.⁵⁸ In these songs, the history of the nation seemed wrapped in the distinctive timbres of Mtukudzi's rich, gravelly voice, in the energetic movements of his angular limbs, and in the warm tones of his nylon-stringed Godin guitar.

"The Struggles Are Going On"

As a sahwira to the nation, Mtukudzi felt a profound responsibility to perform during the war, using song to comment upon unfolding relations of power. Referring to the collective role of musicians during the liberation years, he recalled his conviction that the nation's artists were "born to do this. This is our duty; it's a national duty." Yet although Mtukudzi's songs expressed what he perceived as "the feeling of that time," they were not overtly political. Instead, his strategic use of ngoma music, commitment to playing the role of a national sahwira, and poetic musical imaginaries of hunhu combined to produce polysemic musical utterances capable of supporting multiple readings. Marked by an ability to critique relations of power that both predated the liberation war and would resonate long after, ngoma songs such as "Bganyamakaka" and "Mutavara" refrained from identifying any particular individuals or social groups as subjects of their commentaries. In this way, they deferred any definitive interpretation, placing the burden of kunzwa—or hearing, feeling, and discursively understanding their contextual implications—upon Mtukudzi's listeners. Even at the height of the liberation war, the political implications of Tuku music thus emerged only through dialogic acts of listening. As a result, Mtukudzi's music has assumed enduring power as a form of social criticism, enabling it to articulate, reflect, and comment upon changing political and social relations.⁵⁹

The multivalent nature of Mtukudzi's music proved especially important as the white, Rhodesian settler state ruled by Ian Smith gave way to the newly independent nation of Zimbabwe, led by Robert Mugabe. While the liberation war had ended, a new terrain of social struggle soon began to emerge. In the process, popular music came to acquire different and often unexpected meanings. As one listener observed more than three decades after he first heard Mtukudzi perform "Mutavara" during the late 1970s, for example, the song took on new significance in a postcolonial context, where a variety of competing political interests, individual subjectivities, and collective structures of feeling had become inextricably entangled: "'Play the drum, Mutavara' can be relevant any time—'Play the drums for land,' because people were given land. 'Play the drum, comrades, let's go.' It's a slogan, and the slogan lives, because it is true at any given time. 'Play the drum, boys.' That could be the opposition. 'Play the drum, boys.' The ruling party could be ruling. 'Play the drum, boys.' The struggles are going on."

"Yorire ngoma"
(Let the drums sound)

Baba namai	*Father, mother*
Teerera unzwe	*Listen and you shall hear*
Yorire ngoma	*Let the drums sound*
Jaya nemhandara	*Young man, young woman*
Mhururu nemheterwa	*Ululation and whistling*
Yorire ngoma	*Let the drums sound*
Makwa nehosho zvopindirana	*Handclapping and shakers interweave*
Mhito nemitumba	*High pitched drums and low*
Yorire ngoma	*Let the drums sound*
Shasha yetsuri mira nepapapo	*Master of the flute, your place is here*
Gwenyambira nekokoko	*Great mbira player, over there*
Yorire ngoma	*Let the drums sound*
Yorire ngoma baba	*Let the drums sound, father*
Yorire ngoma chinzwa	*Let the drums sound, listen*

THREE

Singing Hunhu after Independence

On the eve of Zimbabwe's independence—April 18, 1980—a group of global dignitaries assembled at Rufaro Stadium, just across the road from the hostels built to house temporary male laborers in Mbare township. Drawing a final curtain over the last act of Ian Smith's Rhodesian regime, the British Union Jack was lowered precisely at midnight. In its place rose another flag, featuring the iconic image of the soapstone birds excavated from the ruins of Great Zimbabwe. Shedding its colonial title of Salisbury, the capital city of this independent nation was renamed Harare in tribute to the Neharawa people, who had occupied the area prior to colonization. Streets were likewise rechristened, with the names of Chimurenga heroes such as Herbert Chitepo and Josiah Tongogara replacing those of prominent British explorers, such as Cecil John Rhodes and Henry Morton Stanley. On the city's western edge, atop the rocky *kopje* previously occupied by Chief Neharahwa, Zimbabwe's new prime minister, Robert Mugabe, lit an eternal flame, its light beckoning the newly liberated citizens of this modern African nation toward what appeared a brightly shining future.

Deeply woven into these rituals of political transformation, music played an important role at Zimbabwe's independence ceremony. Regaling the distinguished crowd with the sounds of a new nation, an elated Mtukudzi was among the many local artists invited to perform at a musical gala that culminated in one of the last public appearances by Jamaican reggae legend Bob Marley. With limited space in the stadium, however, throngs of ordinary citizens, many of them local Mbare residents, were shut out of the festivities. Desperate to get inside, they mobbed the gates when Marley's turn to perform finally arrived, prompting the already jittery police to fire tear gas into the crowd. Wafting onto stage, the stinging fumes disrupted Marley's performance for over an hour, dampening the ceremony's celebratory atmosphere. In the chaos, many of those waiting outside managed to make their way into the stadium, resulting in a decidedly more popular audience for the second portion of Marley's set.[1]

Around the nation, popular musicians joined Mtukudzi in commemorating Zimbabwe's transition to majority rule, raising their voices in song after song of celebration. As scholar Alec Pongweni has observed, their lyrics were "ecstatic, oozing gratitude to the guardian spirits of the nation, who had guided the people and their leaders" during the hardships of the liberation war.[2] Among them were tracks such as The Green Arrows' "VaMugabe Votonga," or "Mugabe is now ruling" (FYF 406, 1980), the Four Brothers' "Makorokoto," or "Congratulations" (1980), and Thomas Mapfumo's "Nyarai," or "Be ashamed," (AS 1104, 1980).[3]

Reflecting the atmosphere of this magical moment, Mtukudzi's fourth LP was called simply *Africa* (1980). As its title track, *Africa* featured a distinctly reggae-inflected version of Zimbabwe's new national anthem, "Ishe Komborera Africa," adapted from the South African choral hymn "Nkosi Sikelel' iAfrika," or "God bless Africa," originally composed by Enoch Sontonga in 1897.[4] With off-beat chords on the rhythm guitar and a syncopated, active bass line, Mtukudzi's rendition seemed a deliberate nod to Bob Marley's involvement in the liberation struggle, which began with the release of his song "Zimbabwe" (*Exodus*, 1979) and culminated in his ill-fated appearance at the nation's independence ceremony. Among other politically minded songs on *Africa* were "Gore Remasimba Evanhu" or "Year of the people's power," which took its title directly from a New Year's address given by the nation's new prime minister, Robert Mugabe:

Gore remasimba evanhu	Year of the people's power
Rega kutya mhandu yaparara	Fear no more, the enemy has been defeated
Rega kutya mhandu yasakara	Fear no more, the enemy has been overthrown
Gore remasimba evanhu	Year of the people's power
Evanhu evanhu	People's, people's
Gore remasimba evanhu	Year of the people's power
Nguva yatanga takamirira	The time we have been waiting for
Gore ratanga takamirira iri	The year we have been waiting for
Gore remasimba evanhu	Year of the people's power
Evanhu evanhu	People's, people's

Joining Marley's song of the same name, *Africa* featured Mtukudzi's own song called "Zimbabwe," with lyrics reminding listeners of the arrogance of their former colonizers and exhorting them to remember the sacrifices of those who died in the liberation struggle.

Singing Hunhu in the Postcolony

Mtukudzi would proceed to release more than a dozen records during the nation's first decade of independence, including *Shanje* (1981), *Maungira* (1981), *Please Ndapota* (1982), *Nzara* (1983), *Hwema Handirase* (1984), *Mhaka* (1985), *Gona* (1986), *Zvauya Sei* (1986), *Wawona* (1987), *Sugar Pie* (1988), *Strange Isn't It* (1988), *Nyanga YeNzou* (1988), and *Grandpa Story* (1989). Occasionally, these albums invoked the nationalistic flavor of *Africa* in tracks such as "Yevatema Africa," or "Africa for black people" (*Zvauya Sei*, 1986), and "Sausi Africa," or "South Africa" (*Nyanga Yenzou*, 1988). Yet for the most part, Mtukudzi chose not to address national governance in his songs. Instead, his carefully crafted lyrics portrayed vivid social imaginaries of hunhu, with its emphasis on negotiation, mutuality, and dialogue. Reflecting on this transition, Christopher Timbe told me:

> During the war, yes, he would sing about the war. You know, the guerillas, *matororo*, the boys in the bush, how they contributed, how people contributed. . . . [5] There came a stage when independence came. The songs mirrored what was happening then, the celebratory message. But . . . he also looked into the family setting, where he never wanted family settings and relations neglected. So, I think he is one guy who never really had one slot of, "*Ino iyi inguva yehondo, ngatingoimbai dzehondo chete. Hondo yapera, ngatingoimbai dzemafaro chete* [This is wartime, let's sing only war songs. The war has ended, let's sing only celebratory songs]." He actually went ahead to look at the wholesome life of a person, life of a community, the livelihood of a nation.

Mtukudzi's commitment to singing about the relational ethos of hunhu was reflected in song after song exploring the complexities of kinship. Often, the titles of these songs spoke to universally relevant themes, inviting listeners into a broadly inclusive social imaginary. Among them were tracks such as "Shanje," or "Jealousy" (*Shanje*, 1981), "Hubaba," or "Fatherhood," (*Wawona*, 1987), and "Nhaka," or "Inheritance" (*Sugar Pie*, 1988).

Yet Mtukudzi did not shy away from the difficulties of negotiating moral kinship. In many songs, he dramatized particular fraught relations, singing, for example, about tensions between *vakwasha*, or sons-in-law, and *vanatezvara*, or fathers-in-law. Recounting the story of a young man faced with the impossible demand of bringing elephant tusks and rhinoceros horns as part of his brideprice payments, or *roora*, for example, the song "Munoshusha," or "You are exasperating" (*Nyanga Yenzou*, 1988) offered a humorous critique of contemporary marriage practices. Widely broadcast on Zimbabwean television, the song's video featured Mtukudzi as an aspiring bridegroom whacking his way through the bush in his attempt to track and kill an elephant and rhino, fleeing in fright after actually stumbling upon them, and dodging a series of blows after failing to satisfy the exorbitant demands of his obstinate in-laws. Serious yet comical, "Munoshusha" portrayed the social conflicts increasingly associated with roora in the context of a capitalist economy. In this way, it echoed the dramatic skits of Mtukudzi's childhood hero Safirio Madzikatire, which often similarly revolved around gender, marriage, and social status.

Mtukudzi's evolving approach to singing hunhu throughout the 1980s and 1990s is the subject of this chapter. Setting the stage, I begin by describing the challenges Mtukudzi encountered as he sought to make a living as a professional musician during the first decade of Zimbabwe's independence. Next, I offer an analysis of "Yorire Ngoma," or "Let the drums sound" (*Zvauya Sei*, 1986), which particularly exemplifies his approach to crafting musical imaginaries of hunhu during this period. As I illustrate, Mtukudzi's lyrics and musical arrangements worked hand-in-hand to generate the type of performance style that music scholars such as Samuel Floyd and Ingrid Monson have described as dialogic, enabling him to pull listeners into a unique musical and social groove. At same time, Mtukudzi moved away from the ngoma arrangements typical of his early years and toward original pieces such as "Baba," which preserved many elements of ngoma—from its distinctive rhythms to its dialogic multipart relationships—yet did not import identifiable ngoma songs wholesale.

As Mtukudzi came to occupy an increasingly audible position within the Zimbabwean music scene, his professional networks quickly expanded, bringing him into contact with local cosmopolitans in the fields of music, dance, and film, as well as public health, journalism, and development.[6] In the final section of this chapter, I illustrate how these relationships both proved critical in enabling Mtukudzi to consolidate an impressive degree of control over his artistry and facilitated his entry into new artistic disciplines such as theater and film. As a result, his vibrant musical imaginaries of hunhu began reaching new audiences and attracting new listeners.

The 1980s: The Promises and Perils of Peacetime

The first, heady days of independence seemed to herald a new era in Zimbabwean popular music. Liberated from the strictures of wartime, local artists were freed from the material shortages of sanctions, the travails of touring a nation torn apart by violence, and the censorship imposed by Ian Smith's Rhodesian regime. Reflecting the energy and excitement of this period, the concept of trad music began losing its currency, and a vast diversity of new musical genres flourished in its place.[7] Foremost among them was jit, a style of music popularized by artists such as the Bhundu Boys and the Four Brothers and characterized by call-and-response singing, a fast-paced, $\frac{12}{8}$ metric framework taken from ngoma styles such as jiti, dinhe, and katekwe, and the I-IV-I-V harmonic progressions of South African popular styles such as kwela. At the same time, artists such as the Khiama Boys, John Chibadura, and Simon Chimbetu were gaining ground with sungura, which featured tightly harmonized lead vocals lines, soaring guitar-work derived from the rhumba music of Central and Eastern Africa, and a $\frac{4}{4}$ metric structure. Joining jit and sungura, the mbira-based guitar music played by artists such as Thomas Mapfumo, Susan Mapfumo, Jonah Sithole, and others came to be called simply chimurenga, in reference to its associations with Zimbabwe's armed war for independence. Other popular musical styles that emerged in Zimbabwe during the 1980s included the rhumba performed by resident Congolese musicians, the largely urban Afro jazz scene pioneered by Louis Mhlanga and Steve Dyer, and the type of local gospel music developed by artists such as Mechanic Manyeruke.

Despite this flourishing music scene, making a living as an artist still proved incredibly difficult. With an excruciatingly small domestic music industry, record companies were able to exercise a near monopoly on music production. As a result, musicians were plagued by prejudicial contracts, high album prices, endemic piracy, high equipment costs, and inferior recording technologies. To some extent, each of these problems would persist throughout the coming decades, placing local artists at a distinct disadvantage in both regional and global markets.[8]

The challenges of making it were readily apparent for Mtukudzi. Shortly after releasing "Mutavara," he split off from the Wagon Wheels in order to form his own group, the Black Spirits. Alongside Mtukudzi's brother Rob on rhythm guitar and keyboard, the Black Spirits featured Bartholomew Chirenda on lead guitar, James Austin on drum kit, Joseph Alpheus on bass, and Kenny Mukwesha on vocals.[9] Full of energy and talent, the Black Spirits nonetheless struggled to eke out a living as professional musicians. As Mtukudzi recalls, their troubles were epitomized by one of their first appearances in Hwange, a remote mining outpost located in the country's northwestern reaches:

> We played for three nights in Hwange—total gate takings, of three shows, was thirty-four dollars. And we owed the guesthouses, and our blankets were withheld because we had to pay for them to release our blankets. . . . And as we were at the service station, VID [Vehicle Inspectorate Department] took our kombi and said it wasn't road-worthy. And we are in Hwange . . . it was tough! The driver of the kombi had another kombi, here in Harare. . . . So he had to hitchhike back to Harare, get the registration of the kombi here, and the number plates, and go ahead and license that one, bring it back, fix it on our kombi. And we drove during the night, to catch up with the next show in Bulawayo. So, we got to Bulawayo. We were so hungry. We got there early in the morning since we traveled in the night. So we parked at the hall. We slept—no blankets, 'cause the blankets had been left in Hwange—sleeping there, waiting for the evening to put up the show.

Soon, the Black Spirits embarked on an equally troubled journey during their first engagement outside of Zimbabwe, on a tour of Zambia. Venturing south from Harare, they performed in Chegutu, Kadoma, Kwekwe, and Bulawayo, then headed back through Hwange to Victoria Falls. Crossing the Zambezi River into Zambia, they played in Livingstone, Ndola, Kabwe, and Kitwe before finally reaching the capital city of Lusaka. Anticipating a huge turnout for their final show in Lusaka, their inexperienced promoter, a Zimbabwean expatriate, had booked the national stadium. Positioned at the base of a tall, sloping hill, it offered a prime vantage point for people to watch the show for free. As Mtukudzi recalled, a large group of people soon congregated just outside the gates, dwarfing the sparse audience within the stadium. Needless to say, the band returned broke and disheartened.

In 1983, Mtukudzi's first tour outside of Africa, with performances in the United Kingdom and Germany, was even more disastrous.[10] Throughout the tour, each band member received a per diem meant for food and other incidental expenses. The Black Spirits' guitarist, bass player, and drummer quickly spent this money on food, cigarettes, and alcohol, while Mtukudzi and his brother Rob, male backing vocalist and dancer Eric "Picky" Kasamba, and the band's female backing singers all managed to save a portion of their per diems. Together with their performance fees, this small savings enabled them to buy televisions and other high-status commodities to take back home. Intensely jealous, Mtukudzi's disgruntled instrumentalists felt they had been cheated out of their rightful income. As Mtukudzi recalled: "They thought I had taken some other monies and favored these other youngsters and not them. So that was the complaint. And I said, 'Hey, look here. You guys have been drinking beer, and these others were not drinking. So how do you think we can be on the same page?'" Unconvinced, Mtukudzi's drummer sabotaged a performance for a group of European promoters by leaving the stage midway through the show. Thinking quickly, Kasamba broke out of his choreographed dance routine with Mtukudzi and made his way to the back of the stage, where he seamlessly took over on drum kit. While Kasamba managed to redeem the performance, the band itself proved unsalvageable, leaving Mtukudzi without a backing group upon his return to Zimbabwe. As he told me: "That's the day I first realized Picky could play drums. . . . And we finished off the song, tried to make it like a style, like that's our performance. So that was it. And when we came back, they were all over newspapers, saying that we never got paid. Well, there was nothing I could do about that one, besides getting the newspaper clip and hanging it in the rehearsal room."

The Zig-Zag Band

Rather than starting over on his own, Mtukudzi joined forces with a series of local groups. At first, he played with the Ocean City Band, whose ever-changing membership included figures such as the legendary guitarist James Chimombe,

On Dance

I had names like "lazy bones," "fox trot," dances like "donkey jump." Yeah, I gave them names. 'Cause whoever I'm dancing with, for him to identify the moves, I would give them a name and then he would know. Like Picky knew, he understood. The railway line, he would understand, "Ok, we're going to do that move." We used to follow each other, like a train. The name would be inspired by the way we are dancing. And I would label it with a name. The donkey jump is—we used to do two moves a side, two moves a side, jumping.

—*Oliver Mtukudzi*

He likes jumping a lot—quite a lot. In most of his dancing there was a lot of jumping. I would say the jumping characterizes most of Tuku's dancing, because he always tries and makes sure he jumps somewhere. And I think also he dances to his music, he hears his music. And it's something that amazes me, 'cause with his music, what he dances to his music is not what everyone else hears.

—*Gilbert Douglas*

as well as Safirio Madzikatire's son Elijah. Yet as Mtukudzi quickly realized, the Ocean City Band "was a band on its own, and it had its own direction. We didn't share the same destiny. So, we split." Next, he recorded a few albums with a group called Rising Power, located in his home neighborhood of Highfield. In 1986, Mtukudzi moved to the mid-sized town of Kwekwe, where he began working with a local outfit called the Zig-Zag Band, featuring Stanley Phiri on drums, Gilbert Zvamaida on lead guitar, Idan Banda on rhythm guitar, Fabian Chikamba on bass, and George Paradza on vocals.[11]

Formed in 1982, the Zig-Zag Band played a style of popular music its members called *chigiyo*, after a version of the muchongoyo drumming, dance, and song genre prevalent in the nation's Eastern Highlands.[12] Similar to the jit pioneered by artists such as the Bhundu Boys and the Four Brothers, chigiyo fused ngoma with contemporary influences such as reggae, producing what one local journalist would describe as "hard hitting dance" music.[13] Upon joining the Zig-Zag Band, Mtukudzi brought in his brother Rob on keyboards. He also introduced a

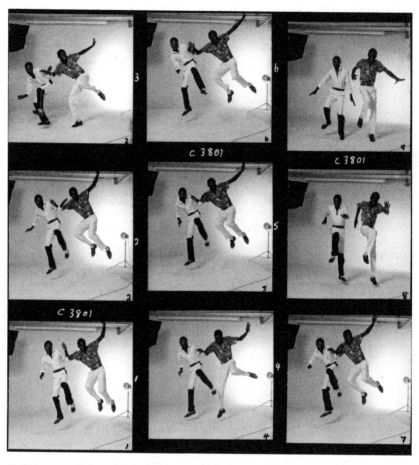

Early images of Oliver Mtukudzi and Picky Kasamba dancing.
Courtesy of MG Wesson Photography.

quartet of female backing vocalists—Anna Phiri, Eva Mbeva, Maureen Mbojelo, and Lois Makoni—called the New Sisters.[14] Rounding out the group was Picky Kasamba, who had been supporting himself by performing with Brave New Sun, a band led by Mtukudzi's childhood musical hero Safirio Madzikatire, since the Black Spirits' disastrous European tour.

Zvauya Sei: How Has It Happened?

While the Zig-Zag Band has largely faded into obscurity, it was once hailed as "one of the best live groups in Zimbabwe" and backed Mtukudzi on several albums during the mid-1980s.[15] Among them was *Zvauya Sei*, or "How has it hap-

Mtukudzi and Kasamba in 2007. *Courtesy of Mary Cairns.*

pened?" (1986), which Mtukudzi would describe many decades later as one of the most meaningful albums of his career. Released during a time of great upheaval in Mtukudzi's personal life, *Zvauya Sei* was dedicated to his father Samson, who had recently passed away. By this time, his father had become one of his most fervent supporters. As Mtukudzi recalled, "When my father died in 1986, even if he finds a broken string, he would keep it for me—'Are you sure you don't need this?'" As Samson's eldest son, Mtukudzi inherited his father's status as head of the family, shouldering a new set of moral obligations. As he would later say:

> Since I'm the eldest son in the family, all problems, now, are facing me.
> . . . He was blocking all those from me. Now that he's dead, I'm facing the reality of life, now. I'm the father now, and it's like I'm now a fool. 'Cause I can't handle it anymore. . . . You see, culturally here, we have extended

families. And it's like, I don't only concentrate on my wife and my kids, but my sisters too, my brothers. I'm also the father to them, since I'm the eldest son in the family. So, you find I end up responsible in a very big family. Now all those things—a sister may have a problem with her husband in her own home, she comes to me to complain—I have to solve that problem, of that family. 'Cause I'm the father, I'm the overseer of the whole family.[16]

Upon inheriting his father's position as household head, Mtukudzi found himself responsible for maintaining the reciprocal relations of hunhu within his entire extended kinship network. In the years after his father's death, *Zvauya Sei* and its eponymous title track were among the many songs and albums Mtukudzi released in response to the difficulties of moving into his father's role, including "Madanha," or "Do as you please" (*Rombe*, 1992), "Vende," or "A gap" (*Ivai Navo*, 1995), and "Masimba Mashoma," or "Little strength" (*Svovi Yangu*, 1996).

Shortly after the Black Spirits' disastrous tour of Europe, Mtukudzi's family life was also thrown into turmoil, and in 1981, he separated from his first wife, Melody. Soon after, he met his second wife, Daisy. Yet he remained legally married to Melody for several years, including a brief period of reconciliation during which his daughter Selmor was born. His first and third children, Sandra and Selmor, were thus Melody's, while his second and fourth children, Samantha and Samson, belonged to Daisy. Finalized during the same year his father passed away, Mtukudzi's divorce from Melody represented a new start for the singer, yet the dissolution of their marriage also resulted in additional friction for all sides of the family.

Mtukudzi suffered yet another loss when his close friend and manager Jack "Jeri" Sadza passed away in 1985. Just as he had done after his father's death, Mtukudzi responded by writing a song about losing Sadza. Titled simply "Jeri," it appeared on the album *Gona* (1986), released during the same year as *Zvauya Sei*. Described in the local press as "one of the most solemn songs he has ever written," its lyrics invoked the ritual friendship of husahwira in order to describe Mtukudzi's exceptionally close relationship to Sadza.[17] Portraying the bonds of ritual friendship as even stronger than those of kinship, the song's lyrics positioned husahwira as an indispensable part of Shona social relations.

Writing songs about his troubles was not enough, however, and Mtukudzi soon developed a stress-related stomach ulcer that left him bedridden for nearly an entire year. This illness proved the catalyst for his decision to move from Harare to the mid-sized town of Kwekwe, located in Zimbabwe's Midlands Province: "I just needed a new environment. 'Cause I'd been sick for too long. And when I was in Kwekwe, there was Zig-Zag, doing nothing. And as a sick person, I didn't want to stay in bed. I wanted to go out. So I used to go and visit Zig-Zag,

"Jeri"

Zvamunoona husahwira	As you see, husahwira
hunokunda hukama	surpasses kinship
Vaitiona vaiziva	Those who saw us knew
mukufamba tiri tose	we journeyed together
Maitiro edu ose nemashandiro	In all our doings, and in all our work
edu ose	
Zvamunoona husahwira	As you see, husahwira
hunokunda hukama	surpasses kinship
Vanondiona vanoshama	Those who see me are astonished,
sahwira wakaisepiko?	where have you left your sahwira?
Kuringaringa ndatoshaya	I search everywhere, but cannot find
sahwira waendeipiko?	sahwira, where have you gone?
Zvamunoona husahwira	As you see, husahwira
hunokunda hukama	surpasses kinship
Amai kani	Oh mother!
Jeri Jeriwo Jeri wakatadza Jeri	Jeri, Jeri, oh, Jeri you have failed, Jeri
Jeriwo Jeri Jeri unodada	Jeri, oh Jeri, Jeri you are too proud,
wakandisiya ndiri ndega	you have left me alone
Jeri wakashata	Jeri you are terrible,
kundisiya ndiri ndega	to leave me alone
Zvamunoona husahwira	As you see, husahwira
hunokunda hukama	surpasses kinship
Amai kani o	Oh mother! Oh
Ndichatamba naniko	With whom shall I play?
Ndichafara naniko	With whom shall I be happy?
Kokushanda naniko	And with whom shall I work?
Ndichafamba naniko	With whom shall I travel?
Zvamunoona husahwira	As you see, husahwira
hunokunda hukama	surpasses kinship
Ndichatamba naniko	With whom shall I play?
Ndichafara naniko	With whom shall I be happy?
Kokushanda naniko	And with whom shall I work?
Ndichasara na . . .	With whom shall I. . .
Jeri wakatadza	Jeri, Jeri, oh, Jeri you have failed,
wakandisiya ndega ndega	you have left me all alone
Jeri unodada	Jeri you are terrible,
kundisiya ndiri ndega	to leave me alone
Zvamunoona husahwira	As you see, husahwira
hunokunda hukama	surpasses kinship
Amai kani o	Oh mother! Oh
Hazvinei wazorora asi	No matter that you have been laid to
mumhepo tiri tose	rest, but in spirit we are together
Zvamunoona husahwira	As you see, husahwira
hunokunda hukama	surpasses kinship

Zvauya Sei. Courtesy of Tuku Music and Sheer Sound/Gallo Record Company.

and of course I would take the guitar and say, 'Come on, let's play this song.' And hey, we came up with something new, and that was a band. It was Oliver Mtukudzi and the Zig-Zag Band." Yet the debilitating pain of Mtukudzi's ulcer hindered his efforts to record *Zvauya Sei* with the Zig-Zag Band, forcing him to work at an excruciatingly slow pace. As he recalled, "I would sing one line and stop the tape and rest. Then roll again. As I go to the next line, I sing that line, and we stop the tape. And I finished the whole album doing that." Reflecting this painful genesis, the album cover featured a pensive photograph of Mtukudzi resting his head against his clasped hands, as if contemplating his many recent misfortunes. Many Shona-speaking listeners would immediately have recognized this pose as a sign of the condition known as *kufungisisa*, or "thinking too much," an idiomatic term for severe feelings of mental, social, or even spiritual distress.[18]

"Yorire Ngoma": Music, Sociality, and Dialogue

Of all the songs on *Zvauya Sei*, its last track, "Yorire Ngoma," or "Let the drums sound," was particularly tied to Mtukudzi's personal suffering. As he would tell the local press, "I was encouraging other artists to continue singing and not to give up. I was convinced that I was going to die and before I departed, I wanted to leave some form of inspiration for other musicians."[19] In this section, I offer a brief analysis of "Yorire Ngoma," which speaks with exceptional clarity to relationships between music, dialogue, and sociality in Mtukudzi's approach to singing hunhu.

Like most of Mtukudzi's songs, "Yorire Ngoma" is structured around a musical relationship found across the African continent, often referred to simply as call-and-response. The theme of call-and-response is also dramatized within the song's lyrics, enabling "Yorire Ngoma" to simultaneously embody and comment upon dialogic musical relationships. Central to its chorus, for example, the word *shaura*, or "call," comes from the verb *kushaura*, which denotes the leading part in a multipart musical ensemble.[20] In particular, the kushaura player is responsible for initiating musical performance, for only after he or she begins do other musicians join in with their corresponding response parts, often referred to by singers as *kudaira* or *mabvumira*, and by mbira players as *kutsinhira*. While call-and-response relationships are particularly fundamental to ngoma songs, they are also found in a broad spectrum of Zimbabwean musical styles, from the harmonized choral music of the liberation struggle to the densely layered texture of mbira ensembles.[21]

The concept of call-and-response is not only musical, however; it is also social. As they negotiate the performance of kushaura and kutsinhira parts, musicians become jointly engaged in producing what might best be described as an interlocking musical groove. In her work on American jazz performance, music scholar Ingrid Monson has suggested that the Afro-diasporic concept of groove is both a distinctly musical form of sociality, and also a dialectical field of musical and social action.[22] In a Zimbabwean context, Monson's emphasis on groove as dialogue, in which each part comes into being through its relationship with a musical other, is particularly important, for it reflects not only the mutually constitutive relationship between kushaura and kutsinhira parts, but also the very essence of hunhu, so succinctly summed up in Mtukudzi's emphasis on "being a person among others."

Yet neither musical perfection nor social unity are required to successfully sustain a musical groove. Instead, the call-and-response relationships of ngoma are capable of accommodating what music scholar Charles Keil has referred to as "participatory discrepancies," in which people may phase in and out of synch with each other, yet remain within the collective experience of the groove.[23]

Elaborating on these participatory discrepancies, Keil suggests that musical grooves offer "the possibility of participation, sensuous immersion in sound, taking pleasure in life (rather than asserting power over it), felicity, grace, surrender of self to save co-cultural others and to a benign primary reality."[24] In Mtukudzi's emphasis on hunhu, we see how the participatory discrepancies of ngoma extend even beyond the frame of the musical event, for tension, friction, and antagonism between individuals is not antithetical to the wider social body's ability to sustain relationships of family, lineage, or community.

With these intersubjective musical and social possibilities, "Yorire Ngoma" is particularly saturated by what music scholar Samuel Floyd has called the principle of "call-response." Through this term, Floyd seeks to foreground the dialogic, conversational, and relational nature of African and Afro-diasporic music making, while moving beyond what has too often been a reductive Western notion of "call-and-response" relationships.[25] For Floyd, call-response is a "master musical trope" that encompasses nearly every aspect of African-derived musical practice.[26] Within "Yorire Ngoma," Floyd's conception of call-response is particularly useful in reminding us that neither kushaura nor kutsinhira parts map precisely onto the roles of "leader" or "follower," for both frequently engage in complex improvisational and signifying gestures. At a larger level, Floyd's work similarly reminds us that kushaura and kutsinhira parts offer more than simply a style of singing or playing together; they also enable participants to jointly participate in negotiating a uniquely musical way of being together in the world.

In the lyrics to "Yorire Ngoma," Mtukudzi quite clearly ties musical relationships to social ones. He begins by invoking gendered reciprocities of kinship, calling upon both fathers and mothers to listen as the ngoma sounds—a phrase that could be interpreted as a reference either specifically to drums, or more generally to music itself. These brief opening lines thus succinctly invoke many of the major themes informing Mtukudzi's musical project, tying the kinship relations of hunhu to the indigenous musical practice of ngoma, as well as to the intersubjective nature of hearing, feeling, and understanding conveyed by the term *kunzwa*.

The song's subsequent verses similarly remain firmly within the conceptual framework of call-response, invoking reciprocal forms of both musical practice and social relations. These include the mhururu ululation done by women, and the complementary mheterwa whistling done by men. Together, these gendered sonic interjections both reflect and enhance song's affective power, offering participants a way to signify upon collective musical experience.[27] Joining mhururu and mheterwa, Mtukudzi includes several other reciprocal pairs in the lyrics to "Yorire Ngoma," such as the gendered figures of young men and women, the complementary rhythmic practices of makwa handclapping and hosho shaker playing, and the interlocking drumming parts known as mhito and mitumba.

In the final section of "Yorire Ngoma," Mtukudzi engages many of the conversational techniques of call-response identified by Floyd—including calls, game rivalry, and individuality within collectivity—by singing the names of several of Zimbabwe's most popular musicians, including Lovemore Majaivana, John Chibadura, Marshall Munhumumwe, Solomon Skuza, James Chimombe, Job Mashanda, Fanyana Dube, Tine Chikupo, Dorothy Masuka, Stella Chiweshe, Doreen Ncube, Susan Mapfumo, and Elizabeth Tadereera.[28] Mtukudzi's mention of Thomas Mapfumo, his closest musical rival, is a particularly compelling example of musical signifying, for immediately after calling out his name, Mtukudzi mimics the style of chimurenga singing so closely associated with Mapfumo, delivering a descending vocable line in a voice similar to Mapfumo's own.

Seamlessly weaving the social ethos of hunhu together with the musical master trope of call-response, "Yorire Ngoma" proved incredibly popular among Mtukudzi's audiences, and was quickly reissued as a maxi-single with the new title "Shaura," or "Take the lead" (XKDZ 209, 1986). In a letter to the editor of *Parade Magazine*, one person praised "Shaura" by invoking the interplay of listening and comprehension inherent in the Shona concept of hearing, or kunzwa. As he enthused, "The song has everything needed for the ears and brain."[29] Nearly two decades after its initial release, Mtukudzi recorded the song yet a third time on his album *Paivepo* (1999), now retitled "Ngoma Nehosho," or "Drums and hosho." Reviewing *Paivepo*, journalist Funny Mashava lauded the way "Yorire Ngoma" and other old hits had been "spiced up to give them a more upbeat and modern beat to make them appeal to both the older and new generation."[30] Responding to the dialogic imperative of call-response, he concluded his review by declaring, "All I can say to Tuku is 'shaura Tuku shaura.'"[31]

Cosmopolitan Collaborations

In the same year that he released *Zvauya Sei*, Mtukudzi encountered music promoter Debbie Metcalfe.[32] A liberal white Zimbabwean who had spent seven years of self-imposed exile in the United Kingdom, Metcalfe returned to Harare shortly after independence. Working with local sound engineer Phillip Roberts and British music producer Chris Bolton, she founded an independent recording venture called Frontline Studio. Reflecting Metcalfe's progressive views, the studio's name came from the political concept of the "Frontline States," a reference to South African apartheid's spill-over effects in neighboring nations such as Angola, Botswana, and Mozambique, many of which had offered "bases, training camps and training for guerillas, logistical support, weapons, food, clothing, medicine and sanctuaries for refugees" during Zimbabwe's liberation struggle.[33] Reflecting this emphasis on political solidarity against apartheid, the first group Metcalfe managed, Southern Freeway, was founded by white South

African saxophone player Steve Dyer, who lived in voluntary exile for many years in Botswana and Zimbabwe.

During Mtukudzi's first visit to Frontline Studio in 1986, he recorded a musical response to the emerging HIV/AIDS pandemic, titled "Stay with One Woman," as part of a musical competition hosted by the World Health Organization. Immediately struck by Mtukudzi's easy-going nature and "bloody good" songwriting, Metcalfe was also impressed by his willingness to tackle difficult social issues, describing him as "prepared to look at the things that were evolving in this year or day of his life . . . health issues, education issues. And he took them on quite willingly and quite openly. He sort of engulfed them, and made something of them." Soon, Metcalfe began organizing and running Mtukudzi's live shows, as well as writing press releases and arranging graphic design work for posters and album covers. After he was invited to perform "Stay with One Woman" at the World Health Organization's headquarters in Switzerland, she also coordinated passports and travel plans for Mtukudzi and his band members.

Further exemplifying his commitment to addressing evolving social issues, Mtukudzi worked actively with the Zimbabwe National Family Planning Council (ZNFPC) during the late 1980s and early 1990s. Godfrey Tinarwo, who coordinated major family planning campaigns for the ZNFPC during this period, described Mtukudzi's participation as integral in enabling the organization to reach key target demographics, particularly during the "Male Motivation Campaign" of 1993–1994.[34] Foremost among Mtukudzi's contributions to family planning was his 1988 release of the maxi single "Rongai Mhuri" (XKDZ 219, 1988), which featured a diverse line-up of guest vocalists, including John Chibadura, Naison and Simon Chimbetu, Fanyana Dube, Solomon Skuza, Busi Ncube, Christopher Shoko, and Ketai.[35] As they traded verses of the song, Mtukudzi and his guest vocalists alternated between Shona, Ndebele, and English, making "Rongai Mhuri" accessible to an exceptionally wide audience. Emphasizing the "deep and rich lyrical content" that listeners frequently cite as a primary part of his musical appeal, Mtukudzi opened the song with a well-known proverb that states, "*Gore mwana gore mwana munovapeiko*," or "Each year, a child, each year, a child, what shall you give them [to eat]?"[36] Released only two years apart, "Stay with One Woman" and "Rongai Mhuri" represented Mtukudzi's first real forays into the world of public health, positioning him to become involved in subsequent initiatives addressing HIV/AIDS, as I discuss in chapter 7.

Shortly after "Rongai Mhuri," Mtukudzi and Metcalfe would embark on their first major joint venture in the form of a pioneering double LP titled *Live at Sakubva* (1989). The first live album in Zimbabwean music history, *Live at Sakubva* was recorded at Sakubva Stadium on the outskirts of Mutare, a peaceful town ringed by emerald hills in Zimbabwe's Eastern Highlands. Enlivening this sleepy

The ZNFPC Male Motivation Campaign

We realized that for family planning to really take root, and be established as the norm among Zimbabweans—men and women and couples—it was important to bring the male factor on board. And so we did some surveys to talk to a lot of men, and we were surprised—to us at that stage, it was late '80s—that they said they had always felt left out. And most of the family planning work—the community-based distributors, the messages on radio and so forth—were really targeting women. But yet men are ultimately responsible, or that's what they felt, for the welfare of their families. And they needed to be involved if there were going to be decisions about family size, fertility, contraceptive use, and so forth. But then we said, "In what form should the message be conveyed to you?" One of the most popular forms, of course, was they liked a musical form. They wanted messages which would come as songs really, which would endear them to the program.

We approached a number of local musicians then. And Oliver, obviously, was already well-established as a music icon in the country, and it was almost natural for us to talk to him and engage him. And we found him more than willing to play a part, and come up with songs which would support the family planning message—the general reproductive health and welfare messages around family well-being, and so forth. So we then met with him, and before we realized, he'd already come up with some ideas on what songs he wanted. He found it almost easy to relate to the message of health.

I think it was one of the first programs he had been asked to come in a meaningful way to contribute towards the general welfare of the people, population, and so forth. And I think when HIV became an issue later on, it became very natural and very easy for him to follow through from the initial stint with family planning into the broader HIV and AIDS issue. They're addressing outcomes with the same act—they deal with unplanned, unwanted pregnancies, and now they deal with HIV/AIDS in the context of, again, the results of sexual activity. So I think there was almost a natural move from family planning to HIV and AIDS.

Even in those early days, we found him a very humble, down-to-earth musician who wants to put his mind to a certain program, or certain idea. He would really work hard to get something of quality out of it. He was just doing it. Not just to pay lip service, but we could feel that he was saying, "Alright. We have agreed we are together. We're going to sit, reflect, come up with something which will suit the occasion." So it was that kind of dedication, that commitment, once he bought into the idea.

—*Godfrey Tinarwo*

hamlet with a burst of musical energy, Mtukudzi's massive show was described by the local press as "the first time in . . . memory that Mutare has been the venue for such a major local outdoor event."[37] An all-night affair, or *pungwe*, it featured many of the nation's top artists, including Andy Brown, Ilanga, Lovemore Majaivana, and James Chimombe, alongside local performers from Mutare. One group with special meaning for Mtukudzi was Pengaudzoke, a band he had first discovered in the rural areas of Chihota, and whose members he mentored throughout their rise to fame.

For Mtukudzi, the process of recording *Live at Sakubva* was simply exhilarating.[38] As he told me:

> I really wanted to record a live album. And I wasn't sure of what I was doing, but I really just wanted to do it. So I had to uproot a studio from Harare to Mutare—hire the stage, the stadium and everything, hire equipment. And I did all that. I wasn't even sure whether I was gonna come up with a good recording. And the night before we were supposed to have set up, there came this heavy rain. And it was very stressful. I wasn't sure whether we were going to put on the show or not. So the next day, waking up, the rains stopped and we set up. And we got about sixteen thousand people. It was a huge show. . . . So it carries lots of memories. Up to now, I will never forget that show.

For Metcalfe, the show was as nerve-wracking as it was exciting. As she related: "We dismantled our whole studio, and drove it down in a little one-ton, a little Bantam truck. . . . I was terrified of dismantling the studio, I mean, that was our entire capital investment going to one show. One riot and, pfft! You know? So I was very anxious about it, but for some reason, once we'd all agreed to it, we really committed to it, and just did everything possible to make it a success. A massive success." With its all-star billing and high-quality sound system, the show confirmed Mtukudzi and Metcalfe's positions as music industry professionals, as well as cementing their working relationship. Of even greater importance, *Live at Sakubva* represented what the local press would recognize as "a new attempt at getting the audience involved in a live recording."[39] Inscribing live performance in the form of a commercial album for the first time in Zimbabwean recording history, *Live at Sakubva* offered yet another example of Mtukudzi's efforts to ground his work in a dialogic musical aesthetic.

Breaking Away from the Zimbabwe Music Company

Thanks to Metcalfe's valuable advice, *Live at Sakubva* was one of the first albums released by Record and Tape Productions (RTP), a new, independent record label. Since Mtukudzi was first signed by producer West Nkosi in the late 1970s, he had

worked with the South African recording house Gallo Records, which had subsequently begun operating in Zimbabwe as Gramma Records.[40] Gradually, however, Mtukudzi began to perceive the terms of his contract, which he had signed
without adequate legal counsel, as unfavorable. As he told me: "When I started,
I didn't think it was my career. It was more like a hobby, more like something
that I loved to do. . . . As I grew up, I then realized, 'Oh! I'm losing out here, it's
supposed to be a business. It's not just for fun.' You see? And the best advice I got
was to have my own company . . . and control my own music." By the mid-1980s,
Mtukudzi's records were topping the Zimbabwean music charts, yet he was receiving only a paltry sum in royalties.[41] More importantly, the title to his songs
was held by Gramma, leaving him without rights to his own recordings. On Metcalfe's advice, Mtukudzi obtained legal representation, broke his contract with
Gramma, and signed a new distribution agreement with RTP.[42]

While Mtukudzi's relationship with RTP was relatively short-lived, his decision to sever ties with Gramma enabled him to assert agency over how his music
was recorded, produced, and distributed. By the end of the 1980s, Mtukudzi had
formed his own record label, called Tuku Music, which enabled him to negotiate
favorable terms with both domestic and international distribution companies.
In addition to the Zimbabwe Music Company, a partner of Gramma Records,
Mtukudzi's music has been distributed by Germany's Shava Records, American
world music label Putumayo, Tower Records' Earthsongs, and the French Label
Bleu/Indigo. Since the late 1990s, he has also maintained an ongoing partnership
with Sheer Sound, an independent record label based in South Africa.

In addition to founding his own label, Mtukudzi would later build his own
recording studio in the town of Norton, freeing him from standard practices in
the Zimbabwean music industry, where artists are expected to record several
songs each day, granting them little time for overdubbing or experimentation.[43]
He also purchased sound equipment and began employing a full-time audio engineer. Giving him an exceptional degree of control over his own music, these
investments would set him apart from the majority of Zimbabwean popular artists, who remain dependent on live shows for their primary income, with mar-
ginal subsidiary income from radio play.[44]

From Jitaj to Tuku Music

Even given the diverse forms of popular music that emerged in the decade after
independence, Oliver Mtukudzi's distinctive style never fit comfortably within a
single mainstream genre. As a result, he struggled to reshape local understandings of his sound after the concept of trad music fell out of common currency.
In the mid-1980s, Mtukudzi sought to reposition himself by coining an entirely
new term for his music, which he began referring to as "jitaj." In a 1988 interview

with the *Sunday News*, he described jitaj as a fusion of two existing Zimbabwean musical genres—the urban jit played by artists such as the Four Brothers and the Bhundu Boys, and the Afro jazz pioneered by musicians such as Louis Mhlanga and Steve Dyer.[45] Yet Mtukudzi's attempt to relabel his music was quickly rejected by listeners, who preferred to call it simply Tuku music. As he recalled: "It was written in a few articles, you know, 'Tuku, his music is called jitaj,' and so on. But people called it 'Tuku music' instead . . . it was like the whole country decided that. 'Cause even in Bulawayo, they would say, 'Ah, Tuku music.' Everyone was just [saying], 'Tuku music, Tuku music.' And I don't know where that came from, you know? Of course I tried to find out, 'cause that was a challenge. Trying to beat 'Tuku music' with my jitaj name, you know? . . . But it didn't work." While it is difficult to identify precisely why Mtukudzi's audiences rejected the term jitaj, it is possible they perceived its characterization of his music as a blend of jit and Afro jazz to be limiting and imprecise. As one journalist would write several years later, "Mtukudzi cannot be labeled as a jazz artist per se . . . Mtukudzi's 'jazz' is not informed by any one dominant sound. There is a place for everything, a fusion of local beats."[46] On his website, Mtukudzi has similarly remarked, "In my research with the fans they said my music was uniquely influenced by the mbira, there is jit, there is tsavatsava, katekwe, there is dinhe . . . it might be a ballad but you can feel those elements. So they labeled it uniquely Tuku Music."[47]

Soon, Mtukudzi abandoned jitaj in favor of Tuku music, which began appearing in his promotional materials and on album covers. The cover of *Strange Isn't It* (1988), for example, featured the words "Tuku music" next to a photograph of Mtukudzi, superimposed over an abstract green spiral with the silhouetted shapes of indigenous instruments and musical practices—from ngoma drums and dancing figures to the single-stringed chipendani mouthbow—rendered in a style reminiscent of prehistoric rock art. By invoking forms of indigenous expressive culture on a commercial album, the visual layout of *Strange Isn't It* signaled Mtukudzi's willingness to move away from the hybrid term jitaj, and toward the more complex, ngoma-based musical identity embodied by the phrase Tuku music. Although Mtukudzi's efforts to name his music jitaj were ultimately unsuccessful, however, the very process of negotiating a new term for his sound with listeners was productive in its own right, serving to project Tuku music into a new discursive framework and to distinguish it from other commonly recognized genres.[48]

Forays into Film

As Mtukudzi solidified his position in Zimbabwe's emerging music scene, he also acquired new visibility as a cosmopolitan figure, thanks partly to his con-

Strange Isn't It. Courtesy of Tuku Music and Sheer Sound/Gallo Record Company.

nections with Debbie Metcalfe. In the process, he became increasingly involved in cross-disciplinary collaborations in fields such as film, theater, and dance. The BBC's 1989 documentary series *Under African Skies*, for example, featured Mtukudzi performing "Zvauya Sei" in the courtyard of the Queens Hotel, one of Harare's most renowned music venues. Shortly after this brief appearance, Mtukudzi was invited to join the cast of *Jit* (1991), the first local feature-length film produced after Zimbabwe's independence. True to its name, the film was packed with popular music, from artists whose names have since been largely forgotten—such as Mandebvu, Tobias Areketa, and Fallen Heroes—to enduring musical legends such as Robson Banda, John Chibadura, and Jonah Sithole.[49] Born in the Congo, Banda contributed "Ngoma Ngairire," or "Let the ngoma sound" and "Farirai Mwana Auya," or "Rejoice, your child has returned," tracks emblematic of his mastery of Zimbabwean genres such as jit and chimurenga. Sungura singer John Chibadura, the son of itinerant farmworkers from Mozambique, offered the reggae-inflected "Zuva Rekufa Kwangu," or "The day of my death," which had already garnered heavy radio play prior to its inclusion in the film.[50] Finally, legendary guitarist Jonah Sithole, whose innovative adaptations of mbira music were instrumental in the emergence of Thomas Mapfumo's chimurenga sound, contributed the song "Samere."

Mtukudzi's contributions to *Jit* included an eminently danceable version of the Methodist hymn "Mumweya," or "In spirit," as well as a trio of songs with a mixture of English and Shona lyrics, titled "Under Pressure," "What's Going On," and "Right Direction."[51] Of the three, "Right Direction" had already been featured in television advertisements for the ubiquitous plastic Sandak sandals marketed locally by Bata Shoes, making it familiar for local viewers. Against a background of syncopated, synthesized handclaps and arpeggiated ostinato guitar work, the lyrics to "Right Direction" invoked the type of comedic social commentary pioneered by Mtukudzi's childhood hero Safirio Madzikatire. Reminding listeners that travelers on the same train inevitably arrive together, no matter which class they travel in, Mtukudzi playfully reprimanded first-class passengers fixated on their social status by calling out, "Slow down, slow down, you're on the wrong direction!" Tying material consumption, social class, and mobility together with the ebullience of local music making, "Right Direction" epitomized the shared optimism of Zimbabwe's heady first decade of independence.

"Neria"

Neria, Neria o
Usaore moyoka Neria Mwari anewe
Usaore moyoka Neria Mwari anewe
Mwari aneweka Neria Mwari anewe

Neria, Neria, oh
Don't lose hope, Neria, God is with you
Don't give up hope, Neria, God is with you
God is with you Neria, God is with you

Kufirwa nemurume hanzvadzi
Zvinoda moyo wekushinga
Usaore moyoka Neria Mwari anewe
Usaore moyoka Neria Mwari anewe
Shinga moyo shinga Mwari anewe

Losing your husband, sister
Requires a courageous heart
Don't lose hope, Neria, God is with you
Don't give up hope, Neria, God is with you
Be strong, take courage, God is with you

Neria, Neria o
Usaore moyoka Neria Mwari anewe
Usaore moyoka Neria Mwari anewe
Mwari aneweka Neria Mwari anewe

Neria, Neria, oh
Don't lose hope, Neria, God is with you
Don't give up hope, Neria, God is with you
God is with you Neria, God is with you

Hupenyu imhindupindu
Ngwarira mhepo dzezviedzo
Usaore moyoka Neria Mwari anewe
Usaore moyoka Neria Mwari anewe
Shinga moyo shinga Mwari anewe

Life is chaotic
Watch out for the winds of tribulation
Don't lose hope, Neria, God is with you
Don't give up hope, Neria, God is with you
Be strong, take courage, God is with you

Vanhukadzi vanobatwa senhapwa
Kugara senherera
Usaore moyoka Neria Mwari anewe
Usaore moyoka Neria Mwari anewe
Shinga moyo shinga Mwari anewe

Women are treated like slaves
And live like orphans
Don't lose hope, Neria, God is with you
Don't give up hope, Neria, God is with you
Be strong, take courage, God is with you

Rufu rune shanje
Kutsaura vanodanana
Usaore moyo hanzvadzi Mwari anewe
Usaore moyoka Neria Mwari anewe
Shinga moyo shinga Mwari anewe

Death is jealous
And takes away those who love each other
Don't lose hope, my sister, God is with you
Don't give up hope, Neria, God is with you
Be strong, take courage, God is with you

FOUR

Neria

Singing the Politics of Inheritance

One of Zimbabwe's premiere movie theaters and performance venues, the 7 Arts Theatre lies off of King George Road in the Avondale Shopping Centre, a collection of upscale cafes, restaurants, and shops just north of downtown Harare. Despite its many amenities, the visual aesthetic of the Avondale complex long seemed straight of out the early 1960s, its lack of updates one more reminder that the ebullient days of Zimbabwe's early independence had given way to a sense of weary resignation. Perhaps no building proved this point more forcefully than the 7 Arts Theatre, a large brick complex gaudily adorned with colored letters forming the words "Rainbow Vistarama" above a small marquee listing movie show times. Yet over the years, the venue has regularly hosted luminaries of the Zimbabwean music and arts scene, from sungura singers such as Sulumani Chimbetu to Ndebele musicians such as Lovemore Majaivana and Busi Ncube.

In September 2002, I arrived at the 7 Arts for Tumbuka Dance Company's tenth anniversary performance, a celebration of the group's continued presence as Zimbabwe's only modern dance company. On the program was a piece set to "Neria," a song Mtukudzi originally wrote as the title track to the film *Neria* (1992), which sought to educate viewers about women's rights to inherit property after the death of a spouse.[1] The vision of director Godwin Mawuru, *Neria* was produced by the Media for Development Trust (MFD), a nongovernmental organization established to increase the availability of media materials "relevant to the development needs of Africa."[2] The MFD's first feature-length release, the film depicts the trials facing its protagonist, Neria, whose husband is killed riding his bicycle home from work. Shortly after the funeral, Neria's brother-in-law seizes her belongings, home, and even children. On the advice of a neighbor, she seeks recourse in the community courts. Despite the absence of a written will, a judge declares her eldest daughter Mavis as heir, appoints Neria as custodian, and orders her nefarious brother-in-law to return her husband's estate. At the end of the film, Neria's victory in the courts is echoed by a subsequent triumph in her husband's village, where she returns to complete the inheritance rite known as *kugara nhaka* (literally, "sitting inheritance"), which marks the symbolic transfer of the deceased's status to a family member, such as a son or younger brother.[3]

Facing the expectation to select one of her brothers-in-law as her new husband, she instead chooses her young son, indicating a desire to remain single and devote herself to her children.[4]

On the night of Tumbuka's tenth anniversary show, Mtukudzi put in a special guest appearance, playing an acoustic version of "Neria" as female dancer Maylene Chenjerai performed a dance solo choreographed by another dancer, Gilbert Douglas. Wearing a black, flowing skirt reminiscent of mourning clothes, Chenjerai began the piece seated on a spare, wooden bench—the only prop on the stage—as Mtukudzi launched into the distinctive, arpeggiated opening guitar lines of "Neria." Large enough for only a single person, the bench seemed to signal a lack of material possessions, recalling Neria's empty home after her dispossession in the film. Alternately clutching her hands to her chest, covering her face and head, and pummeling the bench, Chenjerai gradually abandoned her initially defensive body posture, leaving the bench behind to use the stage, as well as her own body, more expansively. Yet as Mtukudzi's voice washed over her, she occasionally reverted to the emotions that had colored the piece's beginning, falling suddenly to the ground and hitting it with her fists, or returning to sit on the bench with her arms covering her face. As the piece neared an end, Mtukudzi's magnetic musical presence finally pulled her in completely, drawing her ever closer to where he was seated with his guitar. By the time the last notes of "Neria" rang out in the silent hall, Chenjerai was standing immobile next to Mtukudzi with her arms clasped across her chest, as if expecting him to alleviate her grief and pain.

As Chenjerai would later tell me, her interpretation of "Neria" was shaped by her family's long history of collaboration with Mtukudzi. Her grandmother, Susan Chenjerai, sang with Mtukudzi in the Wagon Wheels during the late 1970s.[5] Her mother, Jane Chenjerai, also performed with Mtukudzi, contributing to early recordings such as "Waenda Rosemary" (KDZ 109, 1977). Part of a lineage of powerful female artists, Chenjerai was well-positioned to deliver a moving interpretation of Gilbert's choreography. Reflecting back on her performance, however, Chenjerai described dancing to "Neria" as particularly difficult, saying, "Oliver did it as a movie, so it already talks about a woman that had the husband die. So I just had to put myself as a widow. And how am I going to say that using my body? . . . What goes on in the song is easier heard, and you can understand. But now putting it to dance, I just found it so hard." For Chenjerai, this challenge was intensified by the affective power of dancing to Mtukudzi's live, solo performance: "My heart just went kaboom. . . . It was very emotional, because he was right there in my face. And I felt like he's a father that's telling me not to worry, you'll be fine. At the end of that performance, I promise you, I was the one that was crying, by myself." Like Chenjerai,

"Waenda Rosemary"

Mtukudzi: *Nhai Rozi, mukadzi wangu, wadii wadzoka kumba?*
Chenjerai: *Inini here Baba Tichaona?*
Mtukudzi: *Hongu mukadzi wangu.*
Chenjerai: *Ah, kumba kwenyu handichauya ini.*
Mtukudzi: *Inga wani Mercedes Benz ndinayo, mari ndinayo zvese panapa.*
Chenjerai: *Zvino mari neMercedes Benz ndorugare here?*
Mtukudzi: *Aiwa ka mudiwa wangu. Zvino kwawamhanyira ikoko kusina mari, ndorugare here?*
Chenjerai: *Asi kune rufaro, hakuna kushushwa, ndosaka ndagara hangu kusina mari ini.*
Mtukudzi: *Aiwa kukushusha kwakapera mukadzi wangu, dzoka mhani iwe.*
Chenjerai: *Aiwa, kumba kwenyu handichauya.*
Mtukudzi: *Ah, dai wadzoka mukadzi wangu.*
Chenjerai: *Handidzoke.*

"Rosemary has gone"

Mtukudzi: Hey, Rosy, my wife, why don't you come back home?
Chenjerai: Are you talking to me, Baba Tichaona?
Mtukudzi: Yes, my wife.
Chenjerai: Ah, I'm not coming back to your house.
Mtukudzi: But look, I have a Mercedes Benz, I have money; everything is here.
Chenjerai: Now, money and a Mercedes Benz, is that a good life?
Mtukudzi: Oh, no, my dear. Now, over there where you've run to, with no money, is that a good life?
Chenjerai: But there is happiness, there is no bullying, that's what I've living with no money.
Mtukudzi: The bullying has stopped my wife, return, man!
Chenjerai: No, I'm not coming back to your house.
Mtukudzi: Ah, if only you'd return.
Chenjerai: I won't return.

Mtukudzi's listeners often describe being moved to tears upon hearing him play "Neria." After one live performance, for example, a public health administrator living in Harare reflected, "When he did the Neria thing . . . even as a health worker, I could cry." Upon hearing the first notes of the song ring out at Mtukudzi's HIFA performance in 2008, another audience member similarly declared, "Now it's time to cry."[6]

Music and Moral Kinship in "Neria"

In this chapter, I illustrate how "Neria" has proven particularly effective in drawing listeners in to an imagined social world. A compelling musical narrative of kinship, loss, and bereavement, "Neria" reminds us that funerary rituals are what anthropologist Frederick Klaits has described as a "ground of politics" within the family.[7] As such, the song has resonated with the lived experience of many of Mtukudzi's listeners. From his extensive contact with radio audiences, for example, DJ Richmond Siyakurima observed, "Each time you play 'Neria' the chances are you will get somebody phoning in, [saying it] reminds them of what happened after their father died. The uncle came in and took everything else: 'I'm not going to school, because my uncle took everything that our father left for us. I'm not going to school, because my mother was chased away by my uncle.'" Rather than hearing "Neria" as a fictionalized account of a general social problem, in other words, many listeners felt personally connected to the song, which they saw as narrating the individual circumstances of their own lives. One listener, for example, described "Neria" as speaking directly to "what had happened in my immediate family, my extended family." Following this type of close identification with the song, Mtukudzi's audiences have mobilized "Neria" in a variety of creative ways in order to navigate their own social worlds, bringing the song into new contexts that range from film festivals to poems such as Batsirai Chigama's "Heroes," which contrasts the exalted status of martyrs who died in the liberation war to unsung heroes such as Neria.[8]

As a film, *Neria* advocated for settling matters of inheritance through civil law and written wills, rather than through the customary inheritance practices collectively known as *nhaka*. Yet this modernizing discourse had larger implications, conveying a vision of society in which collectively negotiated identities would cede to individual rights. As such, the film suggested fundamental changes in the production of human relations, replacing the social ethos of hunhu with an individual, rights-based legal framework. As I will argue in the second section of this chapter, however, Mtukudzi's soundtrack complicated this carefully scripted message, asserting the importance of moral kinship in enabling families to navigate struggles over inheritance. I pay particular attention to how Mtukudzi's songs have portrayed rituals such as kugara nhaka, depicted

Neria

I looked at the traditional and the Western interpretation of inheritance, and I found out that both were trying to safeguard the family, but that people were misrepresenting or misinterpreting for their own good and for their own greediness. And I thought, well, why not bring these to a platform where people can think about it, can debate about it? I'm happy that it made the people that were in law really look at the law, and it assisted or ignited that wish to change some of the laws. Indeed, after '92, new laws came into being.

If you can sort out the politics at the family level, I think it's easier to push that into the bigger sphere. And I think that same family politics influences leaders, because they come from families as well. If they think they're the only ones who have solutions for everyone and they're always right, from the family level, it goes up to the highest level in the country. So I think yes, it sounds political, but it starts at the family level.

Looking at the project that we were working on, Oliver's music suited the kind of film that we wanted to produce. I was amazed, because, well, there are times when you meet a musician, and you think he doesn't understand film—which is not a fault—and you think, let me guide the person. But with Tuku, actually, he brought much more than one had asked for. As soon as he understood the story, it became his story.

—*Godwin Mawuru*

in the last scene of the film, as meaningful forms of contemporary social practice rather than anachronistic vestiges of the past.

Writing "Neria"

The storyline of *Neria* closely paralleled the childhood experiences of its director Godwin Mawuru, whose mother was similarly left destitute after his father was prematurely killed in a car accident. While the film took Mawuru's personal history as a point of departure, however, its script was crafted through a process of intensive research, with a team of experts from the fields of law,

women's rights, and the arts advising the MFD on legal and cultural aspects
of the film's screenplay. Intensely involved in the film, Mtukudzi composed its
theme song, compiled its soundtrack, and played a supporting role as Neria's
brother, Jethro.

The centerpiece of *Neria*'s soundtrack, Mtukudzi's "haunting theme song"
was his most significant artistic contribution to the film.[9] Demonstrating his extraordinary abilities as a songwriter, "Neria" was commissioned on an impossi-
bly tight schedule, leaving Mtukudzi only three days to write what would prove
one of his most powerful songs. As he told me:

> Godwin Mawuru came, brought me the script, and said, "Here's the stor-
> yline. . . . But we don't have time. We only have three days. We need this
> theme song in three days. Because the way the theme song is is going to
> guide us, how we're going to shoot this thing." I said, "Fine, OK, I'll do my
> best." And he came to find out how far I'd gone on the second day, and I
> hadn't even read the script. And I was like, "Oh, I forgot to do this thing."
> So at night I browsed through the script, read a few lines on every page,
> just to get the sense of the storyline. And from the way he had explained to
> me, I thought, "The best way to come up with the best song is to involve
> myself in the storyline, and either give advice to my sister, or be the hus-
> band, or whatever." And I thought, "Of the whole storyline, the strongest
> song is to be supportive of the main character. That will bring out best
> song." And I thought, "OK, then I'm going to be the brother of the main
> character." So I wrote my words as the brother to the main character. And
> the next morning I went into a studio, laid down what I thought, and sent
> it to them. And it was just overwhelmingly accepted.

Debbie Metcalfe, Mtukudzi's manager at the time, remembered her amazement
at his ability to write such compelling music under this kind of pressure: "Where
does Tuku get that? Like the writing of 'Neria,' John Riber coming in to say,
'Debbie, you know, it's two days to go, and I thought you were on this.' I said,
'Oh shit John.' You know, Tuku only had that one [phone] line at home, there
was no cell phones in those days, nothing. He's been in Bindura for the week, or
something, and I'm being told he's got two days to write the theme song for the
movie. And look at it!"

Slow and meditative, "Neria" marks a pivotal point in the film's narrative,
just before its protagonist finally overcomes her victimization and asserts her
agency by bringing her brother-in-law to trial. Sung from the perspective of
Neria's brother, Jethro, Mtukudzi's lyrics are meant to empower her to act. A
poignant example of Mtukudzi's reliance on kinship terms to invoke the moral
relations of hunhu, "Neria" uses the words *hanzvadzi*, or sister, and *murume*,

or husband, in order to locate the fictional characters of Jethro and Neria on an imagined social map. As Stephen Chifunyise observes, his lyrics encompass layers of different characters and voices, including "Neria herself, and the way the song talks about Neria, and what people say about it, and what the future holds, and what women should do, and how women have been handled from over the years, and so forth. . . . It's like modernizing a very indigenous art form of topical musicals . . . where you have characters in the songs, and the characters are clearly distinct."

The Reception of "Neria"

Mtukudzi described "Neria" as an attempt to craft a musical narrative that would be relatable for a broad spectrum of listeners, telling me, "It was kind of a personalized song; all the same, I tried my best to make it as broad as possible, so that anyone who listens to the song, who understands what I'm talking about, will use the song, and not end up in the Neria story." He initially doubted whether audiences would connect with it, saying, "Being a soft song like that, would it make any sense to somebody who hasn't watched the film? I wasn't sure about that." Yet listeners have overwhelmingly reported feeling intimately connected to "Neria." This is particularly true of women who have experienced struggles similar to those portrayed in the film. Describing "Neria" as one of her favorite songs, for example, a middle-aged woman in Harare stated, "I'm a widow. So Neria is one [too]. He sings about the trials and tribulations of a widow." Yet the song's appeal has also crossed gender lines, leading one man to observe that its lyrics reflected "how female members had been badly treated" within his own family.

With his nuanced approach to singing about kinship, bereavement, and death, Mtukudzi's soundtrack to the film proved wildly successful. Shortly after its release, the album won a prestigious South African M-NET award for best movie soundtrack. As Metcalfe recalls, this was an impressive accomplishment given that Mtukudzi was up against the musical *Sarafina*, "which was a massive hit in South Africa. And no one could believe that Neria actually . . . went on to win that M-NET award." Ultimately, the popularity of Mtukudzi's soundtrack would eclipse that of the film itself, prompting MFD founder John Riber to suggest that his songs were the primary factor responsible for keeping the film's fictional character and message alive.[10] The soundtrack also proved more commercially viable than the film, prompting Mtukudzi to rerecord the album in a studio with updated technology nine years after its original release. The new disc sold over twenty-five thousand copies, surpassing the original album and earning Mtukudzi a gold disc.[11] Soon, "Neria" was among Mtukudzi's most popular songs not only in Zimbabwe, but also throughout Africa. As one Ghanaian listener told me: "I LOVE this song, partly because I saw the movie and fully understand the story. Whenever I hear the song, I am able to put my feet in the shoes of a widow like Neria and feel her pain. Issues of inheritance and family interference are just as real in Ghana and I understand what the song represents and means . . . I also love the slow rhythm that gradually pulls me into the song and puts me in a different world." In South Africa, one reviewer similarly noted that members of Mtukudzi's audience "did not just sing along with him, but were actually competing, trying to outdo him" as he sang "Neria" at a live show in Pretoria.[12]

By far the most fascinating aspect of the song's reception, however, lies in the way audiences have repurposed "Neria" within the context of their daily lives, using it as a springboard in launching their own, individualized responses to kinship, grief, women's rights, and the contemporary politics of inheritance. Raised in the city of Bulawayo, for example, brothers John and Mpho Mambira are founding members of the neotraditional music group Bongo Love. In a conversation with fellow group member Trymore Jombo, they recalled what happened when their father gave Mtukudzi's album to his recently widowed sister:

> Mpho: Our dad bought her the LP, on vinyl, that, "This is yours, don't be heartbroken."
> John: "Don't be heartbroken," 'cause she was heartbroken.
> Mpho: Also, "God has done his will, but your life has not ended. Do something." So she continued to do something, doing her business, gardening.
> John: And she survived with a good life. But the first few weeks, she was someone who thought her life had ended. But dad bought her the vinyl of *Neria*, saying, "This is your present." So, she used to play it, you know.
> Trymore: It comforted her.
> John: Yes, it comforted her, exactly.

Their aunt identified so closely with the lyrics to "Neria" that she adopted Mtukudzi's title track as a sort of personal theme song, listening to it repeatedly. As John Mambira recalled: "She used to come on the weekends to our house, carrying that vinyl with her. And then when we spent time together—enjoying ourselves, drinking—she would say, 'Oh, play my song for me.' You know? And then upon playing it, you would see our *tete* [paternal aunt] dancing with our dad, and us kids. Dancing, you know? It's life changing. It changed her."

Back to the 7 Arts

Nearly seven years after attending Tumbuka's tenth anniversary performance at the 7 Arts, I visited a company rehearsal at the National Ballet of Zimbabwe.

As it happened, Gilbert Douglas, who had originally choreographed "Neria," had recently dug out an old VHS cassette of the 7 Arts performance, which he was watching with dancer Maylene Chenjerai. The following day, I returned to speak to Douglas, now the company's artistic director, about how "Neria" had inspired him as a dancer and choreographer. In reply, he offered the following story:

> When they did the movie *Neria*, at the same time there was a woman that I knew who lived next to my house. She had the same exact problems that were depicted in the movie; her husband had just died, and she had a stroke. So she couldn't speak, she couldn't walk, she was being carried to go to the loo, and everything.
>
> And the relatives of the husband just came, and collected everything, and left her with eight kids. And the house was a very small, two-roomed house. Eight kids—two boys, and the rest were girls—and they didn't want anything to do with them. They just collected the property, and they left. The man had done a lot for his family. He was extending the house, he had a car, he had lots of things that they could actually live on, but the relatives just collected everything.
>
> And because of the song, what it talks about, it inspired me to do something for that woman. Because the song was very inspiring. It's touching, and it's a very common thing with the Shona culture that the relatives of the husband or relatives of the wife just come and collect everything once their relative passes away. And they never leave anything for the kids.
>
> In a Shona context, when you take someone's property, you say you're becoming the heir. So you have to take the children as well. But because they didn't take the children, it became a burden to the woman. So, the children wanted to go to school, they wanted food, they wanted clothing. And nobody, none of them, was looking after that. They all just disappeared. . .
>
> It's something that was very personal. It's something that I needed to talk about, I wanted to discuss, I wanted to say something about . . . So for me, when things like that happen, I would just like to say something about it. I just comment. And for me, I put myself in her shoes, and tried to think, "What she's thinking, how she's feeling?"

Here we see with exceptional clarity how Douglas's creative response to "Neria" enabled him to articulate and reflect upon social relations in the high-density township of Tafara, where he lived. Among the most interesting aspects of his choreography is how Chenjerai's body becomes a surrogate for that of Douglas's widowed neighbor, symbolically embodying the experiences of a widow who has been rendered physically immobile. Yet Douglas's story also illustrates how listeners launch songs such as "Neria" into new contexts, extending their social meanings.

Much to my surprise, Douglas proceeded to describe his engagement with Tuku music as extending far beyond the individual pieces he has choreographed to Mtukudzi's songs. In fact, Douglas described listening to Tuku music almost constantly throughout his working process, from the moment he initially begins to conceptualize a piece to his subsequent rehearsals with Tumbuka's dancers:

> I always use Tuku's music before I start on anything that I'm going to cho-
> reograph. It's just for me, to inspire me. And then, if I need that same in-
> spiration on the dancers, then I bring it on to the dancers. Even though
> I might not use that music, or I might never use that music at all, in the
> piece. In the final project, there might be no Tuku music at all. But in the
> process, there will be a lot of listening to Tuku music. 'Cause—it's just the
> way he writes that's very interesting for me.
>
> When he writes, he writes things that are relevant. Especially to me,
> 'cause coming from the ghetto, you know what he's talking about. When
> he says something, you know exactly what he's talking about. So it's quite
> easy to relate to that. And then, when he comments like that, then you
> think. You take a step back and look at it, and yeah, there's much more to
> say once you have that kind of inspiration.

Reflecting Mtukudzi's dialogic approach to singing hunhu, Douglas further likened listening to the singer to a conversation, stating, "When I listen to some of his music, it's like discussing with someone. 'Cause when you're listening to it, you say, 'Oh, yeah, yeah, yeah, that's what I'm thinking about, that's what I'm saying.'"

Taking Action in the Diaspora

Yet "Neria" also prompted more concrete forms of social action around the is-sues portrayed in the film. In Philadelphia, diasporic listener Esau Mavindidze told me that Mtukudzi's approach to singing about social issues seemed to "de-mand that people think about these things, and do something. . . . I put Tu-ku's CD in my car. And I'm driving. And so the message is coming again. And so when you are driving, you are thinking, 'My goodness, what can I do about some of these things?'" In Mavindidze's comments, we see Tuku music produc-ing the sense of mutual social obligation situated at the heart of hunhu. Yet as a member of Zimbabwe's growing diaspora, Mavindidze must work harder in meeting this sense of social obligation. One of the ways he has done this is by joining forces with other diasporic Zimbabweans to provide material assistance back home, including a clothing drive he helped organize for a Zimbabwean or-phanage. The largest project he has taken on, however, was organizing a film fes-tival around the theme of women's inheritance rights after hearing Mtukudzi's song "Neria" as a graduate student:

> "Neria," I remember I was in Syracuse. It had a big impact on me, and I started researching, and having a film festival. . . . My sister was quite an activist when she was at the university. And so she was drawing me to all these female, feminist issues. And around that time I think it was quite a big activity in Zimbabwe's civic organizations, around issues of femi-nism. You know, just interrogating the status quo, and patriarchy. And so "Neria," actually, is what drives me to this, and to get interested, and then researching the legal age of majority. I wrote a paper—it was not pub-lished, I presented it. . . . We called it a Pan-African film festival. And I cre-ated that festival, actually. And so the first time we showed *Neria*, I had written this paper around the theme.

Like Douglas, Mavindidze emphasized the dialogic aspect of Tuku music. As he told me, "I've heard a lot of my friends saying, 'But, what was Tuku talking about?' You know, just that statement, when someone asks you, 'What did Tuku mean in this regard?' And then you talk about it."

Navigating "tradition" and "modernity" through law

Reflecting Mavindidze's efforts to enact social change in the diaspora, "Neria" spoke to debates about governance, nationhood, and law in Zimbabwe. As a film, *Neria* sought to engender significant changes in relations of gender and authority within the domestic household. Through its carefully crafted script, *Neria* en-couraged women to make use of Zimbabwe's civil courts to protect their rights as individuals. In contrast to the benevolent power of civil law, the film portrayed customary inheritance practices, or nhaka, as detrimental to the well-being of women, with one internal MFD document suggesting that women were "treated like little children and have no say or control over their very own lives" under customary jurisdiction.[13] The film's bias toward the modernizing influence of law, with its codified and written legal norms, was explicit; as *Neria*'s planning committee concluded, "It is advisable that people be married under Civil Law and that they should write wills."[14]

Members of the film's design team viewed friction between the spheres of "tradition" and "modernity" as the primary factor motivating family disputes over inheritance. As sociologist Joan May suggested during an interim plan-ning meeting, "customary law is functional in its own context, but things have moved quickly to modern life. People's thinking has changed, and the laws must change with it. What is functional in a village becomes non-functional in the city."[15] Accordingly, the film's screenplay depicts Neria, along with her husband and children, living a modern life in the city, while her jealous brother-in-law clings to traditional ways in the rural areas. The schism between rural and urban spheres is also reinforced through Neria's feeling that her rural mother-in-law "just doesn't understand city life." Locating Neria and her children within this cultural conflict zone, the film suggests they are "one of the many families caught between traditional and modern ways of life."[16] In its most egregious and stereotypical portrayal of "tradition," Neria has a dream in which her covetous brother-in-law and his wife appear dressed in the short skirts, feathered *ngundu* headdresses, and patterned *retso* cloth typically worn by spirit mediums and traditional healers. With wrists laden with the copper bracelets known as *ndarira*, long favored as an indigenous adornment, they raise a knife to murder Neria as she lies on her sleeping mat. Illuminated by a diffuse red light, these shadowy figures appear as the very personification of evil, inviting viewers to ponder whether perhaps tradition itself constitutes the most significant threat to Neria's well-being.

Even as *Neria*'s production team sought to mobilize Mtukudzi's music in order to fulfill their objective of enacting modernist reform, however, his songs departed subtly from the carefully crafted messages conveyed by the film's script. While Mtukudzi's lyrics acknowledge that women "are treated like slaves / And live like orphans," for example, he circumvents the film's portrayal of jealous in-laws as the primary threat to women's well-being. Instead, his theme song refocuses attention on the invidious consequences of death itself through lyrics such as, "Death is jealous, separating those who love each other." Replacing the image of covetous in-laws with that of death itself as jealous, "Neria" privileges the intricacies of negotiating moral kinship over the concern with material inheritance foregrounded in the film's screenplay.[17]

Through a series of idioms, the lyrics to "Neria" also encourage the film's widowed protagonist to move away from despair, or "rottenness in the heart" (*kuora moyo*), and toward courage, or a "strong heart" (*kushinga moyo*). A common canvas for the projection of metaphor, the heart is often used by Shona speakers as a platform for expressing sentiments ranging from encouragement to restraint.[18] It is also closely tied to many of the moral qualities of hunhu, such as altruism, or "a pure heart" (*moyochena*), and patience, or "a long heart" (*moyo murefu*).[19] Through idioms of the heart, "Neria" suggests that moral character is a valuable resource in navigating the trials of death. Rather than relying entirely on external mechanisms such as written wills, marriage certificates, or the civil courts, Mtukudzi's songs locate the solutions to problems of inheritance at least partly in the reciprocal moral obligations of hunhu.

Singing the Complex Politics of Lineage Remarriage

Nowhere is Mtukudzi's ability to convey an alternate perspective on customary inheritance more evident than in his approach to the lineage remarriage rite known as kugara nhaka, depicted in the last scene of the film. Often referred to as "wife inheritance," kugara nhaka is among the most contentious aspects of inheritance in contemporary Zimbabwe, eliciting the type of strong reactions typified by the following description: "This custom has invidious consequences in contemporary society. The woman may be expected to become the wife of a man she has never seen in order to keep her children. Or she may have to lose her children in order to retain her autonomy. A social rule which in times past ensured that a widow and her children would be cared for by her husband's kin now treats her as a chattel."[20] In the film's closing scene, Neria and her in-laws are portrayed conducting kugara nhaka, typically held a year after the funeral. Seated in the family's yard on a reed mat, Neria rises to pick up a metal basin filled with water, a ceremonial axe, or *gano*, and a walking stick, or *tsvimbo*, which she is expected to hand to one of her husband's brothers, thereby recognizing him as her new husband and guardian. Instead, Neria chooses an option for women who do not wish to be remarried, passing over her husband's brothers in favor of her own young son. As several generations of her deceased husband's male relatives grumble that her refusal to accept one of them must be "a plot," Neria makes a final declaration of agency, asserting, "I have my own life to live."

Typically held immediately after the postfunerary rite of kurova guva, which symbolically reincorporates the spirit of the deceased within the family's ancestral lineage, kugara nhaka is part of a complex of ritual events conducted after an individual's death, beginning with the funeral, or *nhamo*, and proceeding to the subsequent memorial service known as *nyaradzo* or *ndongamahwe*. Together, this series of rituals serves not only to distribute the material estate of the deceased, but also to restructure kinship relations, marking the symbolic transfer of the deceased's status to a family member, preferably either a child or sibling of the same sex.[21] Because only kugara nhaka is portrayed in *Neria*, however, the interconnectedness of this constellation of rituals, which collectively ensure an individual's transition from a living family member to a spirit elder, or *mudzimu*, is obscured within the film.

An alternate perspective on kugara nhaka, however, surfaces in Mtukudzi's soundtrack to the film. In his song "Kugara Nhaka," for example, Mtukudzi offers an alternate portrayal of the ritual, which differs significantly from the design team's reification of customary inheritance as an ossified set of cultural rules. As Mtukudzi sings:

Kugara nhaka varume	To perform *kugara nhaka*, men
Kuona dzevamwe	Is to observe others performing it
Kudzidza hakupere	Learning never ends
Ruzivo masiyiranwa	Knowledge is a thing inherited
Kugara nhaka varume	To perform *kugara nhaka*, men
Kuona dzevamwe	Is to observe others performing it
Kudzidza hakupere	Learning never ends
Ruzivo maturiranwa	Knowledge is a thing passed down

Encouraging listeners to learn from all aspects of the inheritance ceremonies they have witnessed—both positive and negative—Mtukudzi's lyrics remind listeners that interpretations of customary inheritance are shaped by a variety of influences, voices, and individuals. Through the word *masiyiranwa* (sg. *musiyiranwa*), which refers to inherited objects, values, or ideas, as well as to the very process of passing these down to new heirs, Mtukudzi positions kugara nhaka itself as a form of intangible cultural heritage.[22] His lyrics likewise suggest that the practice of kugara nhaka is subject to constant renewal, reinterpretation, and reinvention as it is modified and refined by each subsequent generation to inherit it.[23]

Through this nuanced approach to kugara nhaka, Mtukudzi's soundtrack departs from the film's carefully scripted messages on gender, law, and individual rights. Indeed, Mtukudzi has explicitly stated his belief that lineage remarriage "wasn't meant to be bad. When it's been done the right way, it works. When one dies, somebody has to take care of that family, to help it out. That's how it was designed."[24] This perspective has put him at odds with prevailing discourses on gender, civil law, and development, leading journalist Funny Mashava to observe, "Tuku dares to go where others, especially women, have been scared to go. He tackles the issue of nhaka which of late has come under attack from all women's groups. But Tuku says there is a positive side to it and that it is people who are to blame and not the culture."[25] Located at the margins of the film's English-language screenplay, Mtukudzi's Shona soundtrack is one of the least regulated spaces within film, granting him considerable latitude in expressing an alternate perspective on inheritance practices. Through his musical contributions to *Neria*, Mtukudzi asserts that rituals such as kugara nhaka, otherwise marginalized by the film's impulse toward modernist reform, continue to play an important role in enabling families to navigate kinship relations fractured by death.

With his nuanced approach to singing about the contested politics of inheritance, Mtukudzi's soundtrack to *Neria* immersed listeners in a powerfully imagined world of mourning, kinship, struggle, and grief. A meditation on death's impact on family relations, Mtukudzi's soundtrack depicted fictionalized versions of experiences common to many of his listeners, enabling it to remain relevant even outside the context of the film. Establishing a vibrant, imagined world of social relations, "Neria" in particular invited listeners of both genders to symbolically position themselves in relation to its lyrics. In turn, Mtukudzi's wildly popular ballad evoked a wide spectrum of creative responses, demonstrating with particular clarity the type of active engagement typical among his audiences.

Beyond Neria: The Perils of Experimentation

Participating in *Neria* soon encouraged Mtukudzi to try his hand at theater, leading to the debut of an original musical play called *Was My Child* in 1993. Produced in collaboration with acoustic guitarist Steve Makoni, *Was My Child* addressed the emerging social phenomenon of street children, once again placing family politics at the heart of Mtukudzi's artistic endeavors. While Mtukudzi's accompanying album *Was My Child* (1993) cemented his image as "a man who carries his social conscience around like his acoustic guitar," however, the play received decidedly unfavorable reviews.[26] Part of the problem lay in its cast, which was made up almost entirely of amateur actors working for minimal pay. Plagued by constant financial difficulties, the company was unable to secure stable rehearsal space, compelling them to relocate every few weeks. Tired of toiling in obscurity, several actors dropped out midway through rehearsals, leaving director Tawanda Kuchera in a panic. By the time *Was My Child* premiered in the mid-sized town of Masvingo, it was so clearly troubled that several audience members shouted and jeered during the performance. Describing the play as a total flop, one reviewer went so far as to call it "Tuku's dumped baby."[27] Plans to turn *Was My Child* into a movie were quietly scrapped, and the production faded into obscurity.[28]

The "Protestant Singer" Turns to Gospel

Shortly after *Was My Child*, Mtukudzi faced more criticism for turning to the emerging genre of local gospel, issuing a flurry of albums with names such as *Rumbidzai Jehova*, or "Praise the Lord" (1992), *Ndotomuimbira*, or "Unto Him shall I sing" (1992), *Mapisarema AOliver Mtukudzi*, or, "Oliver Mtukudzi's Psalms" (1996), and *Pfugama Unamate*, or "Kneel down and pray" (1997).[29] This turn toward Christian songs reflected larger shifts in Zimbabwean popular music, with the rise of gospel artists such as Mechanic Manyeruke and Hosiah Chipanga. From Mtukudzi's perspective, gospel's popularity was linked to the series of economic difficulties facing Zimbabweans in the 1990s, beginning with an extended period of drought:

I think drought has contributed a lot in people turning into gospel music. People never knew whether the rains were going to come, and we all depend on rain here. And, I think it must have contributed to people going in to gospel music. 'Cause the pressure, I got from my fans. Yes, they had the demand for this all along, but this time it was it was a big blow. And, wherever I go, "Why don't you make a gospel song? We should have something religious." So I thought, "Let me do it, let me do it," 'cause the pressure was just too much. But, I think it's the problems people had that contributed them to go into gospel music. It's very popular, it's not only me.[30]

While some of Mtukudzi's gospel songs, such as "Rumbidzai Jehova" (*Rumbidzai Jehova*, 1992) were original pieces inspired by particular Bible verses, many others, including "Ndiri Mwana Wenyu" (*Rumbidzai Jehova*, 1992) were lifted straight out of the Presbyterian hymnal from his childhood church in Highfield.[31] Mtukudzi's arrangements of these hymns ran a gamut of musical styles, from the unaccompanied four-part choral harmonies of songs such as "Hatina Musha" (*Neria*, 1992), to the up-tempo, interlocking guitar lines of "Mumweya" (*Jit*, 1991).[32] Yet almost none of them conformed to the stylistic norms emerging within Zimbabwe's nascent gospel scene, which foregrounded what Ezra Chitando has described as "music using the collective Christian memory that is accompanied by an up-tempo, danceable rhythm or a somber, reflective style."[32] As one listener told me, Mtukudzi's music was "not gospel music, it's more church music. There's a difference . . . Tuku is singing straight Methodist hymns."

Mtukudzi's gospel was a far cry from the vibrant sounds of Tuku music, which listeners were used to hearing as they traveled the streets of Harare in crowded Peugeot "emergency taxis," passed by the ubiquitous record bars of township shopping centers, or attended live shows at venues such as the famed Queens Hotel, with its festive atmosphere and all-night performances, or pungwes. In his gospel albums, the dialogic elements of songs such as "Yorire Ngoma" (*Zvauya Sei*, 1986) gave way to the four-part choral singing introduced by Christian missionaries, and the multivalent musical imaginaries of songs such as "Neria" (*Neria*, 1992) were replaced by biblical quotations. As a result, Mtukudzi's approach to gospel music struck many listeners as staid and old-fashioned, particularly when compared to the more creative songs of emerging gospel artists such as Manyeruke and Chipanga. Further compounding this negative reception, Mtukudzi's gospel albums were marred by particularly low production value. Instead of the interlocking arrangements and ebullient guitar lines they had come to expect, his audiences now encountered poorly synthesized sounds—including a drum machine—that quickly killed any sense of liveness.

Perhaps unsurprisingly, listeners who had fallen in love with the distinctive sounds of Tuku music were disappointed by Mtukudzi's new-found predilection for singing Christian hymns. As journalist Robert Mukondiwa recalled, even loyal listeners began referring to Mtukudzi as "a goner," expressing the growing sentiment that the singer had "gone down. He's singing gospel music. He's singing the United Methodist hymnbook." In comparison with his powerful presence during the liberation years, Mtukudzi now seemed a faded version of his previous self. Around the nation, his fans were left wondering whether the "Protestant musician" had inadvertently lost his way precisely in his own repeated pleas for divine guidance.

"Dzoka Uyamwe"
(Return and be suckled)

Mandiona kusviba mati kuora	You see that I am black, you say I am rotten
Kundiona kusviba mati kuora	Seeing I am black, you say I am rotten
Vandiona kusviba vati kuora	They see I am black, they say I am rotten
Kundiona kusviba hunzi kuora	Seeing I am black, and saying I am rotten
Kwangu vakomana mandiremera	Back home, boys, I'm overwhelmed
Ndoenda kwangu varumewe mandiremera	I shall go back home, men, I'm overwhelmed
Kufunga Dande vakomana mandiremera	Thinking of Dande, boys, I'm overwhelmed
Ndafunga Dande	I think of Dande
Kudzoka Dande	Return to Dande
Ndasuwa Dande	I long for Dande
Kudzoka Dande	Return to Dande
Ndafunga Dande vakomana ndafunga kwedu	I think of Dande, boys, I think of home
Dzoka	Come back
Kufunga Dande varume ndafunga kwedu	Thinking of Dande, men, I think of home
Dzoka uyamwe	Return and be suckled
Ndafunga Dande vakomana ndafunga kwedu	I think of Dande, boys, I think of home
Dzoka	Come back
Kudzoka Dande varume ndafunga kwedu	Return to Dande, boys, I think of home
Dzoka uyamwe	Return and be suckled
Uya zvako gotwe rangu we dzoka	Come my last born, return
Zamu rakamirira iwe	My breast awaits you
Dzoka uyamwe	Return and be suckled
Kukurumura kwandakaita gore riya	That year that I weaned you
Pawakasiyira ndipapo	When you left me here
Dzoka uyamwe	Return and be suckled
Mandiona kusviba mati kuora	You see that I am black, you say I am rotten
Kundiona kusviba mati kuora	Seeing I am black, you say I am rotten
Vandiona kusviba vati kuora	They see I am black, they say I am rotten
Kundiona kusviba hunzi kuora	Seeing I am black, and saying I am rotten
Kuora kwemunhu kuri mumoyo	Rottenness is within a person's heart
Kusviba kwemunhu kuri mupfungwa	Blackness is within a person's thoughts
Kuora kwemunhu kuri mumoyo varume	Rottenness is within a person's heart, men
Kusviba kwemunhu kuri mupfungwa	Blackness is within a person's thoughts

FIVE

Return to Dande

In 1998, Mtukudzi responded to the growing concern over his artistic choices by releasing a blockbuster album, titled simply *Tuku Music*. In the words of one Zimbabwean journalist, the record "broke a five-year jinx for Mtukudzi, whom many had ruled out musically."[1] Lauded in the local press, *Tuku Music* both heralded Mtukudzi's reemergence within the local music scene and catapulted him onto a global stage. A gem of an album, its nine tracks flowed together effortlessly, immersing listeners in the magnetic strains of a perfect groove. As always, the rich, gravelly tones of Mtukudzi's melodious voice were foregrounded within the mix, conveying a soulful, emotional quality even for listeners unfamiliar with Shona. Addressing a wide range of contemporary Zimbabwean social issues, from AIDS to child abuse, the album marked a return to the musical imaginaries of hunhu that had long defined Mtukudzi's music.

Recorded at South Africa's Ikwezi Studios, *Tuku Music* was produced by Mtukudzi's long-time friend and colleague Steve Dyer, now back in South Africa after his many years of self-imposed exile in Zimbabwe. In its lyrics and musical arrangements, *Tuku Music* struck many listeners as the work of a mature artist at the height of his musical prowess. As Zimbabwean poet Chirikure Chirikure, who participated in writing the album's liner notes, remarked, the album "marked a turning point, brought a new dimension to Tuku."[2] Alongside regular members of the Black Spirits, *Tuku Music* featured a number of special guests, including guitarist Louis Mhlanga, keyboard player Keith Farquharson, percussionist Tlale Makhene, and bassist Herbie Tsoaeli. Joining these guest artists, the Black Spirits' backing singers Mary Bell and Mwendi Chibindi contributed tightly harmonized vocal lines, their voices blending together as if woven from a single thread. Throughout, the interlocking melodies of Mtukudzi's songs remained surprisingly spacious, offering listeners a musical texture that never seemed crowded or busy.

In this chapter, I illustrate how Mtukudzi's invocation of his origins in the rural region of Dande imbued *Tuku Music* with a unique historical, geographic, and cultural identity. Emphasizing his Korekore heritage, Mtukudzi put forth a claim to autochthonous identity by positioning himself as a Zimbabwean "son of the soil," or *mwana wevhu*, a phrase widely used to distinguish indigenous residents from outsiders.[3] Through the album's extensive use of Korekore musical and linguistic resources, Mtukudzi also invoked the participatory aesthetics of ngoma performance within a modern form of music making, opening space for active engagement and interpretation on the part of his listeners. My account focuses particularly on the album's first track, "Dzoka Uyamwe," or "Return and be suckled," which was unanimously praised by music critics and ordinary listeners alike for bringing a vibrantly imagined world of social relations to life.[4] As long-time listener Christopher Timbe remarked, the song "touched many people . . . for me, it is deep. It is one of the best compositions he has ever made."

Even as audiences recognized that Mtukudzi was back in the groove, however, few people anticipated just how far the new album would take him. In Zimbabwe, *Tuku Music* attracted the type of elite, cosmopolitan listeners who had previously shown little interest in local music, significantly expanding Mtukudzi's audience base. Outside the nation's borders, *Tuku Music* had an even bigger impact, finally propelling Mtukudzi into the growing market for world music. At the very moment Mtukudzi released *Tuku Music*, however, Zimbabwe entered a new phase in its political history, with escalating conflict between President Robert Mugabe's ruling party, ZANU-PF, and an emerging opposition party known as the Movement for Democratic Change, or MDC, led by former trade unionist Morgan Tsvangirai. Setting the stage for the next chapter, which takes up the reception of Mtukudzi's music in this changing political climate, my discussion of *Tuku Music* concludes with a description of the political, economic, and social turmoil gripping the Zimbabwean nation during the late 1990s and early 2000s.

"Son of the Soil": Claiming Dande in Song

Among the tracks on *Tuku Music*, Zimbabwean audiences responded especially favorably to "Dzoka Uyamwe," or "Return and be suckled," which unites themes of geography, kinship, and moral obligation. Through lyrics rich in metaphor, "Dzoka Uyamwe" conveys Mtukudzi's powerful longing to return to his family's place of origin in Dande, a region located at the base of the Zambezi Escarpment in the remote reaches of Zimbabwe's rural northeast. Far from the nation's centers of power, production, and exchange, Dande is an almost mythical land that anthropologist David Lan has described as "unknown territory. It is 'the bush,' a place of wild animals and backward people, drunkards and witches, left behind by modern times centuries ago."[5] Reflecting on the lyrics to "Dzoka Uyamwe," one of Mtukudzi's urban listeners would elaborate, "When you look at the development of Zimbabwe—in terms of infrastructure, electricity, towns, food, activities, meetings, conferences—none of them have been in Dande."

Several generations ago, Mtukudzi's forefathers migrated away from Dande, ascending the Zambezi Escarpment and resettling in the village of Nyangavi, located in the region of Guruve. Mtukudzi's grandfather then moved once more, leaving Nyangavi for the village of Madziva, located in the Chiweshe region.[6] Yet Mtukudzi remains indelibly tied to Dande, as this fabled, far-off place is still home to his ancestral lineage—the royal clan, or *dzinza*, whose members share the *mutupo*, or totem, of Nzou Samanyanga, or "Elephant, Keeper of Tusks." Clan affiliation remains an important marker of social identity in contemporary Zimbabwean life, and totemic praise names such as Nzou Samanyanga continue to be used as honorific titles in daily conversation.[7] Indeed, Mtukudzi is often addressed as Nzou Samanyanga by listeners, friends, and family alike. Through their continued use, praise names remind people of their place within a larger world of kinship, mapping their identities onto social landscapes that extend back to their families' places of origin.

Since the early days of his career, Mtukudzi has drawn upon associations between territory and clan, symbolically laying claim to Dande in his songs. His adaptations of ngoma music from the rural northeast, from early hits such as "Mutavara" to later songs such as "Wenge Mambo" (*Bvuma-Tolerance*, 2000), are part of this process. Yet even songs that are not grounded in the musical language of ngoma frequently remind Mtukudzi's listeners of his ties to Dande in other ways. In one of his first hits with the Black Spirits, titled "Pamusoroi" or "Pardon me" (KDZ 118, 1978), for example, Mtukudzi repeatedly invoked the musical and social practices of Dande in his lyrics:

Chandakaona muDande	What I saw in Dande,
MuDande, vakomana	In Dande, boys
Chandinoona muDande	What I see in Dande,
MuDande, vasikana	In Dande, girls
Hunzi, "Doro ngarinwiwe,"	They say, "Let beer be drunk,"
"Nyama isigochewa"	"And meat be roasted"
Ndiyo ngoma isirira, varumewe.	There is the drum sounding, oh men.

References to Mtukudzi's status as a member of the Nzou Samanyanga clan have likewise permeated his lyrics, biographical materials, and album titles, and elephant-related imagery has figured prominently on his album covers and posters.

Listening to Dande

Much like Mtukudzi's musical play *Was My Child*, "Dzoka Uyamwe" engaged with the type of complex social forces shaping the contemporary Zimbabwean experience, including urbanization, labor migration, and the fragmentation of

Nyanga Yenzou. Courtesy of Tuku Music and Sheer Sound/Gallo Record Company.

extended kinship networks. As Mtukudzi told me, "The inspiration of that song came after realizing a lot of people in the urban areas, they are suffering. And yet they have homes where they can actually live better. And it's a song that I was trying to inspire people to go back to their roots. And even if they don't have work, but if they remember their roots, they will always have something to do. 'Cause it's their home, it's where they are supposed to be." In the context of combined social, political, and economic pressures, "Dzoka Uyamwe" emphasized that one's home is more than simply a physical place; it is also where one's identity is formed through reciprocal interactions with family, friends, and community.[8]

Years after the release of *Tuku Music*, many Zimbabwean listeners still considered "Dzoka Uyamwe," which some people refer to simply as "Ndafunga Dande," or "I think of Dande," to be one of his most powerful songs.[9] Describing

Promotional poster for *Tuku Music. Courtesy of Tuku Music and Sheer Sound/Gallo Record Company.*

it as deeply philosophical, Christopher Timbe observed that Mtukudzi's lyrics made people "want to listen to the words and look at what he's saying, analyze the song." Similarly, mbira dzavadzimu player Sekuru Tute Chigamba described "Dzoka Uyamwe" as particularly effective in speaking "to what is happening in a place, in a community. . . . What he talks about teaches people how they should behave."

As with "Neria," listeners often described hearing "Dzoka Uyamwe" in relation to their own lived experiences of kinship. As one young university student told me: "I just have a couple of songs of Tuku that I actually listen to. Like, there was this song when I was growing up . . . 'Ndafunga Dande [Dzoka Uyamwe].' Whenever that song was being sung, my mom would always start referring to my little brother, and then I guess I would feel kind of jealous, cause my mom would be like, 'Come back, you're my last born, you should come back and be suckled.'" Interpreting this image of a mother calling her lastborn child, or *gotwe*, to return and be suckled at her breast, Sekuru Chigamba suggested that Mtukudzi's musical imaginaries of kinship also carry profound metaphorical significance: "It doesn't mean you will go back to nurse, to find your mother and nurse. It is an idiom meaning that you have spent too much time in another place, and you must return home for your ancestral spirits to see you. That is what he is referring to as being suckled."

For Sekuru Chigamba, these lyrics held particular significance in the context of the Mtukudzi family's own migration history, for "as a person who has spent a long time in Madziva without returning to see those people who stayed behind in Dande, he is saying, 'I think of Dande, and I will return there to find a new spirit [*mweya*].'" By invoking the concept of "spirit," or mweya, Sekuru Chigamba suggested that this journey of origins is one imbued with spiritual overtones: "If your mother's ancestral spirits are there, or your father's ancestral spirits are there, you must also go. . . . The spirits will take good care of you, and know their child has returned home. When you go back, they clear all the evils. Then you leave. You're clean. So, that is why I refer to a new spirit."[10] Declaring his intention to return to Dande, Mtukudzi thus binds himself within a web of moral relations that extends beyond the living to encompass the ancestral spirits, or *vadzimu*, who represent the true owners of the land. Reflecting the reciprocal ethos of hunhu, Sekuru Chigamba concluded that given Mtukudzi's commitment to his place of origin, "All of the ancestral spirits in Dande will bless him in what he does."

Portraying intimate links among territory, lineage, and kinship, Mtukudzi's lyrics run counter to conventional portrayals of Dande as materially impoverished, emphasizing instead the region's social, musical, and cultural abundance. As Christopher Timbe explained:

Dande would be classified by some people as an underdeveloped area. But is he looking at it like that? Maybe not. It's so developed that it has kept itself to itself, in its natural form. . . . So I think Mtukudzi thought deeper, and said, "Which would be the most underdeveloped piece of area in our land?" Dande would be one of them. And I think he admires it, actually, in that song.

In this way, "Dzoka Uyamwe" offers a reminder that forms of expressive culture, including songs, proverbs, stories, and dream narratives, constitute intangible treasures on earth.[11] Reflecting on the song's opening lyrics, Timbe continued:

He went so deep into thinking. And for me, it is not just about the color black. It is about many other things. The fact that I'm short does not mean that I can't think wider. The fact that I am like this doesn't make me any less of a human being. So, "*Mandiona kusviba, mati kuora. Dande, vakomana.* [You see that I am black, you say I am rotten. Dande, boys]." Like people would shun blackness, they would also shun Dande. But in Dande, how many scholars have gone to Dande to study? How many? And they've found that which is worth studying, which is actually the gold of humanity.

The Musical "Flavor" of "Dzoka Uyamwe"

"Dzoka Uyamwe" also exemplifies Mtukudzi's approach to singing as a sahwira by delivering a serious message paired with the attraction, or *hwezvo*, of a compelling musical setting. As Charles Chipanga, who played marimba with Mtukudzi for several years, observed, Mtukudzi's inherently dialogic approach to voicing places hunhu at the heart not only of the song's lyrics, but also of its musical arrangement: "Alone, he enters, '*Ndafunga Dande vakomana ndafunga kwedu.*' [Then the female backing singers respond], '*Dzoka.*' [Mtukudzi sings by himself again], '*Ndafunga Dande.*' Then we go together, '*Kufunga Dande varume ndafunga kwedu.*' [Then the women sing], '*Dzoka Uyamwe.*' Then you go, '*Uya zvako gotwe*' together . . . It's his own way, which as I see it is that he wants it to be *hurukuro* [dialogue], you know? We're chatting."

Further enhancing the affective power of his musical arrangements, Mtukudzi has paid close attention to timbral relationships in a way that brings his music closer to the aesthetics of ngoma practices. As his former lead guitarist Clive "Mono" Mukundu observes, "Dzoka Uyamwe" relies heavily on the muted timbres of Zimbabwean mbira-style guitar playing, in which the performer dampens the strings with the palm of his right hand.[12] This playing technique is an especially salient feature of Thomas Mapfumo's chimurenga music, where its constant use by both rhythm and lead guitarists produces a distinctive sense of restrained musical exuberance. In "Dzoka Uyamwe," on the other hand, only the lead guitarist uses this dampening technique. Further distinguishing Mtukudzi's sound from Mapfumo's, the muted tones of mbira-guitar playing are featured only during predominantly vocal sections of "Dzoka Uyamwe," rather than throughout the entire piece. In instrumental segments of the song, on the other hand, Mtukudzi's lead guitarist dispenses with this technique, which as Mono notes, functions to "open up the sound" of Mtukudzi's music.[13]

Also on a timbral level, Mtukudzi has traded what he described to me as the "sharp" sound of steel strings for the warm, bright tone of nylon, which he perceives as blending more perfectly with the other instruments in his ensemble, particularly after the mbira and marimba joined the Black Spirits' line-up. Once again invoking the concept of *kurunga*, or "flavoring," he explained: "I'm trying to run away from mbira, 'cause steel strings and mbira, the sound is almost the same. But if it's nylon, then it's now—marimba is wood, I am nylon, and mbira is steel. So, it flavors better." Mtukudzi's preference for the complementary timbres of wood, metal, and nylon reflects the musical aesthetics of various indigenous Zimbabwean ensembles. The *jekunje* music played in eastern regions of Zimbabwe such as Nyamaropa, for example, features the metallic ring of struck hoe blades, the warmer tones of animal skin drums, and the sharp report of makwa handclapping, intended to replicate the sound of wooden clappers, or *zvikeyi*.[14] Similarly, the iron keys of the mbira dzavadzimu are often accompanied by both drumming and makwa. So widespread is this aesthetic preference for the combined tone colors of wood, skin, and metal instruments that music scholar Fernando Ortiz has suggested it is a defining feature of music played throughout Africa and the African diaspora, from the percussion ensembles of Guinea and Ghana to Cuban rumba, Brazilian capoeira, and Haitian rara.[15]

Adding yet another distinctive tone color to this mix, the dense sound of shakers, constructed from gourds, metal, or plastic, is yet another common element in many African and Afro-diasporic music cultures. In Zimbabwe, hosho shakers, made of dried gourds filled with canna lily seeds, or *hota*, play a central role in many performance styles.[16] For mbira and ngoma performers, the hosho are indispensable in keeping an ensemble together. From his perspective as a mbira player, Chigamba explained, "In every kind of music, the hosho must not be left out. It is like lighting a small candle in your house. In response, everyone will say, 'Ah, there is the flame that lights our way.'" Mtukudzi has similarly recognized the hosho's importance. Introducing backing vocalist and hosho player Namatai Mubariki at one live show, for example, he told his audience, "Hosho is a very special instrument, because it complements your mind and the music. It joins your mind and the music. And hosho is so important. It is the one that keeps us on the same page as musicians."

Oliver Mtukudzi, Namatai Mubariki (left), and Charles Chipanga (right).
Courtesy of Esa Salminen.

The most common Shona hosho pattern is a steady series of fast triplets, in which the second subdivision of the beat is accented, resulting in a distinctive swung feel. The hosho's offbeat emphasis also produces a certain musical energy, leading musicians such as Chigamba to describe the hosho player as "the one who makes you dance. . . . If there is no hosho, people do not dance readily, because they are unable to get into the beat." This triplet pattern is played to accompany the vast majority of mbira songs. At a faster tempo, it is also characteristic of many ngoma genres, including dinhe, dandanda, and jiti. It has further crossed over into various styles of popular music, including the chimurenga sound so closely associated with Thomas Mapfumo.[17]

While Mtukudzi was attracted to the sound of the hosho from the early days of his career, he initially found it difficult to incorporate them in his music. As he told me:

I would have liked right from the beginning, to start with the hoshos, because it's a nice instrument. But I didn't have the players who could play the hoshos. And some of these traditional instruments, youngsters wouldn't want to play tradition, they wanted to play modern, to be, you know? So there were very few hosho players then, and the hosho players were old people who could not join the band, who were family men, and so on. Who were not necessarily musicians as such, but they would play hosho for fun. So that's why I couldn't get them. Later on, they started creeping in, and we started using them.[18]

This account echoes the arguments of music scholars such as Hugh Tracey, who concluded that Zimbabwe's indigenous musical traditions, most notably the mbira dzavadzimu, entered into a period of decline with the advent of settler colonialism in the late nineteenth century.[19] Several decades later, Paul Berliner subsequently suggested that the mbira entered a period of revival that coincided with the rise of African nationalism in the 1960s.[20]

This view has been critiqued by Thomas Turino, who has argued that narratives of decline and revival do not adequately capture the dynamics of local musical practice.[21] Indeed, the difficulty Mtukudzi describes in finding a skilled hosho player during the early years of his career seems surprising in light of his close ties to Highfield, where numerous mbira players and ensembles, almost invariably accompanied by hosho, were active throughout the 1970s.[22] The trouble Mtukudzi recalls in finding a skilled hosho player is likely to be related partly to the type of cosmopolitan social formations he frequented, rather than reflecting an absolute absence of hosho players. Yet it is important to bear in mind that musicians frequently interpret their experiences in terms of this modernist discourse of revival, describing what they perceive as the initial popularity, subsequent decline, and ultimate resurgence of indigenous music making.[23]

On a more practical level, the limited recording technologies available to Mtukudzi in the 1970s likewise circumscribed his ability to bring indigenous instruments into the studio. As he recalled:

Don't forget—then, we were recording on a four-track machine. At that time, it couldn't accommodate a lot of instruments. You had to look for the few instruments that you could accommodate. So it was another reason why. . . . We just had a lead guitar, second guitar, bass, and drums. That's all. The whole set of drums would be in one channel. And probably the bass, we would separate it, because it's a bit heavy. And the lead and the second guitar would be in one channel. And voices—all voices, the main voice and the backing voices—would be in one channel. . . . So accommodating a lot of percussion and so on, it was difficult. It wasn't easy at all.

Echoing the observations of ethnomusicologist Louise Meintjes, Mtukudzi's comments remind us that available recording technologies had a defining influence on African popular music in the 1970s, encouraging artists to find creative ways to adapt indigenous musical aesthetics for commercial studio recording projects.[24] Instead of working with live hosho players, for example, both Mtukudzi and Mapfumo would initially transfer the hosho's characteristic triplet pattern to the hi-hat.

An Expanding Audience for Tuku Music

Drawing in the "Nose-Brigades"

Shortly after the release of *Tuku Music*, reports in the local press suggested that the album's enthusiastic reception was tied not only to the affective power of songs such as "Dzoka Uyamwe," but also to a larger shift in local musical preferences as educated, urban elites increasingly turned away from imported sounds and embraced local artists such as Mtukudzi, Mapfumo, and Chimbetu. Jestingly referred to as the "nose-brigades," a reference to the distinctively nasal accents they had acquired at the nation's top educational institutions, these middle- and upper-class listeners increasingly joined the ranks of the township dwellers, mineworkers, commercial farmhands, and rural subsistence farmers who had long been the mainstay of Mtukudzi's audiences.[25] Writing in the *Zimbabwe Mirror* in 2001, for example, Jealous Mpofu attributed this shift in part to the higher production standards of albums such as *Tuku Music*: "Not so long ago, it was not surprising to see the nose-brigades walking away from a party just because too much local music was being played. Now all that has been changed by the likes of Oliver Mtukudzi, Thomas Mapfumo, and Alick Macheso, among others."[26] Following a joint performance by Oliver Mtukudzi and Simon Chimbetu at the Chitungwiza Aquatic Centre in 1999, music critic Vivian Maravanyika similarly remarked, "Only a few months ago this would be a dream. Having local artistes as main attractions, being paid well and provided with a reliable PA system, and local fans forking out $200 [about $5 US] minus a rhumba outfit? You gotta be joking. Well, Zimbabwean music has come of age. For a long time, local musicians were treated as second best. Now they are holding centre stage."[27]

Breaking into Regional Markets

Around this time, Mtukudzi's popularity also began rising in South Africa and other neighboring countries. This was partly the result of his work with Mahube, a collaborative musical initiative spearheaded by Steve Dyer. Taking its name from a Tswana word meaning "new dawn," Mahube featured a line-up of musicians from Zimbabwe, Malawi, South Africa, and Zambia, with Dyer and Mtukudzi lauded by reviewers as "the nucleus of the band."[28] Originally formed to play a festival in Munich, Germany, Mahube billed its purpose as building "meaningful bridges of understanding between African cultures."[29] Echoing Mtukudzi's early interactions with South African producer West Nkosi, this collaborative musical project reflected the type of circular mobility long associated with regional labor migration, as sounds, people, practices, and ideas from around Southern Africa flowed into South Africa, where they shaped the emergence of new musical forms and were subsequently reexported back to neighboring countries.

Joining Mahube dramatically increased Mtukudzi's visibility throughout the Southern African region. Soon, the Black Spirits began touring neighboring countries, playing to sold-out crowds in cities such as Mbabane, Blantyre, Lilongwe, Lusaka, and Gaborone.[30] By 2001, Mtukudzi was appearing at increasingly prestigious venues, such as Cape Town's North Sea Jazz Festival, leading Zimbabwe's *Daily News* to call him "almost a cult figure in the region."[31] In contrast to Mtukudzi's growing popularity, however, journalist Robert Mukondiwa observed that Mahube's hybrid sound was impenetrable for many Zimbabwean listeners: "People were like, this is not sungura, it's not jit, it's world music. And people wondered, do we identify with this music?" For these listeners, Tuku music proved eminently more appealing than the more experimental, transnational sound of Mahube.

Emerging onto a Global Stage

With the release of *Tuku Music*, Mtukudzi also finally captured the attention of audiences in Europe and North America. While he was extremely popular at home during the 1980s and 1990s, Mtukudzi received relatively limited international exposure, especially in comparison to artists such as Thomas Mapfumo or Stella Chiweshe.[32] This was partly due to the fall-out from his disastrous early tour of the United Kingdom. Yet it was also tied to the difficulties of characterizing Mtukudzi's syncretic sound. Reflecting much larger debates about musical authenticity, Afropop Worldwide producer Banning Eyre told me that Mtukudzi's predilection for fusing local sounds with American popular aesthetics initially struck him as less appealing than the more locally grounded sound of artists such as Thomas Mapfumo. As Eyre recalled, "On the first trip we went to Zimbabwe in 1988, we saw him live at the Queens Hotel. . . . I didn't think his music was as original as Thomas's . . . It was nice and it was good, but it didn't seem as surprisingly original; I wasn't as attracted to it. But when I saw that stage show, I realized he was a great performer, and I always loved his voice. And so we went and we interviewed him, and we definitely featured him on that show." Yet Mtukudzi would not fully break into the North American market until the release of *Tuku Music*, which propelled him into a growing pantheon of "world music" artists such as Youssou N'Dour, Salif Keita, Hugh Masekela, Manu Dibango, Caetano Veloso, Gilberto Gil, Ravi Shankar, and Zakir Hussein.[33]

Just as Debbie Metcalfe played a major role in enabling Mtukudzi to break away from the Zimbabwe Music Corporation in the 1980s, so too was she instrumental in catalyzing his emergence onto a global stage. As Eyre observed, Mtukudzi had the incredible fortune "to have someone who was that dedicated, and that together, and that well organized. . . . So often really brilliant African artists never really succeed because they never really have an ally like that." In 1997, Metcalfe made her first foray into promoting Mtukudzi abroad at an African music panel organized by the World Music Expo, or WOMEX, the premier trade fair for musicians, promoters, record companies, journalists, and other industry professionals. During this trip, Metcalfe laid the groundwork for Mtukudzi to tour Europe the following year. Even more importantly, she arranged for him to perform at the next WOMEX fair. As Eyre recalled, Mtukudzi's performance created "a lot of buzz," garnering the singer important new contacts.

Shortly after Mtukudzi's European tour, he made his North American debut with Africa Fête, a musical showcase one reviewer would refer to as a "traveling caravan of top African musicians."[34] Joining Mtukudzi and the Black Spirits, the festival's 1999 line-up featured Senegalese singer Baaba Maal, Malian kora player Toumani Diabate, and American bluesman Taj Mahal.[35] In an interview with Banning Eyre, Mtukudzi described participating in the festival as "a great, great thing for me . . . to get to be with those guys, it's a beautiful thing."[36] American audiences and music critics reciprocated Mtukudzi's enthusiasm, with reviewers such as the *New York Times'* Jon Pareles describing him as "the concert's discovery."[37]

As Eyre told me, the North Americans attracted to Mtukudzi's music were primarily a "college educated, thirty and over, mostly liberal-minded internationalist kind of people," a demographic completely different than the subsistence farmers, manual laborers, and other primarily lower-income listeners who had historically made up much of his audience back home. From Eyre's perspective, these listeners were drawn to Mtukudzi's music in large part because they had become "disenchanted with the direction of American mainstream pop music. They had been alienated by disco, didn't really relate to punk rock. They were looking for an alternative." For them, Mtukudzi's music "was just in that sort of sweet zone where it's different enough to be exciting and clearly alternative, and yet it's familiar enough that you can go there without having to completely rearrange your sense of rhythm or form. So if you can get past the language barrier, it's really easy to get what he's doing." The immediately positive response Tuku music received in North America was a pleasant surprise for Mtukudzi, who later reflected, "I thought it was going to take time for people to really understand my music, but it's like they know the music already."

Coinciding with Mtukudzi's appearance in Africa Fête, Putumayo World Music began distributing *Tuku Music* in 1999, making Mtukudzi's music commercially available in North America for the first time. The album was simultaneously picked up by two European labels, Earthsongs and Label Bleu, and Mtukudzi embarked on a summer promotional tour in Europe that culminated in an appearance for giant crowds at WOMAD, a world music showcase cofounded by Peter Gabriel. Mtukudzi's appearances at WOMEX, WOMAD, and Africa Fête, combined with the widespread distribution of his music throughout Africa, Europe, and North America, soon propelled his career to dizzying heights. In quick succession, he graced the cover of *Time* magazine Europe, appeared on the *David Letterman Show*, and was featured in the documentary film *Shanda* (2002), which told Mtukudzi's life story in what one reviewer called "70 minutes of unbridled joy."[38]

Two of Mtukudzi's songs were also covered by American singer-songwriter Bonnie Raitt, who adapted "What's Going On" as the basis for her track "One Belief Away" (*Fundamental*, 1998), and offered a more straightforward rendition of "Hear Me Lord," on her 2002 album *Silver Lining*. As Mtukudzi related, the film *Jit* was a catalyst in enabling his music to reach Raitt even before he first visited the United States:

> Well, I didn't know anything, you know? Until Debbie said, "Hey, some group in America is looking for you" I said, "Me, why?" "They want to use one of your songs." I said, "Whoa, who's that group?" She said, "Bonnie Raitt." I said, "Bonnie Raitt? Really? Which song is that?" "'What's Going On?'" I said, "Oh, well, how did she get to know the song?" She said, "Oh, she went to watch this film, *Jit*. And from there on she liked the song, so she looked for you all over, and she's been looking for you for the past six months." . . . It was a great feeling, having an artist of her caliber admiring what I've done here. I mean, it made me proud. I'm really proud of it.

As Mtukudzi began touring the United States with increasing frequency, Raitt became a regular fixture at Bay Area venues such as Yoshi's Jazz Club, where she could be found clapping syncopated rhythms, dancing with the crowd, and singing along to songs such as "Hear Me Lord."

Bringing it back home

By the end of the 1990s, the Black Spirits were performing regularly at prestigious engagements around the world, from the London Jazz Festival to the Zanzibar International Film Festival. As music scholar Martin Stokes has observed, the identities of musicians who achieve this type of international stature often change radically as the distinctive characteristics responsible for their rise to global prominence are replaced by an amorphous exoticism, manufactured "under extraordinarily dispersed and fragmented conditions of production" in the world music industry.[39] In Zimbabwe, for example, Johannes Brusila has described how the Bhundu Boys, who emerged onto the global stage at the very moment "world music" was devised as a marketing category, experienced precisely this type of dislocation, coming to occupy "a world music offside position" that prevented them from being fully anchored either in Zimbabwe or in foreign markets.[40] Yet for the most part, Mtukudzi succeeded in avoiding this type of impasse. Indeed, even as *Tuku Music* launched him onto the international stage, it simultaneously revitalized his domestic listenership, kindling a fresh passion for his music among Zimbabwean audiences. In the words of journalist Robert Mukondiwa, "What people had discarded a long time ago as gone has just exploded back to life. And it took a new form and being, and it's beautiful."

Music for Development

Building on previous projects such as *Neria* and *Was My Child*, Mtukudzi remained dedicated to using his music in the service of social change even after becoming a world-renowned artist. Following the release of *Tuku Music*, for example, he participated in a host of social initiatives ranging from development campaigns to public health programs. Among them was a two-year project called Artists Against Poverty, jointly organized by the Zimbabwean Ministry of Culture and the United Nations Development Program in 1998. Intended to encourage musicians, poets, actors, writers, and visual artists to address issues of poverty and development, the campaign culminated in the release of a compilation album called *Bridging the Gap*, which featured a mix of Zimbabwean artists, from established singers such as Busi Ncube and Albert Nyathi to lesser-known performers such as the Ondabezinhle Theatre Group, Pride Germination, the Radiation Band, and Kunzwana Mbira Ensemble. As a key player in the campaign, Mtukudzi judged local artists for inclusion on the compilation album, provided rehearsal space, consulted with musicians and producers during the recording process, and wrote an original song for *Bridging the Gap*, titled "Rega Kuropodza," or "Empty talk."[41] As Doreen Sibanda, the project coordinator, recalled, "We were all very honored by his presence." Over the next few years, Mtukudzi proceeded to lend his music, voice, and image to a stunning number of other development initiatives, ranging from a World Population Day event sponsored by the U.N. Population Fund to the World Health Organization's "Roll Back Malaria" campaign, as well as the type of HIV/AIDS prevention work that is the subject of chapter 7.[42]

Singing Hunhu in New Political Terrain

Yet as it happened, the release of *Tuku Music* coincided with a wave of political instability threatening to engulf the Zimbabwean nation. Even as Mtukudzi's

Tune into the Dangers of Malaria

We wanted to target the community, the lower classes. Because mostly they're just forgotten all the time. The moment you take Mtukudzi out, you have mobilized the whole village, or the whole district. So our focus was mostly the rural communities. And I thought we had good mileage in the campaign. Because the moment they see Oliver, everyone is excited. And as a result, the moment you talk of Mtukudzi anywhere, you are assured of getting support.

Especially for the young generation, and for the elderly people, if you put a song, theatre, role play, drama, it informs. It educates and entertains at the same time. Especially for the rural communities. They don't know how to read, some of them, and plus, you can't just change your behavior by looking. But if you listen to the song, you actually say, "Even my family is affected by this. How best can I assist them?" It touches you. Music touches everyone.

We expected the posters to be at clinics, business centers, like a growth point or whatever. But the problem was that they were so nice! And the health workers wanted to keep them in their houses. Each time you would just go with a poster—I don't think the community benefited a lot. Because the health workers themselves, they wanted the posters, to put it in the house, there. The community might have benefited when they visit a clinic, but definitely the people who benefited from those things were the health workers. Yes, it's a misdirected target, but they benefited. Each time you go out, "Mrs. Ngwenya, do you have a poster for Mtukudzi, Mrs. Ngwenya, do you have a poster for Mtukudzi?"

—*Norah Ngwenya*

musical star continued to rise, he and his listeners soon found themselves confronting a vastly changed social, political, and economic landscape, characterized by raging hyperinflation, political violence, extensive power cuts, and widespread shortages of essential goods such as food, petrol, foreign currency, and medications. As one man told me, many ordinary Zimbabweans increasingly began to despair that their country had "gone from good to worse . . . it's not the same Zimbabwe from when we got independence."

One particularly important event occurred in 1997, when large numbers of war veterans who had fought in Zimbabwe's liberation struggle staged a series of violent demonstrations, demanding long-overdue financial compensation from the government. During the 1980s, both Mtukudzi and Metcalfe supported the war veterans, with Frontline Productions organizing a series of all-night performances, or pungwes, designed to raise publicity and funds for the Zimbabwe National Liberation War Veterans' Association. Explaining the rationale behind this partnership in *Prize Magazine*, Metcalfe described the war veterans as "a much neglected group in the first decade since independence."[43] Boasting an amazing line-up of musical heavyweights, one such Frontline show, timed to coincide with the August Heroes' Day holiday in 1987, featured performances by Oliver Mtukudzi, Thomas Mapfumo, the Marxist Brothers, James Chimombe, Ilanga, Transit, Mudzimu, Leonard Dembo, the Zig-Zag Band, and Robson Banda.

By 1997, the war veterans were no longer satisfied with this type of ad hoc initiative, and the Zimbabwe National Liberation War Veterans' Association's newly elected leader, Chenjerai "Hitler" Hunzvi, began organizing rowdy demonstrations pressuring Mugabe's government for more significant compensation. The state quickly capitulated to the war veterans' demands, designating large sums of money to provide roughly fifty-five thousand former freedom fighters with cash gratuities and other benefits. As anthropologist Donald Moore has observed, these payouts "broke the bank," leading to severe foreign currency imbalances and skyrocketing inflation, which reached over 1,000 percent in 2001.[44]

Facing a sudden increase in basic commodity prices, urban residents staged a series of food riots, foreshadowing the emergence of widespread political discontent. In February 2000, these disgruntled urban voters would finally have the opportunity to express themselves at the polls. Turning out in large numbers, they rejected ZANU-PF's proposal to amend the nation's Lancaster House constitution, drafted with heavy British intervention during the last days of the liberation struggle. As ZANU-PF's first major polling defeat, the referendum marked a turning point in Zimbabwean politics, hinting that the MDC, an emerging opposition party led by labor activist Morgan Tsvangirai, stood the very real chance of gaining a majority in parliamentary elections scheduled for June of the same year.[45] Determined to thwart the MDC's rise to power despite deeply straitened financial circumstances, ZANU-PF played one of the few cards it still held by promising to undertake the type of massive land reform that constituted a paramount issue for many rural voters, yet had been prohibited during the first years of independence under the Lancaster House constitution.

As the politics of land reform assumed center stage in the national political imagination, newly emboldened war veterans embarked upon a wave of land invasions, occupying first dozens, then hundreds of white-owned commercial

farms. Invoking the nation's history of resistance to colonial rule, this movement was soon dubbed the "Third Chimurenga." It quickly met with government support, ranging from tacit acceptance and a lack of police intervention to
the explicit provision of tents and other supplies. In exchange, war veterans cam-
paigned intensively for ZANU-PF during the hotly contested parliamentary and
presidential elections held two years apart in 2000 and 2002, carpeting the nation with campaign posters, compelling local residents to attend political rallies,
and interrogating suspected MDC supporters.

By July 2000, Vice President Joseph Msika announced that the war veterans'
informal efforts at land reform would be superseded by a state-sanctioned resettlement program, dubbed the Land Reform and Resettlement Implementation
Plan ("Fast Track") Approach.[46] As might be expected, the immediate consequences of the "fast track" resettlement program were largely disastrous, provoking what one group of scholars has described as "a widely heralded collapse
in the rule of law, economic meltdown, political instability and a food security
crisis."[47] Among other things, the state's land reform program displaced thousands of commercial farm workers and exacerbated existing food shortages,
placing further pressure on urban residents.[48] It also aggravated Zimbabwe's
already hyperinflationary economy by stalling agricultural productivity. Inflation would ultimately reach the astronomical rate of at least 79.6 billion percent
in November 2008, prompting the government to discontinue printing Zimbabwean currency and adopt the US dollar as a medium of exchange.[49]

As tensions rose between ZANU-PF and the MDC, political violence also
began to escalate, reaching levels unseen in many areas of Zimbabwe since the
liberation war.[50] Numerous instances of torture were reported during the hotly
contested parliamentary and presidential campaigns of 2000 and 2002, with
members of each political party claiming to have been victimized by the other.
Together, these new political and economic realities ended up "normalizing the
abnormal" in ways that beggared belief.[51] Even as resettled farmers were paid
in "Special Agro Cheques" with denominations spiraling into the billions and
trillions, for example, schoolchildren continued learning to add and subtract
long-discontinued two and five coins. With little warning, the government then
chopped several zeroes off in an attempt to reset prices, sending the schoolchildren's currency back into circulation for a few, short days as whole families
scraped in the dirt to locate precious coins discarded months ago, when prices
had first started rising. With time, however, what had begun as an acute crisis
gradually settled into what might be described as a normal state of emergency.
As Mtukudzi's drummer Sam Mataure told a group of students in the United
States, "There is still life—I mean, we live, back home. You know, you do have
the problems. Sometimes power cuts, sometimes no water, sometimes no fuel,

no petrol or diesel. But, you know, somehow we survive. And we're just doing the best we can under these difficult conditions."

Confronting a Breakdown of Meaning

Yet the changes that occurred during Zimbabwe's "Third Chimurenga" were not only political and economic; they were also social. In the nation's new climate of violence and hustle, for example, the authority historically wielded by elders was undermined as youth progressively gained power, with teenagers and young adults cashing in on shady business deals, interrogating their elders at road blocks, and lobbying for parcels of land on the resettled farms.[52] As life in Zimbabwe became increasingly marked by what music scholar Kofi Agawu has described as the "incongruities, contradictions, antinomies, and hybridity" typical of postcolonial experience, meaning itself became cast into shadow.[53] As one middle-aged man living in Harare observed shortly after the nation's 2008 elections, "We've reached a stage where many things are meaningless, or the intended will not be realized."

As people confronted the contradictions, disjunctures, and paradoxes of the late 1990s, a series of colorful new words entered the popular lexicon. In the early 2000s, for example, the word *jambanja*, which literally means "a violent argument," was appropriated to describe the lawless disorder associated with the war veterans' movement.[54] Similarly, by the time of the 2008 "harmonized" parliamentary and presidential elections, the word *kukiya-kiya*, slang for a lifestyle increasingly dependent on backdoor dealing, ingenuity, and constant hustle, had become a touchstone of urban conversations.[55] Echoing the fragmentation of Zimbabwe's political, economic, and social order, kukiya-kiya signaled the increasing importance of ad hoc survival strategies. Reflecting on this time, one person told me, "We are an improvising nation. . . . We can't do anything about the leadership, we can't. . . . We deal with our issues on a grassroots level, and the state continues to fail."

Hearing Tuku Music in a Changing Political World

As Zimbabwe entered this new phase of its history, Mtukudzi's listeners began interpreting his musical imaginaries of hunhu in relation to unfolding political, economic, and social developments. His changing audience base after the release of *Tuku Music* also played a role in these interpretations, for the educated urban elites who had recently begun listening to Tuku music were precisely the people most likely to support Zimbabwe's emerging opposition party, the MDC. Soon, the impassioned political sensibilities of these listeners crested in a wave of political controversy over Mtukudzi's song "Wasakara," or "You are worn out," from the 2000 album *Bvuma-Tolerance*.

"Wasakara"
(You're worn out)

Bvuma	Admit
Bvuma iwe	Admit, you
Bvuma	Admit
Bvuma chete	Just admit
Bvuma wasakara	Admit, you're worn out
Bvuma wahunyana	Admit, you're wrinkled
Bvuma wasakara	Admit, you're worn out
Bvuma wahunyana	Admit, you're wrinkled
Kuchembera	Growing old
Chiiko kuchembera	What is growing old?
Kuchembera	Growing old
Chiiko kuchembera	What is growing old?
Chii kuchembera	What is growing old?
Chiiko kuchembera	What is growing old?
Imi mai makwegura	You, mother, you're elderly
Hamucharugona machembera	You cannot manage, you're old
Makuraka musazoramba	You're elderly, don't deny it
Nemi baba tarirai muone	And you, father, look and see
Mwana yave mhandara	Your daughter is of marriageable age
Makuraka musazoramba	You're elderly, don't deny it
Kuchembera mucherechedzo	Growing old is a sign
Wenguva yakareba	Of a long time
Kuchembera mucherechedzo	Growing old is a sign
Wenguva yakanaka	Of good times
Kuchembera ndizvo ndizvo	Growing old, that's what it is
Nenguva yakawanda	A long time
Kuchembera ndizvo ndizvo	Growing old, that's what it is
Nenguva yakawanda	A long time
Chizokuhunyana mweya imhandara	You're wrinkled, yet your spirit is a young girl
Kunze kusakara ndochiiko vakomana	Outside you're worn out, what is that?
Chizokuhunyana mweya imhandara	You're wrinkled, yet your spirit is a young girl
Kunze kusakara ndochiiko vakomana	Outside you're worn out, what is that?

Just after Independence Day in April 2008, the Black Spirits shifted restlessly on clanking metal seats as their borrowed bus made its way toward Chimanimani, a quiet hamlet nestled on the slopes of a spectacular mountain range in Zimbabwe's Eastern Highlands. Across the valley, the slate-gray cliffs of the Chimanimani National Park rose from a verdant canopy of moss-draped *musasa* and *munhondo* trees, their foliage plunging skyward through tendrils of traveling clouds. Here, the stunted shrubbery of subalpine slopes gave way to a flat plain carpeted unexpectedly by a layer of sand, its particles as fine and white as the far-off seashore. Huddled in the fog, eroded granite obelisks stood sentinel as the terrain plummeted downward to reveal a thin ribbon of stream glistening between grassy banks far below.

Seemingly lost in time, Chimanimani has long offered refuge for an eccentric collection of farmers, artists, hippies, and wanderers. Yet its residents have also become entangled in the politics of the present. In the wake of the government's "fast-track" resettlement program, Chimanimani's commercial plantations of fragrant eucalyptus and pine trees were repeatedly subject to arson, killing farm-workers who labored desperately to stop the raging flames.[1] After the discovery of gold in nearby Chiadzwa, the region faced a sudden influx of smugglers and wildcat miners, or *makorokoza*, who struggled to stay one step ahead of a growing police presence. Long a hotbed of political opposition, Chimanimani was also home to a regional office of the Movement for Democratic Change, or MDC. In a brazen display of opposition to the government's fast-track land reforms, constituents in Chimanimani even elected a white commercial farmer, Roy Bennett, as their representative in the parliamentary elections of 2000.[2]

Just as elsewhere around the nation, the vagaries of Zimbabwean politics significantly affected the social and artistic life of Chimanimani. Central to the town's social calendar, for example, the Chimanimani Arts Festival was held annually from 1998 until 2003, when it was suspended in the face of mounting political and economic challenges. Over time, however, resilient local residents adapted, reviving the Chimanimani Arts Festival in 2007. By 2008, the festival boasted an impressive line-up of both local and national acts, including Oliver Mtukudzi and the Black Spirits, sungura singer Nicholas Zacharia, bohemian

Afro-jazz artist Victor Kunonga, female vocalist Busi Ncube, pioneering Ndebele musician Albert Nyathi, former street-kid singer Willom Tight, and neotraditional performing ensemble Bongo Love.

Road-weary, the Black Spirits pulled up at a grassy square in the center of
town, where a makeshift stage had been constructed of roughly hewn wood.
Tumbling out of their bus, they greeted Mtukudzi, who had arrived a day earlier for the festival's opening ceremony, where he appeared alongside other invited dignitaries. While the Black Spirits earned barely enough to cover their
travel costs, Mtukudzi was particularly enthusiastic about performing at this
free, open-air event, which he described as bringing "the festival to the people."

By the time the Black Spirits took to the stage, what was initially a slow trickle
of festival-goers had become a massive swell of men, women, and children, sporting an assortment of homemade sweaters, patched overcoats, and balaclavas to
protect them from the cold mountain air. Mtukudzi's drummer Sam Mataure,
who grew up in the nearby town of Mutare, noted that this crowd was decidedly
different from Mtukudzi's usual listenership: "These are people from the farms,
OK? It's a forestry area, so people from the farms. The workers, the really bot-
tom of the range . . . 99.9% were people from the neighboring farms. And that's
what the festival is all about. To entertain the farm workers, the women, the children; let me say, the community." After walking for miles to attend the festival,
many people would spend the night in the open air, with whole families unfurl-
ing blankets and bedding down amid the crowd.

Far from the cosmopolitan hub of Harare, where habitual concertgoers regularly attended Mtukudzi's shows, these laborers and their families rarely had the
opportunity to see him perform. In comparison with the energy emitted by his
legions of fans in Harare, most listeners in Chimanimani appeared subdued,
with only a few people engaged in the rhythmic dancing, improvisatory handclapping, or participatory singing so widespread among urban audiences. As
Mataure later recalled: "The audience was not responding at all. They just stood
there and looked. They were not dancing. . . . People were happy to see Oliver
when we were introduced. You know, loud applause, everything. But to move
them, we couldn't move them."[3] Halfway through the Black Spirits' set, however, the crowd was finally roused from its lassitude when Mtukudzi launched
into his massive hit "Wasakara," or "You're worn out." As soon as they heard
the song's distinctive opening riff, a short, stuttering phrase played on Mtukudzi's acoustic guitar, they began dancing energetically, waving their hands in the
air and animating the night with their whistles and cries. Invoking the unique
combination of listening, feeling, and understanding encapsulated by the Shona
word for hearing, or *kunzwa*, one man cried out simply, "Friends, hear the tune!
[*Inzwai tune shamwari*]."

Hearing "Wasakara" as political dissent

"Wasakara" had reverberated throughout Zimbabwe since it first appeared as the title track of Mtukudzi's album *Bvuma-Tolerance*. Released during a watershed year in Zimbabwean politics, the album hit local markets in November 2000, a few months after the MDC fell just short of attaining a majority in parliamentary elections, representing the first real challenge to ZANU-PF's uninterrupted rule since independence in 1980. In this politically charged atmosphere, the lyrics to "Wasakara" exhorted elders to recognize their limitations, step down from positions of authority, and allow a new generation to take up the mantle of their work.

Mtukudzi has insisted that "Wasakara" was nothing more than a personal reflection on growing old, commenting, "The song really started when I noticed how my daughters were growing up. I thought, if I can have such big daughters, then where am I?"[4] Yet listeners quickly came to their own conclusions about the song, interpreting "Wasakara" as a metaphorical critique of President Robert Mugabe's seemingly endless rule. Even before the song was released, the nation was abuzz with talk about its political implications. As one journalist wrote in the *Zimbabwe Independent* after seeing Mtukudzi perform the song live: "I have no doubt the album will be a success judging by the crowd's response. I did not quite catch the lyrics but I think it has a message directed at those who want to cling onto power beyond their sell-by date. The song is called 'Wasakara.'"[5] Just as this anonymous reviewer intuited, Mtukudzi's audiences overwhelmingly heard "Wasakara" as political, interpreting his lyrics as a carefully coded message for an aging Mugabe to respect the popular wish for change and relinquish the presidency.[6] From the perspective of a disenchanted populace eager for change, the song's lyrics offered a rare opportunity to express socially sanctioned political dissent. As one listener told me:

> My opinion was, this song was aimed at our president at that time. Because at that time there was a climate to say, "I think you've spent a lot of time there, just step aside, let somebody else come in and do the job. You've done your bit. Let somebody else take over. You rest, you be the elder statesman, people come to you for advice, etc. etc." And in my mind, that's what I thought Tuku was saying. Saying "Admit it, you're an old man, you can't be running around all the time. Take a rest, go and chill."

Even at the album's release party, held in the bohemian atmosphere of the old Mannenberg nightclub in downtown Harare, audience members were already reportedly changing the song's lyrics, inserting direct references to President Mugabe by replacing the phrase *"Bvuma wasakara,"* or "Admit, you're worn out," with the improvised line *"Bob wasakara,"* or "Bob, you're worn out."[7] Soon,

"Wasakara" was adapted as a de facto political anthem by members of the MDC. As one of Mtukudzi's band members told me, "The opposition basically took it, and said to the president of Zimbabwe, 'You must accept that you are old.'" During live performances of the song, MDC members began engaging in overtly political gestures, flashing red cards to signify dissatisfaction with ZANU-PF and waving their open palms in the air in a symbol of support for the MDC.[8] As Debbie Metcalfe would say, "It was electric, the sense of excitement."[9]

Hunhu and the Political Imaginary

In this chapter, I offer a reception history of "Wasakara," asking how a song that does not explicitly address issues of state governance comes to acquire such astounding political force. Weaving archival and ethnographic sources together, I begin by showing how the metaphorical lyrics to "Wasakara" catapulted the song to the forefront of the Zimbabwean political imagination shortly after *Bvuma-Tolerance* was released. I am particularly interested in how Mtukudzi's assertions that "Wasakara" was not intended to be political have clashed with the perspectives of his listeners, from ordinary citizens to the music critics, radio DJs, and other cultural figureheads involved in mediating the song's popular reception.

The reception of "Wasakara" both reflects a particular postcolonial sensibility and returns us to how the concept of ngoma as social commentary has proved so fundamental to Mtukudzi's approach to singing hunhu. Reflecting on the problem of asserting political agency during the 2008 electoral process, for example, one person told me: "You laugh at everything, even things that are not funny. Like when Mugabe is speaking, we all laugh and think he's funny. . . . And then you play music, to reflect your mood. Like people singing 'Bvuma [Wasakara],' pointing at someone, or saying something in addition to the song, you know? And it always starts a conversation. 'Ha, zveshuwa, bvuma! [Yes, really, admit!],' You know? And then you find someone who is, like, not *bvuma*-ing. *Kuti achembera* [that he has grown old], or whatever. So, you play music." Grounded in the dialogic aesthetics long familiar to Mtukudzi's listeners, "Wasakara" quite clearly demonstrates how song's license as a privileged form of social criticism has crossed into the realm of contemporary Zimbabwean popular culture, including the mass-produced, commercially mediated music played by Mtukudzi and other popular artists.

Even in the face of widespread political interpretations of "Wasakara," however, both Mtukudzi and his audiences have rejected attempts to reduce the song's meaning to a single reading. On the contrary, they have demonstrated an investment in allowing multiple, even contradictory interpretations to stand side by side. The history of "Wasakara" thus firmly resists what Nigerian novelist Chimamanda Adichie has called the "danger of a single story," moving instead

toward the "balance of stories" advocated by Adichie's forbearer, Nigerian literary giant Chinua Achebe.[10] Reminding us that artists and listeners are bound together in a web of both mutuality and difference, the popular reception of "Wasakara" embodies the dialogic ethos of hunhu, which has the coexistence of diverse
viewpoints, subjectivities, and identities at its core.

What is growing old?

In the lyrics to "Wasakara," Mtukudzi employs one of his favorite rhetorical
strategies by posing questions meant to engage listeners in a musical form of dialogue. Throughout the song, he repeatedly asks, "*Chiiko kuchembera?*" or "What
is growing old?" Yet Mtukudzi's own response remains ambivalent at best, leaving a definitive interpretation up to his listeners. On one hand, he lauds growing
old as "a sign of good times," or "*mucherechedzo wenguva yakanaka,*" and compares
the spirit, or *mweya*, of an elderly person to the figure of a youthful, adolescent
girl, or *mhandara*. On the other hand, Mtukudzi takes elders to task for failing
to meet their obligations in lines such as "*Hamucharugona machembera,*" or "You
can no longer manage, you are old," and acknowledges the physical ravages of
old age through words such as *kusakara*, or "to be worn out," and *kuhunyana*, or
"to be wrinkled."

In Zimbabwe, as throughout much of the African continent, the seniority of
age has long been a fundamental principle of social organization.[11] Family elders, or *vakuru* (sg. *mukuru*), who hold responsibility for the well-being of their
extended kinship networks, are widely seen as vested with the moral authority
of the ancestral spirits, or vadzimu (sg. mudzimu).[12] As Mtukudzi explained:

> Vadzimu, it's like our parents. There's no way you can avoid them. There's
> no way you can run away from them. It's a reality. You are also going to
> be a mudzimu to your great-grandchildren. So vadzimu, it's like a chain
> of the family. Christians translate vadzimu wrongly. They think vadzimu
> is something bad, something that's not holy. But no, that's not it. Vadzimu
> simply means your ancestors. Where you came from. You are just part of
> that chain. . . . You die, and you become a mudzimu. And you are part of
> the chain of your family. The family tree will always refer to you as one
> of its branches.

In order to guide the behavior of junior kin, elders have historically been tasked
with maintaining communication with the vadzimu spirits, brewing ceremonial beer, presiding over prayers, and initiating the performance of mbira and
other forms of sacred music. Authors such as Stanlake and Tommie-Marie Samkange have observed that, given their ritual responsibilities and proximity to
the vadzimu, "inordinate respect" for the elderly is central to the interpersonal

ethos of hunhu.[13] As mbira player Patience Chaitezvi Munjeri elaborated, "Hunhu means being a person who lives well and respectfully with others. You humble yourself. You don't act heedlessly in front of elders. You put yourself on a lower level, you have respect for elders."

Literary scholar Silindiwe Sibanda has suggested that given this respect for age, elders are seldom criticized by their juniors. Rather, "the elderly are treated with the utmost respect, and for a younger person to inform their elder that they are old and must act accordingly is not something that would be undertaken lightly."[14] Qualifying Sibanda's statement, however, Mtukudzi has observed that it is possible to correct elders, provided that criticism is delivered through an appropriate channel, or *hurongwa*. As he stated shortly after the release of "Wasakara":

> In my Shona culture, criticizing is not illegal, not at all. It's not that you
> don't criticize the leaders. Leaders can be criticized. That's how they learn
> in our culture. Criticizing in Shona culture—it's done, but we have chan-
> nels. There is some degree of respect. You can criticize, but it has to be
> respectful . . . You don't just talk to one person. When you criticize one,
> you're not criticizing him only; you're criticizing everybody else who falls
> into that same category. So you also listen when others are being criticized,
> and you learn from there.[15]

This perspective has remained remarkably consistent from the early days of Mtu-kudzi's career, as reflected in songs such as "Bganyamakaka," which drew on ngoma's license as a privileged form of social criticism in order to indirectly re-buke a short-tempered, difficult elder, or mukuru.[16] It is also a perspective Mtukudzi shares with many of his listeners. As long-time listener Esau Mavindidze told me: "What Tuku is doing is not really quite different from the Shona tra-ditions. . . . In our traditions, it's almost cultural, this approach to elders. You don't just confront an elder and fight him, just like that, especially in words. You find a way of saying it, which does not mean that the people are docile. But the people have a certain way of expressing themselves, which maybe to some cul-tures might not be as direct."

The Lighting Incident

Yet ngoma's privileged status as a form of social commentary was not the only factor contributing to politicized readings of "Wasakara." Less than a month after *Bvuma-Tolerance* was released, popular interpretations of its title track would be indelibly marked by an incident that occurred on December 29, 2000, during a joint billing between Mtukudzi and Ringo, a popular South African singer. As Mtukudzi played "Wasakara" for a massive audience at the Harare

International Convention Center, an enormous hall with a seating capacity of over four thousand, many people in the audience began waving their open hands in the air and flashing red cards, both signs of support for the MDC. This time, however, lighting engineer Stephen Schadendorf, a white Zimbabwean, responded by shining his spotlight on a portrait of Robert Mugabe, which hung above the stage. As one person who attended the show later told me, it seemed apparent that Schadendorf was timing this gesture to coincide precisely with the lyrics, "Admit / Admit, you." As Banning Eyre has recounted, the lighting engineer "kept it there, even moving it around to draw the attention of the crowd. People went wild. After the show. Schadendorf was arrested, and spent the next four days in a cell with fourteen arrested criminals and a bucket, by his own account, the worst four days of his life."[17] Although Schadendorf, who does not speak Shona, claimed total ignorance that his actions could be construed as political, charges were brought against him under the Law and Order (Maintenance) Act, a repressive piece of colonial legislation originally intended to counter black nationalism by making it an offense to "excite disaffection" against the Rhodesian government.[18]

Schadendorf's arrest provoked an overwhelming response in the popular press, which characterized his persecution as "living testimony of our leader's dementia."[19] In an anonymous letter to the *Standard*, an independent weekly newspaper, one reader mused, "What will Steve Schadendorf be charged with, I wonder . . . trying to assassinate a Presidential portrait with a light beam?"[20] As another anonymous reader observed, it seemed futile to single Schadendorf out for punishment in a nation of listeners enamored with "Wasakara," for in his words, "if the State insists on proceeding with this case, we would advise here and now that it better start preparing another 11 million dockets, judging by the antics being staged by Zimbabweans in homes, bars, workplaces, churches, schools, theatres, farms—everywhere."[21] While Schadendorf was eventually acquitted, the lighting incident both demonstrated just how widely popular disaffection with ZANU-PF had spread and indelibly shaped emerging political interpretations of "Wasakara."

Political Repercussions

After Schadendorf's release, audiences sympathetic to the MDC met "Wasakara" with feverish enthusiasm at performances throughout the country. After one show in Mutare, a reporter with the *Daily News* recounted witnessing "a frenzy when the controversial song 'Bvuma' was played at a packed Queens Hall. The wildly excited crowd sang in unison with The Superstar as he chanted 'Bvuma Bvuma, Bvuma Wahunyana.'"[22] On the other hand, many Mugabe supporters turned against Mtukudzi, leading a listener from the singer's home region of Chiweshe to describe how ZANU-PF party members "hated him and singled him out when he sang, *'Bvuma kuchembera.'*"

Rising tension over "Wasakara" soon led to violence at a show in the Mutoko rural areas, long a ZANU-PF stronghold. As reported in the *East African*, a regional newspaper published in Nairobi:

> On February 9, 2001, Mtukudzi played in Mutoko, a small town northeast of Harare, where he encountered the most hostile of Mugabe supporters. It was reported that "war veterans" invaded the show and forced everybody to wear the ZANU-PF T-shirts and peak caps. The "veterans" then told him not to play the political song "Wasakara," but Mtukudzi had decided that he was going to play the song anyway. At the end of the concert, the audience was beaten up and the musician was only saved by the fact that the cameras were near him and the "veterans" did not want to risk being filmed.[23]

Describing this incident, Mtukudzi's manager Debbie Metcalfe would recall, "It was very intimidating. Oliver says it was the worst night he's ever spent performing live."[24] Several months later, the specter of additional violence forced Mtukudzi to cancel a performance scheduled in the town of Chinhoyi. As Metcalfe recounted to the local press, "The information we had was that a group had been hired to cause mayhem at the show. The group was armed with teargas canisters and we just couldn't take the risk . . . we had to take the threats seriously."[25]

The Question of Censorship

While "Wasakara" was never officially censored, it abruptly stopped receiving airplay through the Zimbabwe Broadcasting Corporation, a state-owned parastatal and the nation's only broadcaster.[26] As one local DJ explained to me, ZBC employees were required to submit playlists for approval prior to each radio program, resulting in what he described as a culture of "gate-keeper journalism." In his words, "Nobody ever told us at ZBC not to play the song . . . But, you must understand that even up to this day, as we're speaking today, on March the 11th, 2009, there is a culture of self-censorship. It has been there. Nobody really says it to you, but you just feel, 'Oh, I couldn't go there, I shouldn't go there, let me leave that. Let me talk about, let me play something else, that's a bit more clean.'"

In contrast to the subtle pressures involved in removing "Wasakara" from the air, more explicit attempts were apparently made to thwart sales of *Bvuma-Tolerance*, with state security forces reportedly confiscating the album at flea markets around Harare. As Farai Mutsaka reported in the *Standard*: "Police and plain-clothed men, suspected to be members of the Central Intelligence Organisation (CIO), last week swooped on flea market vendors in Harare and Chitungwiza, seizing copies of megastar Oliver Mtukudzi's latest hot seller, *Bvuma-Tolerance.*"[27] While police chief superintendent Wayne Bvudzijena dismissed these reports as rumors, they served to confirm the song's power as a political statement, injecting new energy into listeners' impassioned responses to "Wasakara." As one person told me simply, "If I want to piss off Bob [Mugabe], I would play him 'Bvuma.'"

"I Am Not a Politician"

Even as "Wasakara" cemented his reputation as a revolutionary singer, however, Mtukudzi insisted that the song was not intended as a form of political critique. Instead, he sought to distance himself from politics entirely, stating flatly, "I am not a politician."[28] As he elaborated in an interview with the *Standard*: "I cannot help it if people interpret my songs to mean whatever they want, but this song is not political. In the song I am talking about elderly men and women who do not want to accept the fact that they are now old and, for example, old men who continue to propose love to girls young enough to be their own daughter."[29] As journalist Jealous Mpofu observed, however, it proved increasingly difficult for Mtukudzi to maintain this stance, particularly after the lighting incident: "Mukoma [Brother] Tuku is having a torrid time in trying to explain the contents of his hit song *Bvuma-Tolerance*. He insists that the song is not political, but his fans are not buying it. He gave *The Standard*, what I thought was not a very convincing answer last week when asked about the chart-buster. Tuku went on to say he was singing about old men who cuff-up young girls, to realize that they are over-the-hill and should refrain from doing that. I am one of those who believe that the master of music meant something else."[30] Compounding matters was the album title *Bvuma-Tolerance*, which appeared superimposed over a handshake, an image apparently taken from Mtukudzi's early recordings with the Gramma label Kudzanayi. Returning firmly to the ethos of hunhu, Mtukudzi told me, "My translation of tolerance is to respect the next person. And a handshake means respecting each other." Yet, "tolerance" is a decidedly unconventional translation for the Shona word *bvuma*, which might better be rendered as "accept" or "admit." As Debbie Metcalfe observed, the word *tolerance* seemed deliberately misleading: "Why did he put tolerance? . . . It's terribly significant, and it's ambivalent. And that's the reason he went and put tolerance. To me, it qualified the 'admit' thing in the wrong way. . . . He didn't want to be seen to be saying, 'Admit,' so he said he means tolerance—he's not telling the government, the president, to admit to anything."

Despite what seemed a deliberate attempt to obfuscate, listeners refused to cede political interpretations of "Wasakara." With respect to the album title, one person told me, "*Bvuma*, in Shona, means 'agree,' right? Tolerance? You know,

Promotional poster for *Bvuma-Tolerance*. *Courtesy of Tuku Music*
and Sheer Sound/Gallo Record Company.

enigmatic, but not that much. You can see what he meant." Many others simply discounted Mtukudzi's statements to the press. As a second person told me: "People in Zimbabwe, as you've probably noticed, are very scared of their own government. And so if somebody's brave enough to come and sing a song like 'Bvuma,' they know exactly what it means, or what he means, despite what he says to the press." Yet Mtukudzi's professed political neutrality struck some listeners as disingenuous, particularly in the tense atmosphere of Zimbabwe's post-election environment. As one listener reflected:

> I felt we needed our popular musicians to sort of take the lead, to have a leadership role in this. To sort of try to direct people's anger, frustration. . . . I think it may be a cop-out, to hide and say, "No, I didn't mean that, I meant this. You're the ones who are translating all of this, I never said that, I meant this." But I wanted him to stand up and say, "Yes, that's what I meant. Yes." And people—everyone—would have listened. And it would have been like a rallying point, a rallying cry.

Hearing "Wasakara" Abroad

The most scathing critiques of Mtukudzi's refusal to speak out about failures of national governance, however, came from listeners outside Zimbabwe. After a live concert in Delaware, for example, a development worker who had recently returned from a post in Harare told me: "I believe Tuku could be more political, even noting 'Wasakara.' His more 'political' songs are always open to interpretation, and maybe he feels he has to do that to stay in Zimbabwe and not get hassled by the authorities, but I believe he has greatly let the Zimbabwean people down on that front." Similarly, an American who had lived in Harare for many years observed: "If he doesn't want to write about people being abducted, or homes being burned down in the 2008 elections, or Mugabe refusing to step down after he's been defeated, if he doesn't want to write about that stuff, there are a lot of social issues going on that he should be writing about. Like schools not opening, cholera, just all the stuff that's been going on lately. . . . I just have a little bit of resentment." Yet another North American related these comments to emerging news reports about Zimbabwe's growing political unrest, saying, "People know about Zimbabwe. They know that things are really screwed up there. . . . And so to have this engaged, passionate, soulful artist perform for you for two hours and sing nothing about that feels strange. You feel like there's an elephant in the room that's not being acknowledged."

Expectations that Mtukudzi would stake out a firm political position were also shaped by a long-standing discourse of Zimbabwean popular music as inherently revolutionary. Together with his musical contemporaries Comrade Chinx and

Thomas Mapfumo, Mtukudzi had long been depicted as a liberation singer whose messages of social and political protest played an important role in shrugging off the yoke of colonial rule. This narrative began to emerge even before Zimbabwe won its independence; as Christopher Muzavazi wrote in *Illustrated Life Rhodesia* during the last year of the liberation war: "The rediscovery of Shona music and its current success is the effect of both talent and commercial initiative in the music business but the political climate in the country in recent years has contributed significantly to its success. Musicians have found it expedient and desirable to add political notes in their lyrics. . . . The Shona singers do not directly advocate violence of revolution but there is a noticeable tendency towards support for the guerillas."[31] Decades later, this view took on new life as the nation became engulfed in a series of postcolonial political and socioeconomic crises. After Mtukudzi rerecorded several early hits on his album *Paivepo* (1999), for example, music critic Leo Hatugari claimed, "The message in these songs is clear: politically, things are almost just as bad as during the traumatic years of the liberation war."[32]

In the wake of Zimbabwe's food riots, hyperinflation, fast-track land reform program, and contested elections, the international press likewise picked up this thread, describing Mtukudzi's message as "clear to those who long for change in the region."[33] Before long, Mtukudzi's image was emblazoned on the cover of *Time* magazine's European edition, which boldly declared him "The People's Voice" in a country "wracked by famine, AIDS, and tyranny." In an article titled "Singing the Walls Down," the magazine lauded both Mtukudzi and Mapfumo for their ability to "remind the powerful and the powerless of the possibility of change."[34] Steeped in this discourse of music as resistance, international audiences found Mtukudzi's reluctance to articulate his political position not only troubling, but somewhat incomprehensible.[35]

The Political Safety of "Deep Shona"

Back home, on the other hand, the masses of local listeners waving red cards during performances of "Wasakara" seemed to have no trouble at all reading between the lines of Mtukudzi's songs. For these listeners, Mtukudzi's ambiguous political stance was one of his greatest musical strengths. Invoking the idiomatic expression *kurova imbwa wakaviga mupinyi*, or "beating a dog with a hidden stick," Leo Hatugari wrote, "Want my own opinion of Mtukudzi and politics? Well, when it comes to criticizing the government Tuku does what the Shona people of old termed as *kurova imbwa wakaviga mupinyi* or *kuruma uchifuriridzira* [biting while you have covered yourself]—he does it in a hidden way."[36]

Indeed, the metaphorical nature of Mtukudzi's musical imaginaries largely enabled him to escape the type of harassment experienced by his more politically outspoken contemporaries. Foremost among them is Thomas Mapfumo, who has been particularly direct in singing about Zimbabwean politics. Reflecting on Mapfumo's songs during the Chimurenga struggle in the 1970s, journalist Robert Mukondiwa told me, "Mapfumo says, 'Vana kuhondo, garotumira vana kuhondo [Children to war, send the children to war].' It's very direct, you are sending children to war." Illustrating the dangers of this deliberately provocative approach, Mapfumo was arrested and held for several months during the liberation war, although no charges were ultimately filed against him. After independence, he resumed this type of explicit political criticism, releasing songs with titles such as "Corruption" (*Corruption*, 1988) and "Disaster" (*Chimurenga Explosion*, 2000).[37] Soon, Mapfumo was arrested once more, this time for allegedly purchasing several stolen vehicles. Calling the charges an illegitimate attempt to silence him, Mapfumo and the Blacks Unlimited fled to the United States, where they were granted refugee status and resettled in Eugene, Oregon.

In contrast, Mtukudzi's deliberately ambiguous songs granted him an important measure of political safety. In large part, this ambiguity derived from Mtukudzi's exceptional mastery of the Shona language. As Stephen Chifunyise observed, "His Shona is outstanding. There are very few musicians who would handle Shona language the way he has handled it, with the idiomatic expressions, the riddles, the parables, the proverbs." Sometimes referred to as "deep Shona," or *Shona yakadzama*, the metaphorical register of Mtukudzi's lyrics is clearly separate from everyday speech. As one young woman explained: "You don't speak like Tuku sings. I mean, if I started speaking like he sings, I would look a little bit weird. 'Cause there are some words that he uses, and you have to do research to know what they mean ... It's deep." Another listener observed, "There are some songs with Shona that is complex. ... You cannot easily capture what he was trying to say." For Shona-speaking audiences, Mtukudzi's predilection for singing in deep Shona is clearly linked to his desire to communicate the moral ethos of hunhu to his listeners. As one person told me: "When he speaks to us in Shona, his language is so deep. It has got this cultural meaning. ... Our African culture is, when somebody is older, like the age of Tuku and above, your duty is to help the young generation to grow. But you help them using what you call *tsumo* [proverbs]. You know *tsumo nemadimikira* [proverbs and allusive speech]? Those are very strong words, which build character."

Listening to "Wasakara"

Questions of interpretation have loomed large in the reception history of "Wasakara," particularly since Mtukudzi's skillful use of Shona rhetoric appears to be among the "clever strategies that he uses to criticise the government without seeming to do so."[38] Yet I suggest that Mtukudzi's attempts to downplay the political implications of "Wasakara" must be understood as more than simply a form of artistic subterfuge. Exceeding conventional boundaries of the political, "Wasakara" speaks to moral social relations in multiple contexts, from the family to the nation-state. From this perspective, Mtukudzi's refusal to limit "Wasakara" to a single, political reading was not only an attempt to ensure his own personal safety; it also serves as a trenchant reminder that the musical imaginaries of his songs are capable of supporting multiple interpretations, bringing questions of listening and reception to the fore.

For poet Chirikure Chirikure, songs such as "Wasakara" encourage audiences to become actively involved in deciphering musical meaning. Reflecting on the difficulties of translating Mtukudzi's lyrics into English, Chirikure, who participated in writing liner notes for several of the singer's albums, told me: "One straight line can be interpreted in so many different ways, depending on where and who is listening. But then, there are also some nice twists he puts into his lyrics. For example, instead of just making the song say one thing, he can throw in reversed lines, which can give you a new twist altogether to the ideas he's putting through. So you can easily get tricked. By interpreting the chorus, for example, but the rest of the body of the song could have also these other innuendoes." For Chirikure, the lyrics to "Wasakara" are a perfect example of this kind of double-speak: "Take 'Bvuma' as an example. You would have '*Bvuma wasakara, bvuma wachembera*,' which is very straightforward—it's, 'Accept you are old.' But then you have '*Bvuma wasakara, mweya imhandara* [Admit you are worn out, your spirit is an adolescent girl].' So in a lot of ways, he's saying, 'Be proud of age, because even if you are wrinkled, your soul is still good, and belongs to the Lord. To the Lord, you are a small baby.'" Journalist Robert Mukondiwa similarly observed, "You sit down and you ask yourself, is he saying something negative about old age, or is he saying something positive? You know? And some were saying, 'It's saying so-and-so is too old.' And others were saying, 'No, he's saying celebrate age.' You know? But again, as I said, he doesn't impose himself. So it's left to open interpretation."

Echoing this perspective, ordinary listeners similarly read "Wasakara" in different ways. As one told me, "There are so many things it can mean. You can use it politically, or regarding long life, or even right there in the domestic home, right there in the household." As another said, "For me, yes, politically it means a lot. But also, as a story told by the fires at home, in the homelands, it's equally at home." Yet a third reflected, "He could have meant the president of Zimbabwe, that, 'You're an old man, leave.' But also, it could apply to a multitude of other instances. . . . To even patriarchy. To just people not acting their age. So it's a social commentary, which can be interpreted in many ways by many people, and so on. To me, that is great. So I can not judge him, to say, 'Why is he not saying "Down with ZANU-PF?"'" Even people frustrated by Mtukudzi's refusal to identify "Wasakara" as a political statement acknowledged his multivalent musical imaginaries as a major artistic strength. As one listener concluded, "We were looking for someone like Tuku to take the leadership and say, 'Hey, I'm the first one to have said, "You know, what you guys are doing is wrong."' And we all knew that's what he meant. You know? But I suppose that's one of his strengths, isn't it, that his songs are always open to interpretation?"

From Mtukudzi's perspective, the mounting pressure to pin "Wasakara" down to a single political reading was counterproductive. As he told me, "When you find a journalist who comes to ask you about that question, then already he's biased. . . . He's not looking for the meaning of the song, he's looking for me to confirm what they want the song to mean. . . . You can tell that he's got an answer already, that he wants you to confirm, that's all it is." In contrast, Mtukudzi sought to hold space for multiple interpretive possibilities, asserting, "Because Shona is beautiful, and clean, you can have three meanings in each song." With their messages about what it means to live well with others, he perceived his musical imaginaries as capable of speaking across political boundaries:

My songs are not periodical, as I said before. They work yesterday, today, and tomorrow. If you use one of the songs against me, I can use the song against you. Because it doesn't support one person, it supports the inner self of a human being. It's a song about how we should live. It's about who we are. . . . And I think that's the role of an artist. We do have politicians in music. They're not really artists, you see? You can tell from their messages that their messages are partisan; their messages are of a particular class. It's not for everybody.

Despite widespread political readings of "Wasakara," many listeners concurred with Mtukudzi's views. As one told me, "What is good about Tuku's music is its agelessness. You know, it was relevant in 1978, it's relevant in 2007. And there's no political statement which is bigger than that, which can make that kind of impact in a community. No political commentary can beat that." Another eloquently argued, "People might construe these songs to mean one particular thing, but I think that's wrong. People should leave these songs to be interpreted in different ways. Me, I would interpret them in different ways. And I shouldn't be said to be sidelining what other people think. Anybody should be free to interpret them the way they do, and the way they want." For both Mtukudzi and for his listeners, the reductive search for a single musical meaning threatened to undermine the dialogic nature of his songs. Read in this light, Mtukudzi's insistence on political neutrality was not simply a way to dissimulate hidden political messages; it was also a conscious attempt to preserve space for multiple, even competing interpretations of his music to coexist.

Beyond *"Wasakara"*

Catapulting to the forefront of the Zimbabwean political imagination, "Wasakara" offered a particularly compelling example of how listeners have perceived Mtukudzi's musical imaginaries of moral personhood as critiques of national governance. Yet "Wasakara" is but the most prominent example of countless songs that Mtukudzi's listeners have heard as political in an extended process dating all the way back to the liberation war of the 1970s. As Mtukudzi observed, many of his earliest hits were widely heard as political: "Songs like 'Dzandimomotera,' 'Mutavara,' 'Ziwere,' you know, all those songs, they were talking about what we are. 'Nyarara Mwanawe,' 'Chido Chenyu Here,' 'Ndirangarire,' all those songs were used by the freedom fighters. 'Cause they made sense of the way we lived then." Several decades later, audiences would continue to interpret Mtukudzi's songs in the context of contemporary social, political, and economic conditions. Reflecting on "Madiro" (*Tuku Music*, 1997), for example, one person observed that criticisms of Mtukudzi's supposed political apathy were missing the point: "When he's talking about how hard things are—'*Ndovayemura ava baba vakaenda kani* [I pay homage to my father, who passed on long ago]'— you just kind of think back, and see. And think of the difference between, for example, now and then. When someone is commenting about those things and you say it's not political, I don't know what you want him to do. That song, it's a political commentary, when it is making you reflect on the differences in different time periods, and so forth." Extrapolating outward from the household as a microcosm of social organization, audiences similarly interpreted Mtukudzi's portrayal of domestic violence in "Baba" (*Shoko*, 1993) as an allegorical critique of postcolonial governance. As Murenga Chikowero has observed, "The brutal father who abuses his wife in the presence of their children mirrors an irresponsible leader who resorts to violence rather than negotiation."[39]

Joining these emerging political readings of Mtukudzi's older songs, audiences heard other tracks on *Bvuma-Tolerance* as thinly veiled political statements. As illustrated in the preface to this book, "Ngoromera," which advocates for resolving conflict through dialogue rather than physical force, was likewise interpreted as a critique of escalating political violence between ZANU-PF and the MDC. Yet a third track on the album, called "Murimi Munhu," or "A farmer is a person," was also widely heard as political. With terse, almost proverbial lyrics, "Murimi Munhu" acknowledges that farmers play an indispensible role in sustaining the social body. As one person told me, "He's just saying, 'Everything comes from the soil, everything comes from the farmer. For you to do anything, you will have to have had a meal that will have passed through the hands of a farmer.'" Mtukudzi claimed to have written the song far before it was released on *Bvuma-Tolerance*. As he told Banning Eyre: "'Murimi Munhu,' I wrote that song in 1992, when the Musengezi cooperative came. And they wanted their song to uplift, or to promote, or to encourage young farmers to farm. So that's how I wrote that song. It's talking about, people should learn to plow for themselves. 'Cause to be whatever you are, make sure you're going to eat something that has been planted by somebody who has farmed it. So that's how the song came to me."[40]

Yet "Murimi Munhu" was almost immediately interpreted as a critique of ZANU-PF's fast-track land reform program. As one listener reflected:

> This was the time of land invasion, or land reform program in Zimbabwe. And he came up with themes, which I wouldn't say were negative to the land reform, but had different thinking from the government's perception. And the majority of people—especially the urban people in Zimbabwe—had the same kind of thinking. So, that clicked. He would say, "*Murimi munhu*," you know, "A farmer is also a human being." So why are you persecuting them? That was one of the songs on the album, and it clicked with the people. He says, "Even you, president, or minister, or *tsotsi* [thief]. Whoever you are, you depend on the farmer's food, that's why you're alive. So, whatever you do, don't forget that the farmer is also a human being." And that's all he said, in the album! And people, especially urban people, were very much against this land reform program. As you can see, the situation in Zimbabwe now, the majority of the people don't have food because of that disturbance, we call it.[41]

Journalist Percy Zvomuya similarly observed in the Catholic magazine *Moto*:

> In a seemingly ambivalent song, Tuku observes that the farmer is important, that land is nationhood, and nationhood is the land. He advises the farmer to take up his hoe and farm. Everyone depends on the farmer: the writer, the musician, the not-so-honest dealers and even the king. But what good is soil/land which is not in the hands of a farmer, or which is not being used or is underutilized. "Murimi Munhu" teaches us to recognize the sacredness of the farmer's work. Let us recognize the farm labourer and acknowledge him as the vital cog in the economy's engine. Without him we are done for.[42]

As with "Wasakara," "Murimi Munhu" was quietly taken off air at Zimbabwe's state-owned radio stations.[43] Yet it, too, proved equally capable of supporting multiple interpretations. Writing in the *Southern Times*, for example, one anonymous journalist suggested that the song's praise for "the small farmer" was in fact evidence of Mtukudzi's support for land reform.[44] Commenting on these radically divergent interpretations, one of Mtukudzi's band members told me:

"Every person has always wanted those songs to work in their favor. If you are a ZANU-PF person, you think this message, 'Murimi Munhu,' means, 'Let's go on with taking land.' And if you an MDC person you think 'Bvuma [Wasakara]' is saying this and that, you know? Of which, that's not the meaning of the song. So people have really taken the songs to be, 'OK, he does the songs for the people.' And they own them. And then, anybody uses the songs they way they feel."

Less than a year later, Mtukudzi's next album, *Vhunze Moto*, or "Burning embers" (2002), was also interpreted as political. Seizing upon the album's title, the local press called its reference to smoldering coals an appropriate metaphor for a nation "wrecked by horrific political violence, economic meltdown and one of the worst Aids [sic] crises in Africa."[45] As with *Bvuma-Tolerance*, audiences read politics into more than one song on *Vhunze Moto*.[46] Yet the most heated controversy revolved once more around its title track, "Moto Moto," or "Fire is fire." As Zvomuya wrote: "'Vhunze Moto' asks why people wait for a small fire to become big for them to call it a fire. 'Do not ignore this insignificant ember,' Tuku says, 'for it can burn all we have worked for.' This is a camouflaged message for the leadership of this country not to ignore legitimate rumblings for these can flare up into an inferno."[47] The original album cover, with flames superimposed over an outline of the Zimbabwean state, seemed to support this reading. As one person drily remarked, "The album title—*Vhunze Moto*. And you see the album cover—Zimbabwe in flames. I mean, there you are, right there."[48]

Listeners would continue to hear political messages in subsequent songs, such as "Chikara," or "A predatory wild beast," released on the album *Tsimba Itsoka* (2007). Explaining the song's lyrics, which warn against following the track of an unknown beast, lest it turn out to be a dangerous predator, Mtukudzi told an audience at one live show: "The inspiration came to be after realizing that people underestimate the meaning of a footprint. A footprint represents who you are. And each time you see a footprint it means somebody has been there before you. And a footprint will never tell a lie. No wonder why we can tell a footprint from a bird, a footprint from an animal, and a human print. You can tell the difference, 'cause footprints never lie." Once again, however, listeners resoundingly interpreted "Chikara" as a metaphorical critique of the predatory postcolonial state, which threatens to cannibalize and consume its subjects.[49] As one person told me: "*Chikara* is like a fierce, wild animal. . . . So it's like the president's legacy. What legacy are you leaving? For you to follow that footstep, you need to know what sort of animal leaves a footstep like that. You see what I mean? Because you might follow a *chikara*. So, I mean, you could also say he's talking about ZANU-PF people. You know? You keep following, but it has become a *chikara*. You know? What is it that you are following?" Writing on the moral education of Shona children, Carol Pearce has observed that hunhu

Independence Day, Mutare

Vazhinji navazhinji takavafushira	We buried multitudes and multitudes
Nepamusana pekuda nyika yedu	In our longing for our country
Yatakatorerwa nevapambepfumi	Seized from us by the imperialists
Nehanda kombererai mhuri yeZimbabwe	Nehanda, bless the family of Zimbabwe
Kana ndikatondera nehama dziri pasi	When I remember our buried relatives
Misodzi inobva yabuda a-ha	Tears begin to well up
Ndikacherechedza handina chimiro	When I reflect upon it, I lose my strength
Nehanda kombererai mhuri yeZimbabwe	Nehanda, bless the family of Zimbabwe

"gains its force in contrast with pre-human or animal behaviour. A person has moral attributes not granted to a wild animal."[50] Given Mtukudzi's emphasis on singing about moral personhood, the imagery of "Chikara" seemed to intimate that immoral leaders risk losing their human qualities, metaphorically reverting to a nonhuman state.

Back to Chimanimani

By the time Mtukudzi appeared at the 2008 Chimanimani Arts Festival, nearly a decade had passed since the release of *Bvuma-Tolerance*. Yet political sentiments were running high once more in the uncertain aftermath of the recent "harmonized" elections, imbuing "Wasakara" with renewed political significance. The previous day, on April 18, Zimbabweans had commemorated twenty-eight years of independence. With a presidential winner yet to be declared, ZANU-PF seized the occasion to publicly assert its continued hold on power. In between shows, the Black Spirits had spent the day in the town of Mutare, where they watched ZANU-PF party members stream out of an enormous rally held at Sakubva Stadium, the very place Mtukudzi had once recorded the nation's first live album. Clad in outfits emblazoned with Mugabe's image, they raised their fists determinedly in salute, chanting ZANU-PF party slogans and singing Chimurenga anthems praising the nation's martyrs in four-part harmony, in a determined attempt to revive the spirit of the liberation war.

For listeners in the MDC stronghold of Chimanimani, Mtukudzi's performance offered a much-needed musical counterpoint to these displays. Reflecting
on "Wasakara," for example, one member of the Black Spirits observed, "Songs
like that, that have got political things attached to them. They can be like sea-
sonal songs. They can well be played even in the time, like this set-up, that we're
waiting for the [election] results." Seizing the opportunity to express collective
political dissent, thousands of listeners raised their hands in the air as Mtukudzi
played "Wasakara," flashing their open palms in what had become the MDC's
trademark gesture, intended as a symbol of transparency, accountability, and political change. As one listener would later observe, "When he played that song,
they changed, and started doing politics. Because every person was making the
MDC wave, you know? They were waving the MDC hand." From their position
onstage, the Black Spirits looked out over thousands of people with palms held
high, forming a vast ocean of waving hands.

Even here, however, the inherent multivalence of Mtukudzi's imaginaries of
moral personhood enabled "Wasakara" to accommodate other readings. Bringing this point home quite clearly, a high-ranking ZANU-PF minister from a
nearby constituency made a sudden appearance onstage at precisely the moment Mtukudzi began to sing "Wasakara."[51] Exhibiting a rare flash of charm,
the minister and his wife danced energetically alongside the Black Spirits, seemingly impervious to the overwhelming political will of the massive crowd gathered in front of them. For those in the audience, however, the sight of a ZANU-
PF minister dancing to "Wasakara" was not as incongruous as it might seem. As
one person who attended the show later told me, "Probably the minister thinks
something different about the song . . . Maybe he's thinking it's about soccer.
Maybe he thinks it says 'admit' in another way, not that the president should
admit. You see?"

Indeed, several similar occasions have been reported in relation to "Wasakara." After a performance in Harare, for example, one anonymous reviewer
wrote in the *Zimbabwe Independent*, "There was a political message throughout
the show and one that the crowd loved to hear. It was interesting to see Munyaradzi Kajese, the Chief of Protocol in the President's Office thoroughly enjoying himself!"[52] On yet another occasion, posters advertising the Zimbabwe Republic Police's annual funfair touted that Mtukudzi would perform "Wasakara"
at the event, suggesting that even the state security apparatus was not immune
to the song's infectious charm.

While Mtukudzi's lyrics speak primarily to moral personhood within the domestic sphere, they resonate on much larger levels of social organization, making his musical imaginaries powerful metaphors for nation governance. As listeners have actively participated in interpreting songs such as "Wasakara," they

have entered a musical domain in which the household and the nation-state are intimately linked, forming what anthropologist Marilyn Strathern has described as a world of "encompassing morality."[53] The reception of Tuku music thus exemplifies postcolonial struggles over musical meaning, reflecting Richard Werbner's observation that "the political cannot be meaningfully studied apart from the moral."[54]

From politics to HIV/AIDS

Yet escalating political conflict between ZANU-PF and the MDC was not the only trial facing Mtukudzi's audiences during the late 1990s and early 2000s. Even as they grappled with the fallout of escalating political tension, listeners were also confronting Zimbabwe's largely unchecked HIV/AIDS epidemic, with a wave of new infections throughout the 1990s cresting in massive numbers of AIDS-related deaths in the early 2000s. Reflecting his commitment to effecting social change, Mtukudzi began writing songs about AIDS as early as the mid-1980s. As Zimbabwe was increasingly decimated by AIDS, he proceeded to step up his efforts by writing several more songs about the disease, and by lending his voice, image, and presence to public health initiatives designed to combat the growing pandemic. Just as "Wasakara" prompted listeners to engage with Zimbabwean politics, Mtukudzi's songs about HIV/AIDS challenged them to reflect upon and respond to the disease, both individually and as a collective social body.

"Todii"
(What shall we do)

Ho todii?	What shall we do?
Senzeni?	(Chorus in Shona, Ndebele, and English)
What shall we do?	
Tingadii?	
Senzenjani?	
What shall we do?	

Zvinorwadza sei kurera rufu mumaoko?	How painful is it to raise death in your hands?
Ungadii uinawo hutachiwanawo?	What will you do now that you have it, the virus?
Zvinorwadza sei kuchengeta rufu mumaoko?	How hard is it to care for death in your hands?
Ungadii uinawo hutachiwanawo?	What will you do now that you have it, the virus?
Bva zvapabata pamuviri pasina raramo	A pregnancy has taken hold with no future
Ungadii uinawo hutachiwanawo?	What will you do now that you have it, the virus?
Bva zvapatumbuka pamuviri pasina raramo	A pregnancy has germinated with no survival
Ungadii uinawo hutachiwanawo?	What will you do now that you have it, the virus?

Chorus

Zvinorwadza sei kubhinywa newaugere naye?	How painful is it to be raped by your husband?
Ungadii uinawo hutachiwanawo?	What will you do now that you have it, the virus?
Zvinorwadza sei kubhinywa neakabvisa pfuma?	How painful is it to be raped by your husband?
Ungadii uinawo hutachiwanawo?	What will you do now that you have it, the virus?
Achiziva unawo hutachiwanawo	While he knows that you have it, the virus?
Ungadii uinawo hutachiwanawo?	What will you do now that you have it, the virus?
Endi uchiziva unawo hutachiwanawo	And you know that you have it, the virus
Ungadii uinawo hutachiwanawo?	What will you do now that you have it, the virus?

Chorus

Seri kweguva hakuna munamato varume tapererwa	Beyond the grave no prayer can reach men, we have been decimated
Hutachiwanawo	The virus
Dondipai mazano	I implore you, give me advice
Ungadii uinawo hutachiwanawo?	What will you do now that you have it, the virus?
Seri kweguva hakuna muteuro Mambo tapererwa	Beyond the grave no ritual offering can reach, Lord we have been decimated
Hutachiwanawo	The virus
Dondipai mazano	I implore you, give me advice
Ungadii uinawo hutachiwanawo?	What will you do now that you have it, the virus?

Chorus

SEVEN

What Shall We Do?
Music, Dialogue, and HIV/AIDS

In December 2008, the National Gallery of Zimbabwe hosted the Auxilia Chimusoro Awards, an annual event named after one of the country's first women to publicly disclose her HIV-positive status. Timed to coincide with World AIDS Day, observed internationally on December 1st, the award ceremony brought together a diverse array of approaches to HIV/AIDS. At a display of herbal remedies, representatives of The Centre, a local organization that supports people without access to antiretroviral medications (ARVs), mingled with employees of the US Agency for International Development, one of the event's major sponsors.[1] Nearby, invited guests browsed an exhibit of AIDS posters from around the world, accompanied by a set of banners reflecting Zimbabwean experiences of the disease. Echoing the connections between hunhu, self-discipline, and moral relations, one read simply, "It has made me a whole lot more disciplined than I would have expected of myself." In the gallery's light-filled mezzanine, guests passed between white columns adorned with red ribbons, widely recognized as symbols of support for people infected and affected by HIV/AIDS. Filtering between rows of chairs, they seated themselves in front of a small stage, where Mtukudzi performed two short sets bookending the ceremony. Behind him, a large banner emblazoned with Auxilia Chimusoro's image hung above a row of posters featuring Mtukudzi himself, accompanied by the slogan "Don't be negative about being positive."

For radio DJ Leander Kandiero, who was among those honored with an award for his pioneering radio show *Aid on AIDS*, Mtukudzi's performance proved the most powerful moment of the ceremony:

> I walked in. It was actually overwhelming . . . When you see that this is Auxilia Chimusoro awards, HIV and AIDS is the issue. And people who work towards an HIV free generation, who work around HIV and AIDS, have been invited. And you think, someone as big as Oliver, who has taken the message not only across Zimbabwe, but even outside Zimbabwean borders, is there, and he's performing, and he's sitting right in front of you. And you think, "Wow . . . there's a man who has said so much, and done so much to do with HIV and AIDS. And he's an icon, an international icon, and he's

The 2008 Auxilia Chimusoro Awards at the National Gallery
of Zimbabwe. *Photo by Jennifer W. Kyker.*

sitting in front of me." For me as a broadcaster who understands the power
of music, that was amazing. And it was just so relevant that he was there.

While Mtukudzi did not perform any of his many songs about HIV/AIDS at the
ceremony, Kandiero perceived this as a sensitive move, reflecting that the singer
"was conscious that there were people living with HIV and AIDS in the auditorium. And he was also conscious of the fact that there were people who might
not be infected, but are affected."

Bringing us back to how listeners tend to read themselves into the musical
imaginaries of Mtukudzi's songs, Kandiero observed that hearing him sing about
HIV/AIDS can be particularly challenging, uncomfortable, and even painful. Indeed, the tendency to hear one's own private experience reflected in public oral
discourse is so entrenched among Shona speakers that it has given rise to its own
proverb, or *tsumo*, which states, *"Chiri murusakasaka / Chinozvinzwira,"* or "He in
the crowd / Hears for himself."[2] As Kandiero explained:

> It's like church. When the pastor comes up with a sermon on Sunday, it
> usually always sounds like it's aimed at you. And sometimes, you don't
> want to listen to it. Because you feel, "Has someone spoken to this guy

Mtukudzi performing at the 2008 Auxilia Chimusoro Awards.
Photo by Jennifer W. Kyker.

about my situation?" And so some people actually turn off the radio, or take it too personally. . . . And that is the issue. Sometimes when you talk about HIV and AIDS, or play a song to do with HIV and AIDS, people run away from it, to say, "No, that situation that I'm in, I don't want to hear about it." So they turn off the radio.

By comparing popular music to a religious service, Kandiero's comments suggest that although the way people interpret song in relation to their everyday lives may be particularly pronounced in the case of Tuku music, it also extends to other domains, making questions of listening and reception critical to understanding various forms of Zimbabwean expressive culture.

Aid on AIDS

Aid on AIDS actually started when I was doing the breakfast show. I think as a sense of duty as a broadcaster, you can't ignore something as big as HIV and AIDS. In the beginning, there was less info. Ten minutes would be talk, and five minutes would be taken by a song related to HIV and AIDS. Well, gradually, people begin to get used to the idea that there is something called *Aid on AIDS*, and this is what it's about. So people would come through calling. They want to be part of it. The appreciation is amazing. People feel that they have a platform where they're at least considered, and they can speak out.

If I pick up a song on *Aid on AIDS*, I always tell people not to listen to music like they usually do. 'Cause radio, sometimes, is not active listening. Someone is doing something else while they're listening to you, so it's not active listening. I actually urge people to listen very carefully to what is being said in the song, so that they can relate to it and find out why we've chosen this to be the song of the day. You take a relevant song—Oliver's included and other artists' included—and then you say, "Why have I played this song? What's its relevance to the show?" So that's how I use music on the show.

People will say, "I think it's relevant for you to play 'Todii,' or 'Mabasa.'" Yeah, people will say, "Play Oliver's song." That has come through, where people actually ask specifically. Because he has more songs, I think, than most other artists. Maybe you will find that a certain artist has one good song to do with HIV and AIDS, but Oliver has a number of songs. So, yes, I make it a point that I play Oliver Mtukudzi, at least two or three songs within a week.

—*Leander Kandiero*

So powerful is the propensity to hear oneself in song that the audience at the Auxilia Chimusoro Awards appeared visibly tense even though Mtukudzi did not sing about HIV/AIDS. Only a few of them rose to dance, sang along, or delivered the syncopated rhythmic patterns of makwa handclapping. Their reticence to participate was so pronounced that Mtukudzi briefly paused midway through his set in order to remind listeners that his songs are aimed at society at large, rather than at particular individuals, a deliberate attempt to mitigate the propensity to "hear oneself in the crowd." As Kandiero observed: "He went on to, to say, 'Whatever I'm going to sing in my songs, even though it might be relevant to your situation, I'm not really aiming at you. It's just a song that talks about what's happening in society in relation to HIV and AIDS . . . We're all in this thing together, so these are just comments that I'm passing on.'"

Drawing upon the distinctive joking relations inherent in the sahwira's role as ritual best friend, Mtukudzi jested that the least those in the audience could do was to clap after every song, despite whatever discomfort they might feel about its lyrics. By encouraging listeners to connect even as he sought to defuse the tension they felt at an event specifically focused on HIV/AIDS, Mtukudzi closely conformed to the sahwira's expected ability to communicate serious information in a light-hearted manner. From his perspective as a radio broadcaster, Leander Kandiero found this interaction instructive both in illustrating local constructions of listening, and in emphasizing music's power to open up dialogue about HIV/AIDS: "For me, that was a very strong statement. . . . You don't want to listen to it, but it helps for you to actually turn up the volume and listen to it. Because that's the only way we're going to defeat this thing. The more we talk about it, the less power it has over us."

Shaping the National Discourse of HIV/AIDS through Song

In a previous article, I have offered a textual reading of several of Mtukudzi's most significant songs about HIV/AIDS.[3] Building on that foundation, this chapter illustrates how Zimbabwean audiences have interpreted Mtukudzi's songs about HIV/AIDS in relation to the complex and evolving field of public health, bringing his musical imaginaries of hunhu into conversation with biomedical discourse. In the first part of this chapter, I offer my perspective on the role ethnomusicology can play in highlighting the social dimensions of HIV/AIDS and in sustaining a sense of moral urgency in the global response to this ongoing pandemic. Tracing Mtukudzi's history of singing about HIV/AIDS, I then illustrate how he moved away from conventional early messages about the disease and toward a nuanced way of singing that reflected Shona rhetorical expectations concerning illness, grieving, and death.

Drawing on interviews, news reports, and my own participant-observation at public health events, the second part of the chapter turns to Mtukudzi's numerous partnerships with public health organizations. I suggest that Tuku music has proved so appealing for public health work primarily because of Mtukudzi's ability to situate HIV/AIDS within a Shona framework of mutual social responsibility. By incorporating Mtukudzi's songs in a variety of awareness, prevention, and treatment campaigns, public health organizations have sought to ground their initiatives in a musical form of local discourse about HIV/AIDS. In turn, these partnerships have enhanced Mtukudzi's visibility as an HIV/AIDS ambassador, coloring the reception of his songs.

I conclude the chapter by turning to Mtukudzi's work with the Pakare Paye Arts Centre, which he founded in the town of Norton, some twenty miles outside of Harare. I suggest that Pakare Paye, together with Mtukudzi's commitment to singing about HIV/AIDS and his participation in public health work, represents yet another important contribution to the fight against HIV/AIDS. With a unique, collaborative model of arts education, Pakare Paye has empowered local musicians to formulate their own artistic directions, many of them related in some way to HIV/AIDS. In addition, Pakare Paye has hosted a range of workshops, lectures, and programs on HIV/AIDS. Building on Mtukudzi's stature as a trusted local figure, Pakare Paye has been exceptionally successful at mediating relationships between nongovernmental organizations and Norton residents, modeling an exemplary approach to integrating public health and the arts.

HIV/AIDS in Zimbabwe

For anyone with ties to Southern Africa, HIV/AIDS constitutes a new social reality that has quietly but overwhelmingly penetrated every aspect of human experience. More than thirty years after the virus was first identified in the early 1980s, HIV has come to be treated largely as a chronic condition in the developed world, where ARVs are widely available. As a result, the urgent and impassioned political activism that flourished during the early days of the epidemic has all but disappeared, nearly erasing AIDS from the popular consciousness. Yet this now treatable disease continues to rank among the leading causes of death worldwide, killing over 15 million people every year.[4] The African continent has borne a disproportionate share of this burden, accounting for nearly three-quarters of all the people who have died from AIDS, as well as over 70 percent of new infections.[5]

Even in comparison to other African nations, Zimbabwe has been particularly hard hit, experiencing one of the world's harshest HIV and AIDS epidemics.[6] After the country's first AIDS case was reported in 1985, new infections increased exponentially. By the late 1990s, HIV prevalence was estimated at over 25 percent of the general population, giving Zimbabwe one of the highest infection rates in the world.[7] Dropping precipitously, life expectancy plunged to an abysmal low of only thirty-six years.[8] As one person after another succumbed to AIDS, many Zimbabweans experienced the collapse of extended kinship networks, which have historically contributed to the formation of social identity, political authority, economic stability, and ritual life.

Acknowledging an urgent need for improved access to treatment, the Zimbabwean government declared ARV shortages a national emergency in 2002, a move intended to reduce drug costs by permitting the local production and purchase of generic ARVs under international law. Over the following years, the number of people receiving treatment rose significantly. By 2012, one national policy report suggested that 79 percent of people who needed treatment were receiving it. At the same time, Zimbabwe began making strides in reducing its HIV prevalence rate, which dropped to an estimated 15 percent of the population in 2013.[9] Although this decline has been widely lauded as a success story, it is also partly tied to exceptionally high mortality rates during the late 1990s, when scores of people unable to access ARVs simply died.[10] Even after this drop, nearly 1.5 million Zimbabweans were still living with HIV in 2013, and almost a million children had lost one or both parents to AIDS.[11]

Anthropology in a Time of AIDS

Far from the largely treatable condition it has become in the developed world, the contours of Zimbabwe's epidemic remind us that HIV/AIDS continues to be a matter of both moral urgency and global inequality. One of the leading voices of public health, Paul Farmer, has argued that anthropology can play a critical role in bringing HIV/AIDS back to the forefront of global consciousness, as the disease's path is tightly intertwined with the very social forces that have long constituted the discipline's primary target.[12] Foremost among them are the type of structural inequalities that result in both suffering and erasure, creating the conditions necessary for HIV/AIDS to thrive even as they mask the voices of those affected by the disease. Anthropology can work toward changing these conditions by developing new ways of knowing illness that acknowledge the humanity of those affected by HIV/AIDS, integrating lived experiences of the virus alongside its larger structural causes and implications.[13]

In Zimbabwe, HIV/AIDS has often been deeply stigmatized. In the words of one young secondary school student: "Stigma and discrimination has killed people more than the HIV virus itself. People are encouraged to come out into the open, but the problem lies there after disclosing their status. People start gossiping and mocking them. You hear them say, *'Akarohwa nematsotsi, chabvondoka* [he was beaten by thieves, things blew up].' Even the HIV and AIDS orphans are mocked as if they are the ones responsible for their parents' status." As community health worker Barb Ncube explains, this stigma is directly related to the scare tactics used to discourage unsafe sexual behavior in the early days of the epidemic: "They should have started by giving out the facts about HIV and not starting with lines like, 'AIDS kills.' Because that already made it a taboo. It was like the fear factor, 'This is a subject we shouldn't discuss.' If someone is

HIV [positive] then they wouldn't even say, because AIDS kills. We would reject them. They made it like a huge mystery, something really scary. They used the wrong tactic." While stigma has been significantly reduced by the growing availability of ARVs, it continues to discourage people from being tested for HIV, disclosing their serostatus, and even accessing treatment. One woman I spoke to, for example, knew people so worried about being spotted at an AIDS clinic that they refused to enroll in ARV treatment programs even after testing positive for HIV.

Throughout the African continent, music has consistently offered communities affected by HIV/AIDS a way to sing aloud experiences that all too often still cannot be said. Describing her experience as a support group coordinator in the town of Chinhoyi, Ncube recalled: "They loved to sing. In fact, when you sing, something happens. The women's support group, I even remember some of the songs. Like, 'Knock, knock, knock, *usarambe kutestwa* [don't refuse to be tested], knock, knock.' They would make all these songs about HIV themselves, and it helped them to live. Music, actually, that's all they had to hold onto. So they used to sing a lot." An important part of what historian of medicine Steven Feierman has described as the "everyday knowledge that living people hold in their heads and bodies, and even speak about, but that does not enter the process of scientific discovery, or health care practice," music is one among many local strategies for dealing with HIV/AIDS.[14] Alongside other approaches—including indigenous ritual therapies, evangelical faith-based healing, nutrition and herbal medicine, and other forms of expressive culture such as poetry, drama, and dance—music has played an important role in both reflecting and structuring local understandings of HIV/AIDS, whether in Zimbabwe or elsewhere in Africa.[15]

More than thirty years after AIDS was first discovered, public health work has increasingly turned toward other causes of mortality such as heart disease and stroke, which kill more people per year than HIV/AIDS. Yet the social effects of AIDS are substantially different than those of any other disease, robbing societies of an entire productive class, and destroying the fabric of communities. As Mtukudzi sings in his song "Mabasa" (*Tuku Music*, 1997), "The worker leads the way / Leaving elderly men and women / Now who will look after whom?" In a time of AIDS, anthropological approaches are more necessary than ever, for they enable us to engage with precisely the type of lived experiences marginalized both in the sweeping scope of grand theories, and in the minutia of statistical surveys. In the face of stigma, discrimination, and fear, those infected and affected by HIV/AIDS frequently turn to the modality of song in order to give voice to their experiences of the disease. Musical ethnography in particular thus has a particularly important role to play both in highlighting the costly social effects of HIV/AIDS and in sustaining a sense of moral urgency into the fourth decade of the epidemic.

Mtukudzi's Songs about HIV/AIDS

Mtukudzi's commitment to singing about HIV/AIDS dates back to the 1986 release of his song "Stay with One Woman," placing him among the very first musicians to respond to the disease worldwide. In the coming years, Mtukudzi would proceed to record several other songs about HIV/AIDS, including "Ndakuyambira" (1988), "Mupfumi Ndiani" (*Svovi Yangu*, 1996), "Todii" and "Mabasa" (*Tuku Music*, 1997), "Akoromoka Awa" (*Bvuma-Tolerance*, 2000), "Tapera" (*Vhunze Moto*, 2002), "Dama Rinetapira" (*Tsivo*, 2003), and "Handiro Dambudziko" (*Nhava*, 2005). Playing upon the expressive qualities of Mtukudzi's voice, these songs both described the devastation wrought by HIV/AIDS and urged audiences to formulate a collective response to the epidemic.

1986: "Stay with One Woman"

Recorded just one year after Zimbabwe announced its first case of HIV infection, "Stay with One Woman," was Mtukudzi's entry in a musical competition organized by the World Health Organization in response to the growing pandemic. Written primarily in English, "Stay with One Woman" was intended for an international audience still largely unfamiliar with AIDS, which was only starting to be understood even within the scientific community. Based largely on the informational materials Mtukudzi had been given by the WHO, the song's lyrics depicted prevention as a matter of individual responsibility, placing particular emphasis on the importance of monogamy:

> But now there is a new disease called AIDS
> And it's getting right out of control
> Stay with one woman
> Keep to one woman
> Stay with one woman
> One woman, one woman for a man
> Keep to one woman
> Stay with one woman
>
> With AIDS there is no cure
> Prevention is the only way
> Keep yourself and your woman pure

Invoking the standardized language of early public health literature on HIV/AIDS, these lyrics portrayed the disease as an individual problem rather than a social one, situating prevention within the private domain of sexual relations.[16]

As Mtukudzi told me, "Stay with One Woman" reflected his own extremely limited initial understanding of HIV/AIDS: "I did not yet have any real knowledge about AIDS. I didn't understand. But I did have the information I had been given. So, okay, if there is such a thing as this, then probably 'Stay with One Woman' would be helpful. . . . So I just wrote this in order to be able to compete, thinking, 'I really must write something that makes sense about HIV and AIDS, about protecting oneself from AIDS.'" After recording "Stay with One Woman," Mtukudzi was selected by the WHO to travel to Switzerland to perform the song with the Black Spirits. Back home in Zimbabwe, however, his audiences were likewise struggling to understand the disease. As a result, "Stay with One Woman" brought no return in terms of sales.[17]

1988: "I Have Warned You"

Marking a dramatic shift in his approach to singing about HIV/AIDS, Mtukudzi wrote a second song about the growing epidemic shortly after his return to Zimbabwe, titled "Ndakuyambira" or "I have warned you." Sung entirely in Shona, the song demonstrated Mtukudzi's desire to communicate with local audiences about HIV/AIDS. Yet it also reflected how his experience in Switzerland had fundamentally altered his understanding of HIV/AIDS: "After I had gone to Switzerland and I had actually seen people affected, and people infected, and the statistics of people who have died . . . that's when I wrote my second song, 'Ndakuyambira.' I'm warning you. It was from my heart, I'd seen it. . . . Fellow artists, well, they wouldn't believe me, and I wouldn't blame them, 'cause you needed to see it to believe it."

Drawing upon the expressive qualities of Mtukudzi's soulful voice, "Ndakuyambira" begins with a cascading series of vocables, or sung syllabus. Although they hold no lexical meaning, vocables are common to many cultures around the world and are frequently used to heighten a song's emotional impact.[18] Invoking language yet surpassing it, their power lies in an ability to convey feelings that lie beyond the reach of everyday speech. In a song about HIV/AIDS, this quality grants vocables special significance, suggesting that even experiences rendered unspeakable by stigma, discrimination, and fear can nevertheless be sung.

In the verses of "Ndakuyambira," Mtukudzi calls for greater recognition of the HIV/AIDS epidemic. Using the metaphorical image of stiff maize porridge, or *sadza*, accompanied by a side dish of meat or greens, he suggests that AIDS has become as common and familiar as the everyday act of eating; no one can claim to be unaware of the disease. Illustrating his facility with the Shona language, he also adapts a proverb, or *tsumo*, which says, "What can be given up is that which is held in the hand / What is in the blood you will die with," or "*Chinonzi rega ndochiri mumaoko / Chiri mutsinga ndechekufa nacho.*" In the context of HIV/AIDS, this proverb undergoes a striking shift in meaning, for while the phrase "what is in the blood" was originally intended to refer simply to innate personal

"Ndakuyambira"
(I have warned you)

Hiyo hiyo hiyo hiyo hiyo	Hiyo hiyo hiyo hiyo hiyo
A hiyo huwowo huwowo huwowo wowowo	A hiyo huwowo huwowo huwowo wowowo
Hiyo hiyo	Hiyo hiyo
Hiyo baba ndoenda	Hiyo, father I am going
A hiyo huwowo huwowo huwowo	A hiyo huwowo huwowo huwowo
Wowo baba ndoenda	Wowo, father I am going
Hiyo hiyo	Hiyo hiyo
Hiyo baba ndoenda	Hiyo, father I am going
Shoko rakafamba	The message has traveled
Ndokufamba rikafamba	Is has traveled around and around
Ruzivo rwapararira nyika wani	Knowledge is dispersed throughout the country
Njere dzapararira ona iwe	Intelligence is dispersed throughout, look here, you
Mave kuziva seri kwesadza kune usavi	You have come to know that relish follows sadza
Seri kwemusuva kune usavi mudhara	After each bite of sadza there is relish, old man
Ukabata vhunze remoto unetsva	If you touch the coals of the fire you will be burned
Iko kutambira murufuse unetsva	There, playing in the embers, you will be burned
Ndakuyambira ndakuyambira ini	I have warned you, I have warned you myself
A hiyo huwowo huwowo huwowo	A hiyo huwowo huwowo huwowo
Wowo baba ndoenda	Wowo, father I am going
Ndakuyambira ini	I have warned you myself
Hiyo hiyo	Hiyo hiyo
Hiyo baba ndoenda	Hiyo, father I am going
Hiyo huwo	Hiyo huwo
Mwana wamambo	Child of the chief
Huwo huwo(etc.)	Huwo huwo (etc.)
Chaunonzi rega ndochiri mumaoko	What can be given up is that held in the hand
Chaunonzi siya ndochawakabvumbata	What can be left is that you hold tightly to
Chagodza mutsinga ndechekufa nacho	What has settled in the veins you will die with

characteristics, it assumes an entirely new and more literal meaning with respect to a virus transmitted through blood and other bodily fluids.

In contrast with the serious tone of its lyrics, the musical setting of "Ndakuyambira" is decidedly danceable. Together, the congas, hosho, and trap set feature prominently in the song, filling the space between interlocking melodic lines played on guitars, bass, and synthesizer. Packed with catchy melodies, "Ndakuyambira" also strikes an excellent balance between lines of sung text and passages of syncopated vocables, adding to the song's rhythmic interest. While these musical choices may seem incongruous with the somber tone of Mtukudzi's lyrics, they illustrate his belief that music is particularly capable of easing the emotional burden of those affected by illness and death. Asserting a unique claim to indigenous moral authority by comparing his role as a popular musician to the familiar figure of the sahwira, Mtukudzi told me: "Even right there at a funeral, those sahwiras, they come singing, and acting happy. Because they're trying to neutralize the tension which is there, and the pain which is there. They want to lighten that pain. . . . If you are suffering, song is intended to alleviate your pain." Despite its dynamic musical setting, however, "Ndakuyambira" proved another commercial failure. As Kandiero observed, "When you begin to talk about issues to do with HIV and AIDS—one, people think it's boring; two, people don't want to listen to it. . . . I don't know if it's stigma, I don't know what it is."[19] Yet despite its lack of popular appeal, "Ndakuyambira" marked an important shift in Mtukudzi's approach to singing about HIV/AIDS, representing his first attempt to use the proverbs and metaphors of "deep Shona," or Shona yakadzama, to raise awareness about the disease among local audiences.

1997: All Alone

As HIV prevalence rates rose dramatically in Zimbabwe during the 1990s, both Mtukudzi and his audiences would be increasingly affected by HIV/AIDS. During this time, Mtukudzi lost several band members to AIDS within the space of few months, including his younger brother and long-time keyboard player Rob Mtukudzi. In response, he recorded his first full-length solo album, *Ndega Zvangu*, or "All alone" (1997). As Mtukudzi would later recall: "*Ndega Zvangu* means 'All alone.' And how it came to be is, it came out of a disappointment that three of the band members had died. . . . It was my drummer, Sam Mutohwa, and the lead guitarist, Job Muteswa, and my keyboard player—my young brother Rob Mtukudzi. . . . And I'd prepared to record these things with them. And I decided, 'I think I should release them as raw as they are before I introduce them to the band.' So that's how this CD came about."[20] Even during what Mtukudzi's former manager Debbie Metcalfe described as "a terribly grave period," Mtukudzi responded in the way he knew best, channeling his grief into music. On *Ndega Zvangu*, his solo acoustic guitar playing and singing are aesthetically compelling yet "sonically incomplete," gesturing toward what anthropologist Alexander Dent has called the "present absences" of late band members and kin.[21]

1997: "What Shall We Do?"

In the face of these losses, the polished sound of *Tuku Music*, which represented Mtukudzi's first recording project after rebuilding the Black Spirits almost from scratch, is even more impressive. Increasingly committed to singing out about HIV/AIDS after losing so many of his bandmates, Mtukudzi included two songs about the virus on *Tuku Music*, titled "Mabasa," or "A difficult task," and "Todii," or "What shall we do?" Drawing upon the expressive power of Mtukudzi's voice, "Mabasa" emphasized the social effects of HIV/AIDS, describing a society robbed of its most vibrant and productive members, a well-recognized demographic pattern in countries affected by HIV/AIDS.[22]

Yet "Mabasa" was far surpassed in popularity by "Todii," which soon exploded into one of the most massive hits of Mtukudzi's career. For Leander Kandiero, this was "one of the most powerful songs that he did.'" Echoing a similar perspective, Debbie Metcalfe described "Todii" as instrumental in Mtukudzi's rise to regional prominence during the late 1990s, particularly in light of a recent increase in awareness about HIV/AIDS: "It had really, suddenly, finally dawned on Southern Africa that we had a major AIDS pandemic. And 'Todii' was a song which, again, has quite a harsh or sad sort of message, but written in a very sort of upbeat manner. Which made it extremely accessible to a very broad population. Across the board, basically."[23] A moving musical requiem, "Todii" interrogates questions of agency in the late 1990s, when infection rates continued to rise dramatically yet ARVs remained largely out of reach. In the song's chorus, Mtukudzi and his female backing vocalists exchange the question "What shall we do" in call-and-response fashion, alternating between Zimbabwe's three major languages of Shona, Ndebele, and English. This dialogic approach likewise extends to the song's verses, in which Mtukudzi's backing singers respond to each of his vocal lines with a second question, "What will you do now that you have it, the virus?"

A common rhetorical strategy in many Zimbabwean popular songs, the use of questions is a lyrical device particularly favored by Mtukudzi.[24] Questioning is especially prominent in his songs about HIV/AIDS, which are intended to encourage listeners to reflect on the epidemic and formulate a meaningful response in the context of their own lives. As Mtukudzi explained to me:

> When I wrote that song, it was designed to trigger discussion. Because it's got lots of questions, no solutions. I just wanted people to talk more about AIDS. Because of the stigma attached to AIDS, people just didn't want to

talk about it. I wrote that song to try and make people talk about it, and hopefully they'll start understanding that this disease really exists, for sure. So okay, well, what are you going to do about it? What would we do, or what should we do, if you hear that your wife is pregnant and HIV positive? What do we do?

As poet Chirikure Chirikure reflected: "That's a very typical Tuku style. . . . He's educating, creating awareness, but without pushing an opinion down your throat. . . . Just painting a picture, throwing questions, and he leaves it up to you to formulate your own opinions, and open up debate." At Population Services International, Zimbabwe's largest counseling and testing provider, spokeswoman Kumbirai Chatora confirmed that this rhetorical approach has indeed stimulated Mtukudzi's audiences to reflect on HIV/AIDS: "It makes you think. It makes you start to ponder. It's not lecture type; it's asking you, 'What shall we do?' So then it makes you start—you get engaged. Yeah. That's why I think it's powerful. Just the questioning mode is what makes people start to think, and try to relate. You kind of think he's talking to you."

Hearing "Todii" at Home and Abroad

"Todii" quickly became a runaway success in South Africa, where Mtukudzi had already begun to attract a growing number of listeners. As the Black Spirits' drummer Sam Mataure told me, "If you go to South Africa, 'Todii' sends people haywire."[25] A major part of the song's appeal was its combination of Shona, Ndebele, and English, enabling many South Africans to understand its chorus. Yet these listeners remained unable to decipher its Shona language verses. As a result, many people did not immediately connect "Todii" with HIV/AIDS, leading Mtukudzi to observe that outside Zimbabwe's borders, the song "didn't serve its purpose. Because people love that song so much, and yet they don't understand what I'm talking about in it." As Debbie Metcalfe elaborated: "It was very fascinating, because 'What shall we do?' could just apply to so many things. And because the song was quite upbeat, a lot of people didn't necessarily apply it to an AIDS thing. They were thinking 'What shall we do?' in terms of— you could apply it even to your love life, or all manner of things that were happening to you. And you weren't understanding the rest of the song, so it didn't matter."

Responding to this disconnect, Mtukudzi released a music video depicting an unvarnished picture of the suffering, decline, and death of a fictional AIDS patient, played by his long-time backing singer Picky Kasamba. The graphic nature of the video, which opened with a shot of mourners releasing handfuls of dirt into an open grave, came as a shock for many South African listeners, who hadn't fully comprehended the song's lyrics. As Metcalfe recalled: "You're sitting on the coffin looking up at the sky, and the earth's being thrown at you. . . . The extraordinary part about it was that all those people who for a year had been thinking 'Todii, what shall we do, na na na na,' you know? Suddenly it was like, 'Oh my God, this is an AIDS song!'" Back home in Zimbabwe, on the other hand, Mtukudzi's largely Shona-speaking audiences had long been ambivalent about "Todii." As Mtukudzi reflected: "It's been a popular song worldwide. Except here in Zimbabwe, it hasn't become as popular as it is outside Zimbabwe. Maybe because Zimbabweans understood what I was talking about in the song. . . . Stigma was even more serious then, to the extent that people didn't want to talk about AIDS. . . . It was so scary to talk about it. And yet, that's why I wrote the song, so that people can talk about these AIDS issues more freely."

2000: "She Has Fallen"

In his next song about HIV/AIDS, "Akoromoka Awa," or "She has fallen" (*Bvuma-Tolerance*, 2000), Mtukudzi would try yet another approach in facilitating dialogue about HIV/AIDS by singing about his own family's experience with the disease. As he explained to me:

> That song, it's a serious song. I wrote it for my mother. . . . Because in my family we were only two boys and four girls. And when Rob passed away, the impact on her was so serious. Because she expected that at least since we are two, we will be able to help each other in life, and so on. And since he died, I was left alone, just one. So, I wrote that song so that she wouldn't lose hope, saying, "No, even if now I have been left by myself, probably I have been left for a purpose."

During the final days of his illness, Rob accepted his HIV-positive status and encouraged Mtukudzi to speak out on his behalf:

> His last few days, he actually spoke to me, and said, "Hey, tell the people that this deadly disease, it's alive and kicking." 'Cause when the doctor told him to get tested, it was way done late. But he really wanted to test him, just to find out why he's failing to treat him, you see? So when we got the results, my brother said, "I don't want to have the results, I want to hear the results from you. You go and collect the results for me, and tell me." I said, "Ah, fine, I'll do that." So we went together to the doctor. He told me to go. And I spoke to the doctor. The doctor told me, "Yeah, this is terminal. He's infected, he's HIV positive." And I had to tell him. So I told him, he said, "Ah, okay." And he took it lightly, you know? Because he had been sick for quite a while, and I guess he was tired. He was tired of it all—going to

the doctors, 'cause he was always complaining that, "Hey, you have lost a lot of money on me, you have lost a lot of money on me." You see? Which means he was tired of it. So when I was open about it, it wasn't about being shy. It was about trying to save the next life.

As a public figure, Mtukudzi saw singing about his own family's experience with HIV/AIDS as particularly important, telling me, "I wanted people to see that even in our family, as a popular family, that doesn't make us any superior from them. We're just like them. What's affecting them is also affecting us. What's infecting them also can infect us, you see?"

Naming AIDS

Mtukudzi's acknowledgment of his brother's death from AIDS was particularly notable in an environment where public disclosure is still highly stigmatized. Yet "Akoromoka Awa" raises an apparent contradiction in his approach to singing about HIV/AIDS, for while Mtukudzi has confirmed his strong desire to facilitate open discussion about AIDS, his songs almost inevitably refrain from explicitly naming the disease, with the sole exception of "Stay with One Woman."[26] This silence is absolute, extending even to Shona terms for HIV/AIDS, from relatively formal words such as *mukondombera*, which originally meant epidemic or plague, to more colloquial expressions such as *matsotsi*, or "thieves," a reference to the indiscriminate way that the virus attacks.[27]

As ethnomusicologist Gregory Barz has observed, terms such as these are frequently used to refer to HIV/AIDS in song, representing a local practice of "languaging" the epidemic that contributes to reducing the stigma often associated with it.[28] Indeed, a myriad of terms for HIV/AIDS appear in many Zimbabwean popular songs, from Thomas Mapfumo's "Mukondombera," or "Plague" (*Hondo*, 1991) to Paul Matavire's "Yakauya AIDS," or "AIDS is here."[29] Yet Mtukudzi's decision to avoid referring to HIV/AIDS was carefully considered, constituting a deliberate attempt to move away from the direct language of public health initiatives based in biomedical models of disease and toward a more characteristically figurative Shona idiom: "I feel like, if you were to say 'HIV and AIDS,' it's like you have been sent either by the government or an NGO or someone, saying, 'Go and talk about AIDS.' I want us to discuss our topic in a way that we are talking together, it is a problem we both share . . . because a person is very sensitive. You can give him good information, but he may fail to accept it. He can refuse it because of the way in which you have spoken. . . . Then it doesn't help at all." Echoing Mtukudzi's perspective, linguistic researchers at the University of Zimbabwe have observed that Shona speakers "consider matters relating to sex, death, illness or the other's misfortune as taboo or unspeakable."[30] These subjects are instead approached through highly stylized modes of indirect speech intended to avoid exacerbating tension, instability, or grief. By favoring this type of figurative language, Mtukudzi's lyrics have reflected the preferences of his listeners, enabling him to bring focus and clarity to a situation of extreme difficulty and distress.[31]

More Problems of Interpretation

Yet the indirect language of "Akoromoka Awa" quickly raised more questions of interpretation for Mtukudzi's listeners. Most importantly, the song's first verse hinged on the meaning of two relatively obscure Shona words. The first, *mukaranga*, is often used to refer to a woman who has married into a particular patrilineage. As Mtukudzi explained, "My wife is a mukaranga of the Mtukudzis. My mother is a mukaranga of the Mtukudzis. But my sister is not mukaranga of my family. Mukaranga is where she is married." Drawn from the Korekore dialect of Mtukudzi's native area of Dande, the second word, *kutakwira*, was even less comprehensible for many Shona speakers: "*Kutakwira*, that's the last breath when you die. My mom, when she was broken-hearted, it was like her last breath. But I'm saying now, 'That's your last breath, but you're alive! You have passed that. That last breath of death, you have already passed that. You have just fallen down. But you can wake up and go again.'" Largely unfamiliar with Korekore, some of Mtukudzi's listeners misheard this word as the more common term *kukwira*, which means to climb or mount. As journalist Robert Mukondiwa explained, this hearing led to dramatic misinterpretations of the song: "The controversy is . . . in his language, *mukaranga* is your mother, one who marries into the family, you see? So, *kukwira* is to climb. And the word has often been corrupted to also mean, um, to have sex. So, what the song eventually meant to the ordinary Shona-speaking person is, uh, so-and-so had sex with a *mukaranga*. And people were like, 'Oh, Oliver is going naughty.' In fact, weirdly enough, the song meant something totally different." Despite Mtukudzi's habitual reticence to clarify his intentions as a songwriter, he did consent to an interview with Mukondiwa, who published an article correcting misconceptions over "Akoromoka Awa" in the state-owned *Herald*. While Mukondiwa told me that only a fraction of Mtukudzi's audience read the article, he perceived the ongoing confusion over the song's meaning as productive in the sense that it succeeded in capturing the attention of a larger share of listeners. As he concluded, "It made for debate, and people now actually appreciate his music more."

Mobilizing Tuku Music in the Fight against HIV/AIDS

Joining Mtukudzi, many other Zimbabwean musicians have released songs about HIV/AIDS. Among them are mbira players such as Musekiwa Chingodza, Beauler

Dyoko, and the Dzapasi Mbira Group; sungura artists such as Leonard Zhakata and The Khiama Boys; the mbube group Sunduza; and famed chimurenga musician Thomas Mapfumo.[32] Yet few artists have become as actively engaged in public health work as Mtukudzi, whom Kandiero described to me as a "music ambassador" of HIV/AIDS. Setting him further apart from the majority of other local artists singing about the disease, Mtukudzi already had a developed reputation for communicating socially progressive messages in his songs. As a result, he has been invited to participate in numerous public health campaigns, ranging from the early family planning initiatives organized by the ZNFPC to later antimalaria campaigns spearheaded by the WHO.

Yet Mtukudzi's involvement in HIV/AIDS prevention and awareness work has been particularly extensive. He has given dozens of live performances, from local events such as a "Together Against AIDS" concert, organized by a consortium of local musicians in response to Zimbabwe's growing pandemic in 1994, to high-profile global happenings such as the BBC World Service's 2003 World AIDS Day concert. He has participated in several antistigma campaigns led by the nation's largest counseling and testing service provider, Population Services International (PSI), including a free concert celebrating PSI's millionth client to be tested for HIV in Zimbabwe.[33] He has also partnered with the International Organization for Migration (IOM), the WHO, and various branches of the United Nations, such as UNICEF, UNAIDS, and the U.N. Population Fund. In honor of his commitment to the rights of children affected by the virus, he was declared a UNICEF Regional Goodwill Ambassador in 2011, further raising his international visibility as a musical voice in the fight against HIV/AIDS.

The growing number of organizations working in Southern Africa has resulted in a deluge of public service messages about HIV/AIDS, disseminated through radio and television adverts; billboards; slogans printed on t-shirts and hats; posters placed in clinics, offices, and schools; and public performances of music, drama, and poetry. In this densely saturated media environment, music is particularly valued for its ability to draw listeners into the type of participatory relationships described in the introduction to this book, giving it an ability to communicate about HIV/AIDS without producing message fatigue.[34] At the IOM's regional headquarters, for example, spokesperson Erin Foster observed, "Instead of just handing somebody a flyer and having them read, I think music really speaks to people, and it's enjoyable. At the same time you're listening, and enjoying music, you get a great message from it."

Overwhelmingly, public health workers described Mtukudzi's music to me as especially effective in reaching local audiences. Commenting on Mtukudzi's participation in the IOM's Safe Journey campaign, for example, Foster continued, "Somebody from Oliver's status—who is hugely successful not only

Population Services International's 2008 calendar
featuring Oliver Mtukudzi. *Courtesy PSI.*

in Zimbabwe but worldwide—it was a really great thing, and a great boost for us and the campaign to get one of his tracks that were already known. It was huge." After working with Mtukudzi on the ZNFPC's family planning campaigns, Godfrey Tinarwo similarly lauded his ability to reach a diverse audience in both rural and urban areas:

> If we went to a rural outlet, it was a source of free entertainment, so naturally we would attract whoever. They would say, "Oliver is in town! And we are going to get this free music and whatnot, from this icon." So it would draw attention from people across all walks of life. . . . Obviously in urban areas, he had already an established kind of following, so there would be people who would just be looking forward to meet him. If it was in Gweru, if it was in Bulawayo, whatever, they would look forward to see him in action, free of charge.

Echoing Tinarwo's comments, Norah Ngwenya, who worked with Mtukudzi on the WHO's Roll Back Malaria campaign in 2003, told me, "The moment you take Mtukudzi out, you have mobilized the whole village."

As well as appealing to both rural and urban audiences, Mtukudzi's music has proved effective in reaching listeners of all ages. Reflecting on her work with the IOM, Erin Foster told me, "Of course, music is one of the best ways to reach youth. . . . They're interested in these different artists, and might look up to these artists for the messages that they have to provide." Yet many of the musicians favored by young Zimbabweans—including urban grooves artists such as Alexio Kawara, Roki, and Maskiri as well as Zimbabwean dancehall singers such as Souljah Love, Winky D, and Mathias Julius—are not widely appreciated by older listeners, limiting their potential to contribute to public health campaigns. In contrast, people regularly described Mtukudzi's music as speaking to both young and old. As kombi driver John Muchena told me:

> The way I see what is happening in his music is that his music has a message. . . . That's why people enjoy it so much. It isn't only the beat, like the way it is in urban grooves. If you want to look at some urban grooves songs, they have no meaning. It's only the beat that people are enjoying. . . . But Tuku's music—from the time he started up to now—if you listen to it, it means something. . . . That's why everyone enjoys it, from the young people to the elders. Because it suits all ages.

For public health workers, Mtukudzi's ability to connect with different age groups has made his music particularly valuable. In the words of PSI spokesperson Kumbirai Chatora: "He cuts across all targets, all age groups; that's what I feel. You know, he appeals to the more mature people, like me, but he also appeals to them [youth], he cuts across. You should see young people dancing to his music, it's a fantastic thing to see."

Finally, development organizations were also drawn to Mtukudzi's long-standing commitment to intervening in unequal gender dynamics through songs such as "Baba," a theme that has likewise carried over into his songs about HIV/AIDS. In the first verse of "Todii," for example, Mtukudzi highlights the plight of mothers raising children infected with HIV in the absence of adequate treatment options, and he draws attention to the predicament of HIV-positive pregnant women confronting the possibility that their children may be born with the disease. In the next verse, Mtukudzi further emphasizes linkages between gender, power, and HIV/AIDS by asking how a woman feels when she is raped by her own husband, even when he is aware that she is infected with the virus.[35] In these lyrics, Mtukudzi suggests that women's abilities to protect themselves from HIV and to access treatment for themselves and their children are severely limited within the institution of marriage.

In "Todii," Mtukudzi illustrates how power dynamics that exist primarily within a private, domestic sphere have highly political repercussions in the public domain, implicitly suggesting that questions of gender and agency must be considered in the context of effective HIV prevention and treatment campaigns. Yet Mtukudzi's sensitivity to women's rights has not diminished his ability to appeal to male listeners, enabling him to address contentious gender issues without alienating men. As PSI's Kumbirai Chatora commented: "We actually feel that Oliver Mtukudzi might actually best be placed to talk to men. Because they are a tough nut to crack. You can't just go in and say, 'Stop it.' You know? You really need to come up with persuasive messages, and a role model like this, I think, would be very ideal."

The Politics of Disclosure

Despite his valuable contributions to public health, Mtukudzi has sometimes been challenged over HIV/AIDS. When the Black Spirits' guitarist Philani Dube died in 2007, for example, Mtukudzi reportedly replied to accusations that he had abandoned Dube shortly before his death by stating that he had given the guitarist money for ARVs. Yet journalists noted that this comment was tantamount to publicly disclosing Dube's serostatus. As Rosenthal Mutakati would write: "By virtue of those words, Mtukudzi had told the world that Dube had succumbed to Aids [sic]. What right had he to talk about other people's illnesses, with some quoting some of his popular lyrics, 'kusimbirira mhopo iri pamusana, iwe uine ziso rine mbonje'" (you focus on the wart on your back, yet ignore that your eye is severely injured).[36] As Mutakati likewise noted, Mtukudzi's own serostatus had been "the subject of endless rumours and innuendo" for many years.[37] These rumors first emerged in 2003, when the *Herald* published an article alleging that Mtukudzi had been involved in an affair with his long-time backing vocalist Mwendi Chibindi, who had recently died.[38] In the article, journalists Garikai Mazara and Robert Mukondiwa reported that Chibindi had "passed away after a long illness," euphemistically suggesting that her death was AIDS-related, and engendering lingering speculation about Mtukudzi's own serostatus.[39] Mtukudzi was subsequently pressed to disclose his own status on several occasions, and while he repeatedly stated that he was HIV-negative, the rumors about his status persisted.[40]

Yet this speculation about Mtukudzi's HIV status was also tied to his very commitment to addressing the disease. As one of the journalists involved in breaking the story of his alleged affair would later write, "Mtukudzi—an energetic composer, dancer and guitarist—has featured prominently on shows promoting the anti-stigmatisation of those living with HIV and Aids [sic], fuelling speculation that he could be living with the virus."[41] In an environment where solidarity with those affected by HIV/AIDS seemed tantamount to disclosing one's own status, the public nature of Mtukudzi's HIV/AIDS awareness and prevention work made his personal health the object of intense scrutiny.[42] Ironically, Mtukudzi's contributions to public health campaigns thus caused him to experience the very stigma he sought to combat in his songs as he was "diagnosed and labeled" positive by fans, moving him from the realm of an activist and advocate to a public figure widely assumed to be living with the disease.[43]

Shortly after his alleged affair was made public, it appeared that Mtukudzi's credibility to speak out about HIV/AIDS would be compromised. As the *Financial Gazette* remarked, "That his alleged lover Mwendy [sic] allegedly died from HIV-related illness, can we still take his songs on AIDS half-seriously? We wonder!"[44] Over time, however, Mtukudzi's "maturity in dealing with the issue" diminished this controversy.[45] Indeed, the most lasting impact of Mtukudzi's reported affair was not its effect on his moral reputation, but its contribution to the popular perception that he was living with HIV. At PSI, for example, Kumbirai Chatora told me, "I don't think it changes much. As long as he's still able to belt out his songs, and dance, I don't think it changes anything."

Even prior to this controversy, Mtukudzi recognized that musicians constitute a conceptual realm in which audiences work through issues related to HIV/AIDS. As he presciently observed in an interview with *Ngoma*, a magazine published by the National Arts Council of Zimbabwe: "We are dealing with two stigmas: the status of musicians and the other HIV/Aids [sic]. The first is Aids itself and the second stigma is the perception of society about 'artists/musicians.' People expect musicians to be sleeping around everywhere, because they are exposed to so many women. The music industry has to deal with two different stigmas. How musicians are viewed by society has to change. . . . Musicians are used as a platform—they think is he negative or positive? People assume many musicians are already positive."[46] Several years later, Mtukudzi restated this position in our interviews, insisting that he would disclose his status if he ever tested positive for HIV:

> Kyker: Is it difficult for you to know that people out there are discussing your status with what might seem like very little respect for you as a person?
>
> Mtukudzi: Well, I mean, that's what stardom is all about, speculation. So, let them speculate. I'm OK, I'm alright. That's part of a being a star, so let them speculate. If they don't speculate, then you're not a star.
>
> Kyker: And then I also wanted to ask you: If, in your life, you were ever to test HIV positive, would you come out to your fans?
>
> Mtukudzi: Oh, yes. Why not? My brother did it. Yeah, I would do the same.
>
> Kyker: And why? What would be your. . .
>
> Mtukudzi: Just to save the next life. Maybe one person would be aware.

"Men Make a Difference": The Limits of Public Health Partnerships

While Mtukudzi's participation in public health campaigns directly contributed to rumors about his serostatus, it also brought his metaphorical approach to singing about HIV/AIDS into conversation with other discourses in ways that were both productive and challenging. Capitalizing upon Mtukudzi's willingness to address gender, for example, the Southern Africa AIDS Information Dissemination Service (SAfAIDS) invited him to take part in a 2003 World AIDS Day campaign with the slogan, "Men Make a Difference." Widely distributed throughout Southern Africa, the campaign posters featured Mtukudzi's image alongside the following quote: "As real men, we should strive to be exemplary and change sexual habits that can ruin our lives, particularly when there is the danger of getting and passing on HIV/AIDS. We have only one life, one chance and therefore it is never too late to change bad habits." Curious about the direct language of the poster, with its explicit reference to sexual behavior, I spoke with campaign organizer Priscilla Mataure. As she explained, this quote was not crafted by Mtukudzi himself, but rather by the public health experts at SAfAIDS:

> We had several quotes . . . And then we gave him these quotes, and we said, "Choose the one that you think you would feel comfortable with, so that it's coming from you, not coming from us. Because we know that you

are interested in the issues of HIV/AIDS, and in involving men in HIV and AIDS. So, these are some of the quotes that we have come up with. So, can you look at them and choose the one? . . . And if you want to make changes out of it, make changes." Now, I'm not sure whether he made any changes or not, I can't remember that, but that's how we did it.

While there is nothing out of the ordinary in an organization crafting quotes for public figures to deliver, this effort risks what jazz singer Dudu Manhenga described to me as "singing the pamphlet" by discarding Mtukudzi's nuanced approach to singing about HIV/AIDS in favor of the type of direct, biomedical messages he abandoned immediately after writing "Stay with One Woman." Further differentiating the "Men Make a Difference" campaign from his own songs about HIV/AIDS, the SAfAIDS poster was printed in English rather than Shona, distancing it from the register of deep Shona, or "Shona yakadzama," for which Mtukudzi is so widely renowned. Intended to be hung in formal institutions such as hospitals, school, and clinics, the SAfAIDS poster risked being most accessible to the very experts involved in crafting its message, rather than to the local audiences it was ostensibly meant to target.

Reflecting on this problem, Mtukudzi expressed a decided preference for communicating about HIV/AIDS in his own songs, rather than delivering messages developed for him: "It's not really Oliver Mtukudzi telling you. It's more like the organization is telling you. It's not like 'Mabasa,' where I am actually telling even those, even the NGOs, I'm also telling them the same thing. You see? That's me, telling them. And that's why they are repertoire in my shows. . . . I would rather give my messages—personal messages—to them, because they had a feeling to them. It's me saying it. It's not something I've been fed to say to them. 'Cause there will always be a difference." By observing that his songs about HIV/AIDS "have a feeling to them," Mtukudzi articulates how social experiences and imaginaries of the disease are shaped through the type of dynamic, emergent, and often indeterminate configurations that literary theorist Raymond Williams has called "structures of feeling."[47] Moving us beyond the realm of lexical speech alone, his songs take us one step closer toward understanding the evolving, subjective nature of social relations and experiences in a time of HIV/AIDS.

Dialoguing Discourses

While this ability to engage local structures of feeling is precisely what has contributed to Mtukudzi's appeal in the context of public health work, his music has resisted being fully captured by the very campaigns that seek to harness it. Yet the tensions between music's multivalent, inarticulable qualities and the

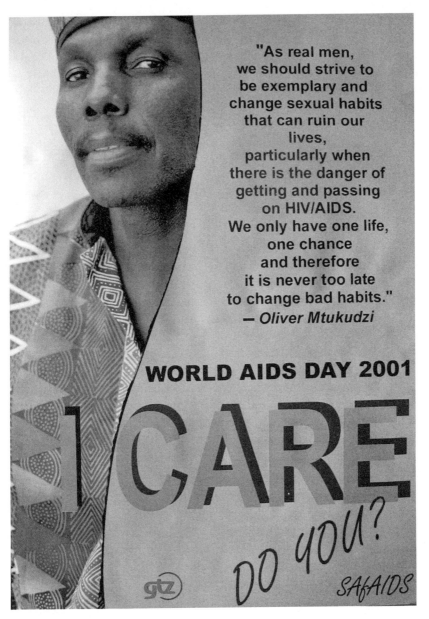

Southern Africa AIDS Information Dissemination Service's
"Men Make a Difference" campaign poster. *Courtesy SAfAIDS.*

digestible, fact-based orientation of public health work can be richly productive, inviting audiences to hear different forms of discourse in relation to each other. As listeners have absorbed Mtukudzi's songs in the context of public health campaigns, his metaphorical, often ambiguous lyrics about the social effects of HIV/AIDS have been thrown into sharper relief as a conscious attempt to influence community responses to the virus. On the other hand, Mtukudzi's music has enabled public health workers to integrate a uniquely relational approach to HIV/AIDS, enabling audiences to interpret the direct messages of public health campaigns within a wider social context. Bridging the distance between different structures of feeling about HIV/AIDS, this dialogue between music and public health has embodied many of the values at the heart of Mtukudzi's project of singing hunhu.

Pakare Paye

Complementing his participation in public health campaigns, yet another of Mtukudzi's contributions in the fight against HIV/AIDS took the form of Pakare Paye, or "That Place," an arts center he built in the town of Norton, where he lives some thirty miles outside the nation's capital. Even before founding Pakare Paye, Mtukudzi had taken part in music education initiatives such as Umoja, which brings young musicians from Southern Africa and Norway together with professional artists. Named Umoja's Zimbabwean patron in 2006, Mtukudzi began attending auditions and workshops, furnishing sound equipment for concerts, and performing with participants in the project's annual arts camp. Over the years, Mtukudzi has also absorbed several Umoja participants in the Black Spirits, including nyunga nyunga mbira player Onai Mutizwa and marimba player Charles Chipanga. Mtukudzi has additionally worked with graduates of Umoja's local host institution, the Zimbabwe College of Music, including Clive "Mono" Mukundu, who played lead guitar with the Black Spirits for several years, and Dudu Manhenga, whose vocal harmonies shaped the hallmark sound of *Tuku Music*.

At Pakare Paye, Mtukudzi has likewise expressed a particular interest in working with youth, many of whom have lost one or both parents to HIV/AIDS. Placing Pakare Paye among the many community organizations that have mobilized local resources in responding to HIV/AIDS, the center has offered aspiring artists space to learn new skills and develop social networks, often leading to more formal apprenticeship or employment opportunities. Reflecting on the center's work with disadvantaged children, Mtukudzi observed: "I was targeting them, cause they are our future, they are tomorrow's artists. Okay, the elderly people are welcome. But if we are to build the future, we need to instill the right things, and give these youngsters the right ammunition to represent

Joining the Black Spirits

I was one of the pioneer members of Umoja when it started in 2003. I was there for four years, because it started while I was at the College of Music. Tuku was made the patron, so he used to come and join us. As a patron, he was supposed to perform, right? So we would do his songs.

When they said, "Tuku is coming, and he's going to perform with you guys," I was so anxious. We just had one rehearsal, 'cause he was on a tour of some sort. Then he came a day before the performance, and he just said, "Okay guys, whatever you rehearsed, that's what we'll do." I wasn't so confident, you know? We're expecting a rehearsal. We thought that as a professional musician he would really take maybe seven hours to perfect one song. Then we performed with him. My heart was beating—I'm performing with Oliver!

He said to me after the performance, "I need to see you. Just come by the center, and we'll talk." Then I went after work. I arrived, and he took his guitar, and we went out back. He started jamming. He didn't ask me whether I knew the song, he'd just play something and sing. We did a whole lot of songs. We did some I didn't know, with him explaining what I should do. And then he just said to me, "I'll call you for our next rehearsal. Welcome on board."

—*Charles Chipanga*

us tomorrow." Complementing this focus on working with youth, Pakare Paye has also hosted HIV/AIDS prevention and awareness activities for adults, ranging from condom demonstrations to a live taping of the Mai Chisamba show, whose gregarious host has sometimes been referred to as the "Oprah Winfrey of Zimbabwe."[48] Displayed prominently at the entrance to Pakare Paye, posters promoting voluntary HIV counseling and testing at the nation's network of New Start Centres likewise testify to Mtukudzi's commitment to making a difference in the fight against HIV/AIDS.

Like the idea of incorporating marimba, mbira, and hosho in Tuku music, Mtukudzi described his desire to build a cultural center as dating back "a long

Marimba player Charles Chipanga. *Courtesy of Mary Cairns.*

"Safe Journey" with Dudu Manhenga

I was born as a performer when I worked with Oliver. I was very shy at the beginning—I started as a soloist for a small band. But you know, working with Oliver challenged me to see there is more that you can do with your music. Your music should be able to speak on your behalf, and you should carry yourself in the way that your music speaks. Before, I was just a voice. And then when I joined Oliver, I became a performer.

With my songs, I speak about things that I stand for. I speak about anything and everything that I feel, really. You know, it's on the same path with my soul—with my beliefs as well. So when I got into the Safe Journey campaign, I thought it was something that was worth doing. Because I had heard stories about women that were going through stuff, of women that are now into prostitution. Of people that are very educated, that went there thinking, "Okay, I'm going to make a way," but without the right papers. And they end up being destitute, yet they've got a degree in their hand.

We wanted to send the message across to say that it's okay to leave home, but it's better to leave the right way. Because that way at least wherever you go, you have a voice. We felt that if the pamphlet has to have that jargon and all those explanations, let it do that. But let the music be so easy in the ears, that when the person hears it for the first time, they laugh and say, "Ah, that song is so funny." But then they've heard what the song is about. They've gotten the message in a lighter way.

—*Dudu Manhenga*

time, since the early eighties. . . . But I didn't have a place to do it, an actual place." After scouting unsuccessfully for locations in Kwekwe and Harare, Mtukudzi finally broke ground on the Norton site in 2004. Within a few years, Pakare Paye had both an indoor stage with seating for two hundred and an outdoor stage with a capacity of over two thousand. Well-equipped with instruments ranging from ngoma, mbira, and marimba to drum sets, guitars, and keyboards, the center also boasted an array of microphones, amps, mixing boards, and stage lighting, as well as a high-quality projector for showing films. As Watson Chidzomba, one of Pakare Paye's leading artists, told me, "We've got the best of the best. We have got the kind of equipment that Oliver Mtukudzi can be comfortable with."

One of the most striking things about Pakare Paye is Mtukudzi's decision to make these valuable resources available to anyone who walks through the center's doors at no cost. After accompanying me to Pakare Paye one afternoon, kombi driver John Muchena remarked that this unusual model reflected a set of values that distinguished Mtukudzi from other local artists:

> What musicians mostly do here is that once they play frequently and become popular—once they make money—they start thinking about having a very elite lifestyle, or even relocating outside the country. But now him, I have seen that he is a person who thinks about the place he was born. That is where he wants to live, and he wants to develop that place. . . . Pakare Paye shows that he is a person who is passionate about his home. That's what I've observed. That is where his thoughts are. He doesn't want to show people that he's made money . . . he wanted to build a place where people who need assistance can come and be helped.

A conscious attempt to shape his artistic legacy, Pakare Paye has extended Mtukudzi's influence within the Zimbabwean popular soundscape by giving rise to several new musical talents, including guitarist and singer Munyaradzi Mataruse. In addition to leading their own bands, many of these musicians continue to participate in the center's own performing group, the Pakare Paye Ensemble.

Echoing Mtukudzi's account of teaching himself how to play the guitar, Pakare Paye privileges informal sharing over formal musical instruction. As Mtukudzi observed, "There's no teacher who builds a gap like, 'I'm a teacher, I know, you're a student, you don't know.' We're trying to kill that gap, and just be artists at work. And it's amazing how that works." In this way, Pakare Paye reflects the widespread Zimbabwean aesthetic of self-directed learning discussed in chapter 2, offering young people the opportunity to pick up skills through relationships with arts professionals such as sound engineer Wonder Mukonowenzou, theater veteran Watson Chidzomba, and Oliver Mtukudzi himself. As Pakare Paye Ensemble member Peter "Poda" Chirima told me, "There were so many people I met here, and shared ideas with. And I was seeing so many people playing, and just learning myself, here and there. So there isn't any one person I can point to as having taught me. I just picked up (*kunonga*) what I could."

Pakare Paye

It if wasn't for Pakare Paye, I wouldn't be a musician. It's a place that was built for people to learn for free, people like me.

I didn't manage to finish my A levels, because I lacked the money. One day, as I was walking around, I saw these posters advertising for people who do music, theatre, drama, poetry, or sculpture. So that's how I came to be here. Since I first arrived, I haven't paid a single cent. The guitars I play, the marimba, mbira, PA system, I haven't paid for anything. Here, it's not a business thing. Really, they are making every effort to help the community.

I love the acoustic guitar. That acoustic sound, it has a certain richness to it; it's natural. That's what I love about it. Before I played guitar, I played marimba. Then after something like three months, I started guitar. I can play any of Tuku's songs. There's a time when I was listening to Nzou's music, and trying by all means to copy what he does. I have the advantage of getting to watch him play.

Whenever he's around, he comes in. And even when he's sitting in his office, it doesn't mean he's not listening; sometimes, he's listening. You'll hear him calling out advice, adjusting those parts of the song he wants to fix.

—*Munya Mataruse*

A Legacy of Hunhu

Beyond simply encouraging musical talent, Mtukudzi is likewise committed to fostering the ethos of hunhu at Pakare Paye by forming young participants into moral citizens who embody values such as mutual respect, tolerance, and togetherness. As he told me: "The vision of this place is to facilitate a place where people could come and showcase what they can do. . . . This is not about money. This is about building a character, building a nation, building the right people to represent us." For members of the Pakare Paye Ensemble, this vision has proved profoundly influential. Reflecting on their relationship with Mtukudzi, for example,

Poda told me, "We haven't only learned music from him. There is so much more, like hunhu." As a result, many of the young people at Pakare Paye have come to refer to themselves as Mtukudzi's "children," or *vana*. As Poda observed, the lyrics to one of the earliest songs Pakare Paye Ensemble members wrote invoked this language of symbolic kinship by referring to Mtukudzi as *baba*, or father: "It says, '*Pakare Paye paruware, baba vatitaridza* [Pakare Paye, located on an exposed granite surface, father is leading us].' The father, that is Mr. Mtukudzi, who is showing us the way, you see? And us, the exposed rock is where we meet, right? So that our music does not die, so that these things continue moving forward." In a similar vein, the band's lead vocalist Chiedza Makaripe described members of the Pakare Paye Ensemble as dedicated to embodying the moral values of hunhu, including love (*rudo*), mutual understanding (*kunzwizisa*), unity (*kubatana*), and listening (*kuteerera*), both in their music and in their own lives. Summarizing the enduring power of these ethical principles, Makaripe told me, "Without love, we can not rise up." Bringing us full circle, Makaripe's words are strikingly similar to the advice given by gombwe spirit Sekuru Musanyange to his followers: "Without love, there is no hunhu."

Without Love, There Is No Hunhu

In his work on music and HIV/AIDS in Uganda, Gregory Barz has suggested two ways in which music can be understood as a medical intervention: first, when it encourages medical analysis; and second, when it "takes the form of medical treatment itself."[49] While Mtukudzi's music has not performed a specific pedagogical function by teaching listeners how to use a condom or disseminating biomedical information about the disease, it has significantly contributed to how AIDS is socially determined in Zimbabwe. Like many Zimbabweans, Oliver Mtukudzi has been deeply affected by HIV/AIDS both professionally, through the successive loss of so many of his band members, and personally, through the death of his brother Rob, as well as the widespread speculation over his own serostatus. By articulating local structures of feeling around HIV/AIDS, his songs have exemplified one of the most important attributes of popular culture, located in its "potential to transform one's thoughts, emotions, and experiences into creations that can be communicated and shared."[50]

Well into the third decade of Zimbabwe's epidemic, Mtukudzi has continued to advocate for an approach to HIV/AIDS that remains consistent with the moral ethos of hunhu. Sung rather than spoken, his metaphorical approach to the disease has differed significantly from biomedical models, reflecting the linguistic preferences of local audiences. In his songs, Mtukudzi has mobilized a range of indigenous rhetorical devices and musical gestures, emphasizing the importance of communicating with local audiences in a way that is sensitive to the dignity, humanity, and agency of those infected and affected by HIV/AIDS. By contributing his voice, image, and presence to public health campaigns, he has placed his songs in dialogue with biomedical approaches to the disease, mutually reinforcing multiple kinds of discourse. Finally, Mtukudzi has emphasized the importance of both artistry and morality in community development at Pakare Paye, articulating his view that health is not simply an individual concern, but also a social one.

"Izere Mhepo"
(Full of air)

Wangu mwana akaenda marimuka	My child has departed for the wilderness
Dangwe rangu riye riri marimuka	My eldest child is in the wilderness
KuLondon	In London
Gotwe rakaenda kwaro	My lastborn child has gone to one place
Mumvana akaenda kumwe	My daughter has gone to another
Gotwe rakaenda kwaro	My lastborn child has gone to one place
Mumvana akaenda kumwe	My daughter has gone to another
Kuenda marimuka kuenderatu vana ava	Gone to the wilderness forever, these children
Kuenda marimuka kuenderatu kuAmerica	Gone to the wilderness forever, in America
Tasara sure sare	We are left behind
Sare vakaringe nzira	Left behind, looking at the path
Nhava izere mhepo	The bag is full of air
Gume nhava izere mhepo	In the end, the bag is full of air
Nhava izere mhepo mukomaka	The bag is full of air, elder brother
Magumo nhava izere mhepo	In the end, the bag is full of air
Ari marimuka uye wofondoka	The one in the wilderness is blunted by work
Hakuna achaziva marimuka, idikita	No one understands, the wilderness is sweat
Ndangariro dzeari marimuka	The memories of the one in the wilderness
Dura rangu razara	My granary is full
Vasare sure sare	They are left behind
Kureme nemusana	Their backs weighted down

EIGHT

Listening in the Wilderness

Half a world away from Pakare Paye, the Kuumbwa Jazz Center sits a few blocks away from the ruggedly beautiful Pacific coastline in downtown Santa Cruz, California. With the intimate ambiance of a dinner club, Kuumbwa regularly hosts worldbeat and jazz shows, drawing precisely the type of listeners who have proved the mainstay of Mtukudzi's North American audience. Pulling up in front of Kuumbwa early one evening in 2007, the Black Spirits were greeted by the sounds of a local Zimbabwean-style band named Sadza Marimba, which played a short opening set in the club's small, outdoor courtyard. In a blur of mallets, the band infused the crisp October air with the warm tones of their wooden keys, launching into an arrangement of the familiar Shona children's song "Sarura Wako."[1] Taken by surprise, several of the Black Spirits lingered in the dusk to listen before heading backstage.

The subdued atmosphere of Kuumbwa seemed far removed from the chaotic energy of Mtukudzi's performances back home, where massive crowds of listeners reveled in his sound. Yet even here, a small group of diasporic Zimbabweans was engaged in the participatory behavior typical of Mtukudzi's shows in Harare. Leaving their tables, they congregated in the tight space behind a row of chairs, where they danced with increasing abandon as the night progressed. Executing complex makwa handclapping patterns, whistling, and ululating, they frequently shouted words of encouragement to the musicians, punctuating Mtukudzi's songs with their calls—"Aiwa, ridza! Ridza!" (Go ahead, play! Play!), "Ona, ona, ona, ona!" (Look, look, look, look!), and "Rova marimba mufana, rova!" (Hit the marimba, young man, hit it!), directed particularly at marimba player Charles Chipanga.

The band played several hits from the 1970s, including "Ndipeiwo Zano," "Mutavara," and "Ziwere," as well as songs from subsequent periods of Mtukudzi's career. Introducing their penultimate song of the night, a fast-tempo dance piece titled "Wenge Mambo" (Bvuma-Tolerance, 2000), Mtukudzi explicitly identified it as an adapted katekwe song, firmly tying Tuku music back to the ngoma music of Zimbabwe's rural northeast. As the Black Spirits launched into the first notes of "Wenge Mambo," its densely syncopated polyrhythms brought the

**Mtukudzi's spoken introduction to "Wenge Mambo"
at the Kuumbwa Jazz Center**

I come from Zimbabwe
Born of the northern part of Zimbabwe
Where I grew up watching elderly people play music
And amongst the different types and different styles of music
  they played
There was this serious music they used to play
When they wanted to communicate with the ancestors
The time of the song is kind of complicated; it's three in one
So, it could be very difficult to find a one
So, when we start playing the song, you just join in
Wherever you join in, that's your one
And the song goes like. . .

entire audience to its feet, causing them to dance until the last notes of Mtukudzi's guitar were finally swallowed by a wave of thunderous applause. Above the din, the Zimbabweans in the crowd could be heard shouting, *"Wagona!"* (Well done!), *Basa sebasa!"* (That's the way to do it!), and *"Ipapo!"* (Just like that!). Invoking an extended usage of kinship terms to express his affinity for Mtukudzi, one listener even called out *"Sekuru vangu uyo!"* (That's my grandfather!).[2]

Tuku Music in a Growing Diaspora

With millions of its citizens currently living abroad, a nascent diasporic consciousness has become increasingly central to the postcolonial Zimbabwean experience.[3] As a result, the nation's popular musicians have begun performing abroad more frequently, compensating for declining opportunities at home.[4] Among them, Oliver Mtukudzi has been particularly engaged in singing the diaspora, releasing songs that speak directly to experiences of migration, performing regularly for diasporic audiences, and participating in initiatives such as the International Organization for Migration's Safe Journey campaign, spearheaded by his former backing vocalist Dudu Manhenga. For the many Zimbabweans who have migrated abroad, the distinctive sound of Tuku music represents what diasporic poet Emmanuel Sigauke has described as "art from an increasingly unfamiliar piece of earth," making it an important part of this new transnational landscape.[5]

In October 2007, I followed Oliver Mtukudzi and the Black Spirits on a tour of the United States, beginning in Wilmington, Delaware, and ending in Oakland, California.[6] As I watched Mtukudzi perform in diverse locations extending from rural North Carolina to Seattle, I observed that diasporic listeners, who ranged from roughly half a dozen audience members in Santa Cruz to almost a thousand in Dallas, responded especially powerfully to his music.[7] As undergraduate student Tariro Mupombwa declared after attending the Wilmington performance, "I felt as if I had actually gone back home."[8]

Turning to interviews with diasporic audience members, as well as radio DJs, poets, and migration officials back in Zimbabwe, this chapter explores the transnational reception of Tuku music, charting how Mtukudzi's musical imaginaries of hunhu have acquired particular social and political meaning for listeners in Zimbabwe's growing diasporic community in the United States.[9] I open with a discussion of one particular song, "Izere Mhepo," or "Full of air" (*Nhava*, 2005), which likens the experience of the migrant to that of an unsuccessful hunter, poised to return home holding nothing but an empty carrying bag. In "Izere Mhepo," I illustrate how Mtukudzi depicts the diaspora as a symbolic wilderness, in which listeners have left behind the civilized space of home, with its expectations of social reciprocity and moral obligation. I conclude by illustrating how audiences have routinely interpreted Mtukudzi's songs about migration and diaspora, ostensibly directed beyond Zimbabwe's borders, as reflecting back within the nation, conveying a powerful yet subtle critique of postcolonial domestic politics.

Changing Patterns of Transnational Migration

Centrally located within Southern Africa, Zimbabwe has a strong history of both internal and external migration, tied in large part to its colonial history.[10] Under British rule, its location at the heart of regional labor networks, together with its strong mining and agricultural sectors, placed it in the unusual position of both sending and receiving migrants.[11] In the postcolonial era, however, it has become a net exporter of labor, with an expanding population of Zimbabweans living abroad, including large concentrations in South Africa and the United Kingdom as well as a growing population in the United States. While Zimbabwean communities have long been translocal, the intensity and expanded geographic scope of recent migration has led to the emergence of a uniquely diasporic Zimbabwean subculture, with its own distinctive linguistic practices, behavioral norms, and forms of expressive culture.[12]

Like Mtukudzi, many Zimbabwean musicians have begun to seek out professional opportunities abroad. These range from mbira players who have taken advantage of niche markets in the United States and Japan to sungura and

Hurry, Tuku in Concert!

If you had been with me
You too would have seen Tuku at Yoshi's.
Premier jazz stylist, giant of Southern Africa,
Tuku has a voice that rouses the dead,
a consciousness that slaps one from

the sleep of forgetfulness.
He lit sparks of memory;
then as we swayed to songs about aging
and not aging, about going away and coming back
(especially coming back),
about stunted love, betrayal, Limpopos of tears,
stories of learning to forget, about forgetting to learn,
we coalesced with the stone soul, the pride of our homeland.

This Zimbabwean musician,
years upon years of rearing the young and the old alike:
Tuku, the King of Shauro, unbruised by Time and Change,
able to keep a smile, when he mouths the legend Zimbabwe:
to some a torn, often deserted, unremembered
chamber of squalor, impossible efforts,
dead spirits of the once caring
dead; to others granite breasts
that feed hearts where they would wilt.

He started with, "We are from Zimbabwe!"
Following this with a rendition
an all-time national, now diasporic, favorite,
one about going away and coming back
(especially coming back);
an unflinching love for the soil
that heaved forth
the very meaning of the poetry of this poetry.
So then there was ululation and dancing,
(especially dancing)

by those who knew and cared,
and those who did not know but learned to care
about an art from a familiar and increasingly unfamiliar
piece of earth, where the worst of the best
are now the best of the worst.

So then there was clapping and dancing
(especially dancing), driven to Chimanimani heights
by earth-possessed, space-dispossessed drums,
then the transfiguring voice of one
who has nursed hearts,
nurtured ambition,
oiled the desire for life
where heads and hearts quiver
when the luxury Life is mentioned.

So then there was crying and dancing
(especially the dancing),
ripples and waves of hearts now damp with hope
until we could not tell
if we had spent only two
or three hours at Yoshi's,
or a non-stopping train of days,
only to be awakened by Parking Lot attendant's Voice,

intoning "One-and-half hours is $4.00."
But even as cars revved their farewell,
and as hearts pulsed to recovery,
we skipped and hopped in glee, celebrating
recovered memories for some,
the start of a new journey for others,
a combination of the two for me.

—*Emmanuel Sigauke*

gospel artists who perform with great success in the United Kingdom, yet have struggled to break into other diasporic settings, including Australia, New Zealand, and the United States.[13] Even contemporary Zimbabwean superstars such as sungura artist Alec Macheso have encountered significant difficulties performing abroad. As media studies scholar Nhamo Mhiripiri has observed, this is partly because many Zimbabwean emigrants in places such as Australia come from relatively upper-class backgrounds and may be "out of touch" with contemporary popular music back home.[14] In contrast, Mtukudzi's ability to appeal to urban elites, particularly after the 1997 release of *Tuku Music*, has contributed to his success among Zimbabweans living overseas.

Rather than relocating permanently, many Zimbabwean migrants make repeated forays abroad while maintaining a primary residence back home.[15] Like many of his diasporic listeners, Mtukudzi is also engaged in this type of circular migration pattern, alternating frequent tours abroad with periods of residence in Zimbabwe.[16] Yet even with this constant cross-border traffic, a shared concept of the Zimbabwean diaspora has begun to emerge, especially among migrants who have relocated outside the Southern African region, and whose position overseas, or *kumhiri kwemakungwa*, places them outside of earlier domestic and regional migratory flows. The political and economic instability of Zimbabwe's last two decades has contributed markedly to this nascent diasporic landscape, leading the South African popular press to observe that Mtukudzi's "shows in the SADC region and in the Diaspora [*sic*] where many Zimbabweans have fled tyranny and economic hardships back home, are always packed."[17] As I illustrate in the final section of this chapter, the political underpinnings of contemporary migration have strongly affected the diasporic reception of Mtukudzi's music, leading many listeners to interpret his songs as subtle critiques of domestic governance.

Listening to Oliver Mtukudzi in the Diaspora

Audience members living in the United States frequently spoke of rediscovering Mtukudzi's music abroad, suggesting that the casual listening habits of home cede to a more active engagement with familiar artists, songs, and musical genres in diasporic settings.[18] In Seattle, for example, Angela Khosa stated, "His music was always in our household, but he only became a household name for me in the Diaspora." As Zimbabwe's proportionately high numbers of educated migrants move outside of the nation's borders, the financial stability they derive from increased economic opportunity may facilitate this process of musical discovery. For Tafadzwa Muzhandu, who spent many years studying in the United States and United Kingdom before returning to Zimbabwe, even an undergraduate work-study position was enough to provide her with a small, yet significant amount of disposable income, enabling her to discover her love of Mtukudzi's music.[19] As Muzhandu related: "For the first time in my life, I could buy my own CD! I had my own radio, and my own discman, so I could play whatever I wanted to. . . . If you're living with your mom . . . sharing a radio with like five other people . . . you don't really have your own music." As diasporic listeners increasingly seek out Mtukudzi's music, they frequently describe themselves as "making up for" what they perceive as a relative lack of involvement prior to relocating abroad.[20] Following a performance in the United Kingdom, for example, one listener posted online, "All these years I couldn't afford a Tuku show because I honestly didn't have the money. Until a few years into the Diaspora [*sic*]. . . . So I can safely say I have been waiting for a Tuku gig for all my life."[21]

In addition to performing for Zimbabwean residents abroad, Mtukudzi has written several songs that speak explicitly to experiences of migration and diaspora.[22] This direct engagement has contributed to his appeal for diasporic listeners such as Angela Khosa, who related, "I clamored for everything Zimbabwean. . . . I listened to everything on Zimbabwean air waves, but nothing resonated within me like Tuku Music." Offering audience members an opportunity to meet other Zimbabweans, Mtukudzi's live performances have also represented a "rallying point" where diasporic networks are forged, strengthened, and made visible as listeners connect with other diasporic residents. In Texas, graduate student Lewis Madhlangobe observed, "There's a big Zimbabwean community. . . . but I didn't know about it. So this morning, we started communicating. So we're just building the networks, starting from here."

Located in what literary theorist Homi Bhabha has described as the interstitial "third space" of diaspora, transnational listeners often describe a heightened sense of engagement with Mtukudzi's songs.[23] Following a live performance at the Shakori Hills Festival in North Carolina, for example, Simba Mutanga observed that Mtukudzi's music "certainly brings more meaning now that I am away from home." As audiences encounter Tuku music in new contexts, they begin hearing it differently, resulting in new musical and social understandings. As Lewis Madhlangobe suggested: "When you are back home, you don't meet Mtukudzi's music the way we met it yesterday, and the way I meet it when I buy it from the shops around here. . . . Usually people don't pay attention when they are in the middle of it. But when you take a step back, then you begin to say, 'Ah, look, there's a problem there, there's a problem there. . . . ' You know, you begin to put so many things together. And now, when I listen to his music from here, it makes greater sense." Incorporating elements of both familiarity and distance, the third space of diaspora, much like that of ethnography itself, grants its occupants a dual status as both insiders and outsiders, opening fresh interpretive possibilities.[24]

Ngoma and the Sonic Evocation of Place

Just like the song "Baba," discussed in chapter 2, "Izere Mhepo" is based in the ngoma genre of mhande, with origins in Masvingo province. As with "Baba," Mtukudzi's creative approach to mhande is readily apparent in "Izere Mhepo." Most notably, the pattern executed by Mtukudzi's conga player, Kenny Nesham-ba, is strikingly similar to the rhythmic motif elaborated by the second drum part in contemporary mhande performance. Yet Neshamba subtly alters this motif by substituting a final eighth note for an eighth note rest. In addition, he reduplicates the motif in order to fill an entire, $\frac{12}{8}$ bar, conveying a rhythmic feel strongly associated with mhande, yet which does not conform to listeners' re-membered hearings of actual mhande performance.[25] Likewise, the second gui-tar, keyboard, and kick drum in "Izere Mhepo" all emphasize a triplet feel with-in the $\frac{12}{8}$ time signature of the piece, evoking the first drum part in mhande, yet without directly rephrasing any recognizable pattern or motif from this indige-nous ngoma genre.

In comparison with Thomas Mapfumo's more literal adaptations of songs from indigenous mbira and ngoma repertories, Mtukudzi's approach to mhande entails more substantial modifications.[26] As his set drummer Sam Mataure ob-served to me, "There is so much room. That's why it's very exciting. . . . It's not straight traditional music like how Thomas puts it. We play it a bit differently, we open up the music a bit more."[27] Indeed, Mtukudzi's listeners frequently cite "fusion" and "mixing" as hallmarks of his musical style, commenting upon his ability "to mix different kinds of music. . . . the fact that he's able to integrate all of those musics then produces something that we can call 'Tuku Music.'"[28] At the same time, however, they suggest that the various influences in Tuku music are woven together to the extent "that right now, you can no longer sepa-rate them away from each other."[29] Mtukudzi's approach to indigenous ngoma songs thus offers powerful sonic markers of place, yet avoids an exaggerated search for precise origins, opening new horizons of possibility for listeners and musicians alike.[30]

Relations and Obligations in the Wilderness of Diaspora

By invoking mhande's signature rhythmic pattern, songs such as "Izere Mhepo" are immediately identifiable as distinctively Zimbabwean, heightening Mtuku-dzi's appeal for diasporic listeners longing for the familiar sounds of home. Join-ing this emphasis on ngoma, the lyrics to "Izere Mhepo" immerse listeners in a particularly vivid musical imaginary of hunhu, encouraging them to symboli-cally reinhabit the social landscapes of a remembered home. Depicting a mu-sical universe populated with migrants struggling to achieve prosperity even as they remain closely connected to the families they have left behind, "Izere

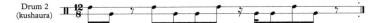

Transcription of the second drum part for mhande.

Kenny Neshamba's conga part in "Izere Mhepo."

Partial transcription of "Izere Mhepo."

Mhepo" has appealed to listeners exiled in the wilderness of diaspora, summoning a world of kinship and moral obligation in which they continue to participate, despite their extended physical absence.

For diasporic residents, home denotes not simply a physical location, but rather
a place remembered in time, a constellation of geography and temporality.[31] As
a result, themes of memory and kinship intertwine in "Izere Mhepo," which explores what Zimbabwean poet Chirikure Chirikure described to me as "a very
sensitive, emotional experience, which the average Zimbabwean family is going through." Invoking as its central image an indigenous carrying bag known
as *nhava*, woven from bark or other plant fibers, the song's chorus features the
repeated phrase *"Nhava izere mhepo,"* or, "The bag is full of air." Juxtapositions
of the familiar and the foreign are reinforced through Mtukudzi's humorous
reinterpretation of a traditional carrying bag on the album's cover, which depicts him reaching into the pocket of a decidedly contemporary backpack.[32] As
Mtukudzi explained in an interview with Zimbabwean journalist Robert Mukondiwa, the image of an empty carrying bag is a metaphor for "the fortunes or
otherwise of a young person who will have left home in search of greener pas-
tures and a better life. However, things are not at all rosy for him, as he has to
feed those he will have left behind who expect that he is leading a life of fortune
and yet his bag is empty."[33]

Speaking directly to experiences of transnational migration, "Izere Mhepo"
has become a favorite among diasporic audiences. In Texas, Lewis Madhlangobe
observed that Mtukudzi's lyrics "bring what is happening here in the United
States and in England to the people back at home." Elaborating further, he noted
that "Izere Mhepo" closely reflected his own personal situation: "The kind of
visa that I'm working on right now, I'm not allowed to work outside [the uni-
versity]. I get so little. And that little is just to pay for tuition. But I support my
family with that same amount of money; I eat less. But when people hear that
you're in the United States, they just think that you just go to the trees and pull
down the green leaves and send them as money. That's not it. So Oliver has actually studied the situation." In Philadelphia, listener Esau Mavindidze likewise
remarked that "Izere Mhepo" took up the experience of many transnational migrants who have "worked very hard to be able to send money back to their families. But there are instances in Zimbabwe where people really think it's all easy
here, and money just comes like that. And so when someone makes that connect-
ing kind of discussion, I think it impacts on people. People start talking about it
and people start reacting to it." Highlighting disjunctures between the lived experiences of migrants and the expectations of their kin, "Izere Mhepo" speaks
not only to diasporic listeners such as Madhlangobe and Mavindidze, but also
to the family members they have left behind.[34] Zimbabwean radio DJ Comfort

Nhava. Courtesy of Tuku Music and Sheer Sound/Gallo Record Company.

Mbofana, for example, described *Nhava* to me as his favorite album, citing his appreciation for "Izere Mhepo" as closely related to his memories of his brother, who had been living outside of the country for the past fourteen years.

In richly figurative language, "Izere Mhepo" plays upon a structural opposition between domesticity and wilderness, which represent the symbolic spheres of "home" and "away." In the words of ethnomusicologist Thomas Turino, the Shona word *musha*, or home, "signifies more than residence. *Musha* is also one's spiritual home; it is the land that a person is tied to because her or his ancestors are buried there."[35] For diasporic residents, the concept of home thus denotes not only a geographic point of orientation, but also a space of social relations where, as Jane Sugarman has similarly observed among Prespa Albanian communities, "one's sense of self as a social being is . . . built up reciprocally through interaction with others."[36] This world of encompassing relations contrasts starkly with diasporic space, which may seem deeply impersonal, even depersonalizing. Recalling her arrival in New York City, for instance, listener Angela Khosa stated, "There were so many people, and I felt lost . . . a feeling that I'd never had before, having grown up in a small town in Zimbabwe. . . . Being so far away from a life that made sense to me, I felt I'd lost my identity."

Reflecting this sense of social alienation, "Izere Mhepo" compares the diaspora to an untamed wilderness. Using the word *marimuka*, which refers to an area inhabited only by wild animals, Mtukudzi names two particular diasporic locations, singing, "My eldest child is in the wilderness, in London," and "Gone to the wilderness forever, in America."[37] This usage reflects greeting practices common in Zimbabwe, where rural kin regularly greet family members returning from an extended stay in the capital in similar terms by asking, *"Kuri sei kumasango,"* or "How are things in the forest?" To describe the cosmopolitan cities of London or Harare as places of wilderness is to metaphorically call attention to their alienation from the kinship networks that define the civilized space of the family home. In opposition to the domestic realm, or musha, the wilderness of diaspora is a condition that, as Homi Bhabha has argued, is particularly "unhomely."[38]

The Politics of Listening in the Diaspora

As in the case of "Wasakara," audiences have interpreted the lyrics to "Izere Mhepo" as a powerful form of commentary on Zimbabwean politics. During a conversation at the National Gallery of Zimbabwe, for example, one artist I spoke with observed: "Ultimately, you're challenging the political system, deep down. Why would someone go there, to go and work in the factories in the UK, for example, when they could make their living and remain united with their families? Or you have the latest experiences in South Africa, at the moment the xenophobia, you know? So you listen to that kind of song, in the diaspora, and in exile, I mean, it makes you question quite a lot of political decisions by the ruling party, by the government." Increasingly, Mtukudzi's songs have been heard by diasporic listeners equally aware of the risks inherent in migrating abroad and the challenges of remaining back home, resulting in what one long-time resident of the United States described as the loss of "romanticized views of a nonexistent utopian Zimbabwe."

As diasporic audiences have come to hear Mtukudzi's musical imaginaries of kinship as political, other symbols of national identity, such as the Zimbabwean flag, have also undergone subtle shifts in meaning. This was evident during a number of live performances I observed in the United States, where the flag was often prominently displayed by diasporic audience members. As local blogger Deborah Sengupta observed following Mtukudzi's performance in Austin, Texas: "It was a packed room at Flamingo Cantina when African legend Oliver Mtukudzi took the stage on Sunday night. 'We are here to take you to Zimbabwe!' the singer declared at the beginning of his set. The crowd was predominantly white, but a strong contingent of African ex-pats flanked the stage waving a Zimbabwean flag. They all roared enthusiastically."[39] Even as it continues to symbolize the proud moment of Zimbabwe's independence, the flag has acquired more recent associations with what Sabelo Ndlovu-Gatsheni calls the "Mugabeism" of ZANU-PF's long-standing rule.[40] At a show in Dallas, Texas, for example, an overwhelmingly diasporic Zimbabwean audience was thrilled to see a young white teenager with family ties to Zimbabwe wearing a t-shirt emblazoned with the Zimbabwean flag. Over and over, other listeners asked to have their pictures taken with him. Complimenting him on his shirt, they proudly declared, "This is one thing that unites us. It is common to us all." As a man who had recently relocated to Dallas from Mbare township told me, however, it would have been much more politically charged for a black Zimbabwean to wear the same shirt, for people might perceive it as a political gesture and take its wearer for a ZANU-PF supporter. Only when clearly disassociated with the nation's postcolonial political struggles, in other words, could the flag be made to stand for something larger, reflecting the heart of an imagined nation capable of encompassing Zimbabweans of all political stripes.

Reflecting the flag's increasingly contested meaning, one person present at Mtukudzi's show in Austin suggested that it had come to acquire a very different meaning for diasporic residents than for those who remained within the nation's borders. As she observed: "Go to Mtukudzi's shows, and try to establish how many seconds—seconds, in terms of time—you will see a Zimbabwean flag being raised there. You will never see any one of those. People right there don't like that flag. But those outside, they want the flag, because they are saying, 'I don't want to be here. . . . I would like to go back home and be more productive. . . . But now, under the current conditions, I can not.'" Strikingly, this audience member proceeded to draw a close analogy between the flag and Mtukudzi's music: "The meaning of Mtukudzi's music outside of Zimbabwe, in the diaspora, that's exactly the same meaning that the flag has got. People raise that flag because Mtukudzi is a symbol of independence also; his music brought our independence. So, we are saying we know exactly the correct benefits of independence, without a dictator." Powerful emblems of national identity, both the Zimbabwean flag and Tuku music harbor contested political implications that undergo striking shifts in meaning as they circulate throughout transnational space, illustrating how diaspora marks both separation and entanglement with the politics of the nation-state.[41]

With political as well as economic roots, the Zimbabwean diaspora is grounded in the structural violence of the nation's history. In recent years, political instability has resulted in widespread internal displacement, as well as migration
abroad.[42] As one listener in the United States asserted, "the people you see in
the diaspora, they are mostly linked to the opposition party in Zimbabwe. And
they ran out, out of the country to flee away from persecution from the government."[43] Back in Zimbabwe, a returned migrant offered an even stronger reading of linkages between diaspora and resistance, suggesting, "The opposition
can not do it from here. . . . They need to have *Chimurenga* [a struggle for libera-
tion] from somewhere else. Like, you can't fight this war in Zimbabwe, or from
Zimbabwe." Producing heightened political sensibilities and expectations, diasporic musical reception frequently becomes a site in which national politics are
contested, negotiated, and worked through.

Circling Back Home

As Zimbabwe's *Daily News* observed in 2002, "So many Zimbabweans now live
in exile in the UK that on the streets back home they refer to London as Harare
North."[44] In the diasporic reception of Tuku music, we see how Mtukudzi's integration of ngoma genres such as mhande, together with his musical imaginaries
of hunhu, have offered listeners exiled in the wilderness of diaspora the opportunity to symbolically return to the social relations of their remembered home.
The kinds of participatory listening practices so closely associated with ngoma
have also shaped the interpretation of Mtukudzi's songs, contributing toward his
audiences' propensity to hear lyrics narrating migration's effects in the domestic realm as metaphorical commentaries on failures of governance at the level of
the Zimbabwean state. On a much larger level of analysis, the social meanings of
Tuku music emerge not only as Mtukudzi's popular songs circulate throughout
the grid work of global geography, but also as they traverse the space between
artists and audiences; the space of musical listening.

"Ndima Ndapedza"
(I have finished my portion of the field)

Pangu pese ndasakura ndazunza	*I have weeded my area, and shaken the dirt off the roots*
Inga wani ndasakura ndazunza	*Look, I have weeded it and shaken the dirt off the roots*
Pangu pese ndasakura ndazunza	*I have weeded my area, and shaken the dirt off the roots*
Ndima yese ndasakura ndazunza	*My portion of the field, I have weeded and shaken the dirt off the roots*
Zvasarire imi kufuka nekuwarira	*It is left to you to do the rest*
Zvava penyu kufuka nekuwarira	*All that is left is in your court*
Zvava kwamuri kufuka nekuwarira	*It is up to you to do the rest*
Zvava penyu kufuka nekuwarira	*All that is left is in your court*
Zvimwe hazvizunzwe	*Some things are not shaken*
Zvimwe hazvizunzwe iwe	*Some things are not shaken, you*

Conclusion

I Have Finished My Portion of the Field

As the Black Spirits' performance at the 2008 Chimanimani Arts Festival drew to a close, the band members launched into "Ndima Ndapedza," which Mtukudzi has regularly played to signal the end of a show. Reviewing one of Mtukudzi's shows in nearby Mutare, for example, journalist Chengetai Murimwa observed that several hours after midnight, the singer "belted out 'Ndima Ndapedza' and fans knew Tuku was bidding them farewell."[1] Back in Harare, regular concert-goers were so conditioned to hearing Mtukudzi end with "Ndima Ndapedza" that they often began streaming out of nightclubs, stadiums, and festivals immediately upon hearing the song's first notes in order to beat the mad rush of people, cars, and security guards clogging the parking lot after his shows. While the song's indexical function in signaling an end to Mtukudzi's performances was largely lost on listeners in Chimanimani, who seldom had the opportunity to hear him play live, the agricultural metaphors of "Ndima Ndapedza" were especially apt given that this audience was overwhelmingly composed of manual laborers from the commercial farms and tree plantations surrounding the town.

Released on Mtukudzi's solo album *Ndega Zvangu* (1997), "Ndima Ndapedza" invokes imagery of agricultural labor in order to suggest that artists are only partly responsible for determining music's social meaning. As Mtukudzi explained:

> When you cultivate and you take off [pull out] some weeds, you don't just take them off; make sure you shake them off, and the weeds' roots are out of any soil. 'Cause if you leave them like that, they'll still grow. So, that's a literal translation of "Ndima Ndasakura." But otherwise the meaning behind the whole thing is, "I've done my work, and I've done it to my best. So it's all up to you now to judge what I've done, whether it's good or bad. It's not for me to tell. But I've done my best. I've done my part, and I've done it to my best."[2]

In the lyrics of "Ndima Ndapedza," Mtukidzi intimates that artists and listeners are inextricably linked. Through phrases such as *pangu pese*, or "my area," and *ndima*, which refers to a portion of a field allotted to one person for weeding, Mtukudzi identifies the musician's role as distinct from that of his or her listeners.[3]

Introducing the image of shaking the weeds he has pulled to loosen any soil clinging to their roots, he suggests that he has executed his role to perfection. Yet he simultaneously calls upon listeners to take up where he has left off, intimating that even the most complete act of artistic creation leave a portion that lingers undone, a remainder that will never entirely be captured within the work itself.[4]

In "Ndima Ndapedza," Mtukudzi suggests that this remainder lies in the space between artists and audiences: the space of musical listening. Deflecting the notion that musicians are wholly responsible for determining the social significance of their work, he implies that artists and audiences are bound together in a dialogic process of determining musical meaning.[5] Mtukudzi's insistence on listening as an interpretive process is underscored repeatedly in the second section of "Ndima Ndapedza," where he calls directly upon his listeners to do "all that is left."[6] Insistently reformulating his appeal through phrases such as "It is left to you," "It is in your court," and "It is up to you," Mtukudzi's lyrics suggest that the endpoint of artistic creation marks another point of entry, as audiences hear and interpret his songs in relation to their own lived experiences.[7]

Living Hunhu in Tuku Music

As I have illustrated throughout this book, Oliver Mtukudzi's audiences have actively participated in shaping the meaning of Tuku music. Based in principles of mutual obligation, reciprocity, and dialogue, the social ethos of hunhu is central to Tuku music, which seeks to convey Mtukudzi's sense of what it means to live as "a person among others." Positioning himself as sahwira to the nation, Mtukudzi has claimed the role of a ritual best friend, counselor, and family advisor, licensing him to speak freely about kinship relations within the domestic sphere. He has also assumed the sahwira's classic role as a mediator who seeks to foster negotiation, reconciliation, and peacemaking.[8] Complementing his ability to convey social criticism, Mtukudzi's engagement with various ngoma genres has both imparted a particular sonic "flavor" to his musical imaginaries of hunhu and invoked the larger participatory aesthetics inherent in ngoma performance. Together, hunhu, husahwira, and ngoma are located at the heart of Tuku music, illustrating how local forms of musical practice and social organization continue to bear upon contemporary experiences of mediated, popular songs.

While they remain underrepresented with respect to the mbira dzavadzimu, for example, Zimbabwe's legion ngoma genres are by far the nation's most common indigenous performance styles, and they have likewise strongly influenced Zimbabwean popular music. As I have suggested, Mtukudzi's affinity for ngoma was partly related to his rise to prominence during the liberation years of the 1970s, a period when many of the nation's popular musicians deliberately experimented by incorporating local languages and sounds within the somewhat diffuse genre known as trad music. During the struggle for independence, Mtukudzi's ngoma-based popular songs, such as "Bganyamakaka" and "Mutavara," functioned as powerful, yet veiled forms of political resistance. Yet the multivalent qualities of his musical imaginaries of hunhu enabled Mtukudzi's songs to transcend the initial moment of their release, maintaining social relevance not only during the liberation struggle, but throughout the shifting political terrain of the postcolonial era.

In the years immediately following independence, Mtukudzi continued to refine his approach to singing hunhu even as he solidified his position within the nascent Zimbabwean music industry. At times, Mtukudzi's relentlessly innovative spirit—his desire to rebrand his music as a fusion of jit and Afro-jazz, his experimentation with emerging genres such as gospel, and his short-lived forays into the realm of musical theater, for example—provoked friction with his listeners. For the most part, however, Mtukudzi's dialogic performance style invited listeners to symbolically inhabit his vivid musical imaginaries of hunhu. Epitomizing his ability to unite themes of kinship, social reciprocity, and moral obligation, for example, "Neria" spoke powerfully to his audiences' own lived experiences of losing loved ones. Yet even as Mtukudzi lent his voice in support of women's rights to inherit, his soundtrack to *Neria* simultaneously ascribed value to the very customary practices marginalized within the film. Complicating dichotomies of "traditional" and "modern," Mtukudzi's songs called attention to the contemporaneity of customary practices such as the kugara nhaka lineage remarriage rite, which continues to represent one among many resources as families renegotiate kinship relations within a lineage fractured by death.

By the mid-1990s, these struggles would intensify in the face of Zimbabwe's growing HIV/AIDS epidemic. Rending the nation's social fabric, HIV/AIDS both destroyed bonds of kinship and robbed the nation of its most productive citizens—its parents, teachers, and workers. In this context, Mtukudzi's songs about HIV/AIDS have exemplified his desire to dialogue with listeners, offering audiences the possibility of singing out loud an epidemic long characterized by silence, stigma, and erasure. Narrating the effects of the disease within the private lives of individuals and families, Mtukudzi's songs about HIV/AIDS, exemplified in his iconic hit "Todii," have addressed issues of agency, gender, and disclosure. Like the soundtrack to *Neria*, however, his songs about the effects of HIV/AIDS within the domestic sphere of the family simultaneously speak to larger social constructions of illness, health, and healing. Among the nation's artists, Mtukudzi has been particularly influential in public health work, participating in multiple campaigns that have capitalized on his dialogic approach in order to bring awareness, prevention, and treatment messages to a wider audience.

Hearing Politics in Hunhu

Approaching the household as a microcosm of society, Tuku music brings to life a vibrantly imagined universe of moral social relations. Speaking simultaneously to what one listener called the "life of a person, life of a community, the livelihood of a nation," Mtukudzi's musical imaginaries of hunhu have resonated at multiple levels of social organization. As Mtukudzi himself has observed: "Like my songs, I'll be talking of one individual. But that individual doesn't end there, 'cause he makes a family. And the whole family is being told about this. And the family makes a community, and the community makes a nation. You see? That's how the structure is in a Shona culture."[9] As illustrated in the reception history of "Wasakara," Mtukudzi's audiences have frequently interpreted his kinship imaginaries as powerful metaphorical critiques of other levels of social organization, extending to national governance. In an increasingly troubled political environment, "Wasakara" in particular offered listeners a powerful way to express popular dissent through musical participation. These politically charged responses to "Wasakara"—as well as songs such as "Moto Moto," "Handiro Dambudziko," and "Chikara"—illustrate with exceptional clarity how Mtukudzi's musical discourse of hunhu, while not overtly political, has taken place in contexts that have larger political implications.[10]

These political implications now extend to a growing Zimbabwean diaspora, where Mtukudzi has built a substantial following through frequent performances in countries with significant migrant populations, including South Africa, the United States, and the United Kingdom. Depicting the space of diaspora as a symbolic wilderness, songs such as "Izere Mhepo" have suggested that migration entails not only spatial, but also social distance, separating migrants from the kinship relations of their remembered home, or *musha*. Mtukudzi's musical imaginaries of hunhu have exerted particular appeal for diasporic subjects, enabling his listeners to symbolically recreate the kinship networks of a remembered home. As with "Wasakara," however, Mtukudzi's songs about migration have reflected back upon issues of national governance, acquiring important domestic political implications.

Exceeding conventional boundaries of the political, Mtukudzi's approach to singing hunhu exemplifies how the moral and the political are inextricably bound together in the context of postcolonial struggles.[11] At the same time, however, Mtukudzi's metaphorical narratives of domestic relations cannot be reduced to a singular, political reading. Rich in ethnographic possibility, they have offered multivalent meanings for audiences, creating the interpretive ambiguity that, in the words of journalist Robert Mukondiwa, "has been his power." Indeed, while it is possible for governments to ban a single song or album perceived as critical of a repressive regime, it would be nearly impossible to do away with Mtukudzi's musical discourse of relational politics, which represents an entire way of "thinking about politics" for his audiences.[12] Tying the major themes of this book together, I conclude by suggesting that hunhu, with its distinctive ethos of moral obligation, holds forth the possibility of conceiving an alternative political vision that departs from conventional discourses of democracy.

Democracy and Dialogue

In recent decades, Zimbabwe has increasingly been viewed as a paradigmatic example of postcolonial political regimes, in which democracy and the rule of law are fetishized even as their autonomy is undermined or ignored.[13] Seeking to monopolize the deployment of signs, for example, the nation's competing political parties, ZANU-PF and the MDC, have each deployed familiar symbols of democracy to bolster the legitimacy of their respective claims to political rule. Extending across multiple sensory domains, this system of signs binds together elements of the visual, audio, tactile, and even kinesthetic, exemplified by the vibrant cloth printed with the president's image and worn by ululating, dancing women whose presence continues to be requisite at many official events. In the process, the trappings of the electoral process come to comprise a simulacrum of signifiers that stand in for democracy, constituting a highly visible yet unreal display.

In this context, questions of how postcolonial subjects approach problems of political agency, subjectivity, and meaning become particularly urgent. Yet as they proliferate, depictions of the postcolony as a palimpsest of disorder, contradiction, and senseless violence risk becoming what Chimamanda Adichie has called a "single story," rendering the postcolonial experience incoherent, illogical, and incomprehensible. As Adichie so trenchantly reminds us, "The consequence of a single story is this: It robs people of dignity. It makes our recognition of our equal humanity difficult. It emphasizes how we are different rather than how we are similar."[14] Tracing the contours of Tuku music as one particular form of postcolonial expressive culture, I have suggested that Mtukudzi's musical imaginaries of hunhu enable us to move from a singular understanding of the postcolony and toward the "balance of stories" advocated by Chinua Achebe.[15] Invoking an indigenous ethos of moral obligation, social reciprocity, and dialogue, Mtukudzi's songs illustrate how an ability to "maintain difference and insist on incompatibility even while keeping all the elements of experience in juxtaposition with each other" is central both to Shona conceptions of social and political relations, and to aural poetic forms from across the African continent.[16] Writing on the cusp of Zimbabwe's independence in 1980, Stanlake and Tommie-Marie Samkange argued that the very idea of declaring a single party victorious at the polls is distinctly Western in orientation.[17] Nearly two decades later, philosopher Mogobe Ramose would similarly suggest that "adversarial politics—the hallmark of the Western-style multiparty system of democracy—is rather foreign to African traditional political culture."[18] By exposing democracy as necessarily contingent, these authors sought to establish the conditions of possibility for envisioning an alternative political process grounded in hunhu, with principles of social reciprocity, dialogue, and reconciliation at its core.[19] Indeed, less than a year after Mtukudzi performed "Ngoromera" at the 2008 HIFA, protracted deliberations between ZANU-PF and the MDC resulted in the formation of a Government of National Unity. Brokering a fragile peace between these adversarial parties, the unity agreement was politically expedient for both sides, allowing ZANU-PF to lay claim to a rhetoric of compromise and granting the MDC access to government after the party's failures to capitalize on its own early successes. Yet it also echoed the Samkanges' call some thirty years earlier for a "Government of National Unity in which . . . we can all, with dignity, set about rebuilding and healing the wounds we have inflicted on ourselves."[20]

Since the unity accord, Zimbabwean residents have experienced tangible gains, as previously shuttered hospitals and schools reopened, HIV/AIDS treatment programs expanded, the adoption of the US dollar led to the end of hyperinflation, electricity and water supplies improved, and roads were repaired and rebuilt.[21] Even in the face of these improvements, Zimbabwe's political climate has continued to prove fractious, and the nation's future remains deeply uncertain. Yet almost a decade after it was signed, the tenuous unity agreement reached between ZANU-PF and the MDC has continued to hold. As Zimbabwe clings tenaciously to a political process governed by negotiation, rather than ruled by clenched fists and raised palms, we both see traces of the relational ethos of hunhu and hear echoes of "Ngoromera," with its repeated refrain, "We don't want war / We don't want senseless violence."

In this work, I have argued that Oliver Mtukudzi's songs are located within a political third space, governed neither by ZANU-PF's revolutionary fist, nor by the MDC's postrevolutionary palm. From the late days of the Rhodesian regime to the recent postcolonial era, Mtukudzi has consistently viewed song as the single best way to express how selves are made only by and through others, weaving the moral bonds of hunhu into a social fabric that will bend, but not fracture, in times of stress. As he told me: "We can only do that through art. Art represents who we are. And if we can have the right artists who do the right thing, that represent the right people, we will always get the right people, and we will always have the right nation." All too often, the efforts Zimbabwe's ordinary citizens—teachers, healers, kombi drivers, public health workers, subsistence farmers, students, cross-border traders, dancers, and musicians—have made to grapple with the quicksand of the nation's shifting postcolonial political terrain have gone unsung. Yet these responses from below are among the most powerful ways of moving beyond a single story of postcolonial collapse and disorder and toward a more balanced understanding, capable of accommodating continuity and reason alongside illogic and disjuncture.

Among these popular responses, forms of expressive culture—from the participatory aesthetics of ngoma to the mediated, commercial sphere of Tuku music—are particularly salient, making them critical to the ethnographic endeavor.[22] With their rich imaginaries of kinship, compelling musical settings, and invocations of the participatory aesthetics of ngoma, Mtukudzi's songs have articulated an indigenous ethos of social reciprocity that establishes moral bonds between the past and the present, revealing what ethnomusicologist David Coplan has called "the articulation of relations of meaning with relations of power."[23] Questions of listening are central in understanding this process, for it is only through acts of *kunzwa*—hearing, feeling, and understanding—that Mtukudzi's songs have acquired their enduring social significance. In the reception of Tuku music, we see Mtukudzi and his audiences jointly engaged in articulating, negotiating, and reimagining an evolving social world with dignity, creativity, and passion. In Mtukudzi's words, "Song is always in between us and our passion, between us and our suffering and pain. The song is always between us."

NOTES

Epigraph

The Papers of Martin Luther King, Jr., Volume V: Threshold of a New Decade, January 1959–December 1960, ed. Clayborne Carson (Berkeley: University of California Press, 2005).

Introduction

1. For a historical account of the nyunga nyunga, see Tracey (1961). For more on the Zimbabwean marimba, see Axelsson (1973) and Jones (2006).

2. Directed by South African Brett Bailey, "Dreamland" featured Bernie Bismark as musical director, Marie-Laure Soukaina Edom as choreographer, and Sue Powell as production manager.

3. "A Dream with a Message (HIFA Opening Concert)," http://www.fungaijames .com/bloggen/2008/04/29/a-dream-with-a-message-hifa-opening-concert/ (Accessed 20 July 2012).

4. Diawara (1997), 41.

5. Operation Murambatsvina, which literally translates as "Drive out filth," was a state-sponsored urban clean-up campaign with devastating social and economic effects, conducted in May 2005. See for example Vambe (2008).

6. For one account of how the ngoromera charm was used in Bulawayo during the 1920s, see Msindo (2006).

7. Terence Ranger (2006) has suggested that the rise of "mangoromera culture" in Matabeleland was a response to changing social relations in the mid-twentieth century. As Hove has similarly observed, the "wayward, the stubborn, the disobedient and several other anti-social elements, used the Mangoromera craze as a backhand blow on established conventions, which their elders religiously adhered to without question. Faction fights, that had hitherto been confined to urban and industrial areas at weekends and on holidays, had moved to villages out in the rural areas. Many slight arguments and disputes quickly developed into duels or faction fights . . . many people resorted to talking about their ability to box and the sharp sting of their boxing" (1985, 121).

8. *NADA* (1933).

9. In his description of the song, for example, Murenga Chikowero observes, "The concluding refrain *ngatiwirirane* (let us deliberate and come to an agreement) captures the ever-evolving nature of political and social relationships, that is, they are constantly shifting and as such, can only be maintained by being regularly and carefully re-negotiated" (2006, 41).

10. Hunhu can alternately be spelled as unhu. Throughout this manuscript, I opt to spell hunhu, as well as other words such as husahwira, with an initial "h" in order to facilitate pronunciation, as well as because this is the way that some of my primary informants in Zimbabwe have encouraged me to spell these terms.

11. See for example Ndlovu-Gatsheni (2009).

12. Chikowero (2006), 40.

13. As local journalist Percy Zvomuya (2004) similarly observed, "The clenched fist does not achieve anything. It does not resolve disputes. The song 'Ngoromera' says it all. We don't want war. If we have differences let's talk things over. Some people have said that they have a long successful history of violence while others have stated, boldly that they have degrees in violence. But violence has never succeeded." Political readings of "Ngoromera" may likewise have been heightened by the song's inclusion on Mtukudzi's controversial album *Bvuma-Tolerance* (2000), discussed at length in chapter 5.

14. Fabian (1998).

15. These quotes are taken from fan mail held in the personal archive of Debbie Metcalfe, Mtukudzi's former manager. The first letter was written by Farai Dafter (2003), and the second by Manase Muguti (2003).

16. Despite growing recognition of its importance (see, for example, Bendix 2000, Cohen 1993, Erlmann 2004, Wong 2001), musical listening has seldom been at the heart of ethnographic study, which has historically focused primarily on musical performers and producers. Only in recent decades has this situation has begun to shift, as ethnomusicologists and anthropologists have begun to recognize the importance of "situating the expressive arts within an acoustic environment in which listeners are active social participants" (Samuels et al. 2010, 335). Within this emerging body of work, approaches to listening and reception include cognitive research (Becker 2009), phenomenological inquiry (Downey 2002), quantitative and statistical methods (Mauerhofer 1997, Um 2000), and studies of cross-cultural listening (Hopkins 1982, Krüger 2011). For other ethnographic accounts of listening and reception, see Cavicchi (1998), Schulz (2002), and Wong (2004).

17. A small but growing body of work suggests, for example, that musical listening is instrumental in the formation of Asian American identities in the United States (Wong 2004), the maintenance of kinship relations among Brazilian migrant workers (Dent 2007), and the ability of Aboriginal Australian communities to maintain familial ties with imprisoned relatives (Fisher 2009).

18. Erlmann (2004), 2.

19. See Corbett (1990), 84.

20. In their discussion of soundscapes, for example, Samuels et al. firmly locate listening "as a cultural practice" (2010, 330).

21. As Robert Kauffman has observed, "The verb that means 'to hear' is much more comprehensive in its meaning than are the other sense verbs. It is *kunzwa*, and it means 'to perceive by touch, sight or hearing; to understand'" (1969, 508).

22. Perman (2011), 242. While Perman's primary focus is on the coterminous nature of ethics and aesthetics in the Shona conception of *kunaka* (to be beautiful/good),

these semiotic elements map precisely onto the set of interrelated sensory domains encompassed by the multivalent term *kunzwa*.

23. Kauffman (1969), 508. In a Venda context, Charles Adams has similarly observed that "'aurality,' sounding and hearing, is a necessary condition of becoming conscious and the principle mode for the production of significant interpretation of the circumstances of living" (1979, 318).

24. The intersubjective nature of listening extends beyond a strictly Zimbabwean context, as reflected in recent scholarship emphasizing how work that incorporates "Bakhtinian notions of dialogism, polyphony, and the chronotope presents the voice as an utterance shaped and sounded in relation to other voices and to situated events" (Samuels et al. 2010, 332).

25. My discussion of the meaning of *kunzwana* and *kunzwanana* draws from Hannan ([1959] 2000), Chimhundu (1980), and Chimuka (2001).

26. As Tarisayi Chimuka observes, "For the Shona, life in the *'nyika'* [a territory or administrative political unit] was inconceivable without *kunzwanana*. Good relations were characterised by mutual understanding and respect" (2001, 35).

27. Samuels et al. (2010), 338–339.

28. Now deceased, Dumisani and Mai Chi Maraire were the parents of the late mbira player and singer Chiwoniso Maraire, whose HIFA performance is described earlier in this chapter. "Mai Chi" is in fact a teknonymic name meaning "Chiwoniso's mother."

29. See Berliner ([1978] 1993). See also Berliner (1975), Kauffman (1969, 1976), Tracey (1961, 1970, 1972), Tracey ([1932] 1969).

30. My research in Zimbabwe was supported by a Fulbright-Hays Fellowship.

31. See Kyker (2013).

32. These phrases are respectively drawn from Samkange and Samkange (1980, 34), Ramose (1999, 52), and Pearce (1990, 146). Ramose in particular suggests that hunhu has both epistemological and ontological dimensions as it is oriented both toward the nature of existence itself and toward the way human subjects conceptualize and understand this existence.

33. The Zulu version of this aphorism, *Umuntu ngumuntu ngabantu*, forms the basis for Brenda Fassie's song "Umuntu ngumuntu ngabantu" (*Brenda*, 1991). In Uganda, J. S. Mbiti likewise uses the similar formulation, "I am because we are; and since we are, therefore I am" (1994, 141).

34. Indeed, Mandivamba Rukuni has described hunhu as "love for one another and love for our Great Creator" ([2007] 2010, Kindle loc. 343–344).

35. Personal communication, Musekiwa Chingodza, 26 March 2014. Musanyange's current medium, Kajawu George Chingodza, is Musekiwa's father.

36. It is not unusual for male artists to sing from a female perspective in Shona music, and Mtukudzi himself performs several similar songs.

37. In a Brazilian context, Alexander Dent has similarly argued for "the continued efficacy of kinship for understanding social relations and cultural production in varied domains. . . . In the singing of it, rural music reaches out towards other fields of social life—not only family and romance, but commerce and politics as well" (2007, 458–459).

38. Mutamba (1999) similarly describes Mtukudzi as "the best on lyrics, no doubt" among Zimbabwean musicians.

39. As linguist Pedzisai Mashiri explains, "Two male strangers or acquaintances who have not yet established a form of relationship between them may address each other as *Tsano*, literally 'Brother-in-law.' The terms *sahwira* 'ritual friend,' *mukadzi wangu* 'my wife,' *shamwari* 'friend,' uncle and aunt, among others, are also used for marking out and expressing of social relationships" (1999, 106).

40. Barber (1991), 249.

41. In recent years, Zimbabwe's growing diaspora has led to an offshoot of the original program, known as *Kwaziso Kubva KuDiaspora*, or "Greetings from the diaspora." For the largely rural listenership of programs such as *Kwaziso*, the pealing guitar lines of *sungura* music, popularized by artists such as Alec Macheso, Leonard Dembo, and Nicholas Zacharia, have recently risen to prominence, dominating request letters. Yet Mtukudzi's songs are regularly requested alongside those of sungura artists.

42. For an analysis of similar themes in the context of Aboriginal radio programing in Australia, see Fisher (2009).

43. In a group interview I conducted, three members of the neotraditional popular band Bongo Love—Trymore Jombo, Godfrey Mambira, and John Mambira—concurred that "Hazvireve" reflects a common experience for many Zimbabwean men. Godfrey Mambira in particular suggested that Mtukudzi's song has inspired men to try to reestablish relations with their distant children, telling me,

> "The Tuku song '*Hazvireve rudo handina mwanangu* [It doesn't mean that I don't have love, my child]'—you find some men who leave. They get divorced, whatever. But he still has love for? For his child. Frequently, some men have children, but don't see them; they don't care for them. The mother is who is caring for the child, but the father is doing his own things. But some of them, they have been changed, to say, 'But, I have what? I have a child. Let me do what? Let me show my love for my child.' He [Mtukudzi] has changed many people."

44. Many thanks to Lloyd Munjanja and Tonde Mufudzi for assisting me in translating several idiomatic expressions in this letter. Interestingly, with the exception of Mtukudzi, all of the other songs and artists mentioned in this request appear to be fictional inventions.

45. This letter in particular might fruitfully be read in relation to another letter, sent in 1951 to the Central African Broadcasting Station in Lusaka, in which a disgruntled husband similarly invoked song in order to "call upon the radio audience to join him in humiliating his ex-wife for her indecorous behavior" (Bessant 1994, 44).

46. Thomas Turino (2000), for example, offers a four-part categorization that divides musical activity into "participatory," "presentational," "hi-fidelity," and "studio audio art," and would place popular musicians such as Mtukudzi and Mapfumo firmly within the presentational and high-fidelity domains.

47. *The Standard* (2001c).

48. I take the concept of music's role in producing a social life "in excess of mere survival" from the work of Darien Lamen (2013).

49. Werbner (1998), 15.

1. *Hwaro*/Foundations

1. According to mbira player Patience Chaitezvi Munjeri, mafuwe is often heard at ceremonies honoring the ancestral spirits of women who performed the dance during their lifetimes; indeed, this kurova guva ceremony was held for an important female spirit medium who had recently passed away.

2. Thanks to Rumbidzai Chipendo for assistance in transcribing this phrase.

3. Ignatowski (2006), 276.

4. The First Chimurenga occurred from 1896–1897. As Maurice Vambe observes, "The term *chimurenga* comes from the name of a legendary *Shona* ancestor, *Murenga Sororenzou*. Believed to be a huge man with a head (*soro*) the size of an elephant's (*nzou*), *Murenga* was well known for his fighting spirit and prowess, and legend has it that he composed war-songs to encourage his soldiers to continue the fight against their enemies in pre-colonial Zimbabwe" (2004, 167).

5. Huffman (1985), 70.

6. Fontein, for example, refers to the ruins as "an intricate part of the spiritual and historical basis of the state of Zimbabwe" (2006, 782).

7. See, for example, Eicher (1995), Made and Whande (1989), and Tumwine (1992).

8. Documenting Zimbabwe's emerging political and economic climate, a growing body of scholarship has focused on issues of violence, displacement, and conflict in the aftermath of the liberation struggle (Werbner 1991), the implications of ZANU-PF's controversial land reform program (Hammer, Raftopolous, and Jensen 2003), and the continued role of war veterans (Kriger 2003).

9. Karin Barber has similarly recognized the particular salience of aural poetics at funerals in a Yoruba context, observing that the funeral "is a highly complex event inviting a much wider and more subtle range of expressive acts" than other collective social events, such as marriage (1991, 118).

10. Mashiri (1999).

11. Mafundikwa (1999).

12. Unpublished interview with Banning Eyre (1993).

13. Paul Berliner, for example, recounts that "in the court of Chitungwiza a man named Dandara was Pasipamire's acolyte and Zhanje, Mpawose and Muchaonwa were among the most important mbira players. In the accounts of Mujuru and Pasipamire's descendants, a group of mbira players accompanied the great medium on his journey to meet Lobengula. In the confrontation with the Ndebele, Pasipamire's mbira players performed the music which enabled Pasipamire to become possessed by Chaminuka and thereby to elude his assailant" ([1978] 1993, 48). The mbira also plays an important role in rituals contexts such as the *bira,* where it is a primary means of summoning the *vadzimu* ancestral spirits responsible for protecting social health, who may then speak with their living descendants through a spirit medium, or *svikiro.*

14. See, for example, Berliner ([1978] 1993) and Turino (2000).

15. Azim (1999) and Brusila (2002). This burgeoning international Shona music community is the very way that I initially became involved in studying Zimbabwean music, as a young person growing up in Eugene, Oregon.

16. Reflecting this particular combination of elements, Diane Thram describes the genre of dandanda as "an indigenous form of ritual dance with its own song repertoire and distinctive *ngoma* (drum) and *hosho* (gourd rattle) style" (2002, 129).

17. Ngoma can also be used to designate events at which drumming or other forms of music are played.

18. Thram (2002), 136. For more on ngoma as healing ritual, see Janzen (1992). In a South African context, Louise Meintjes has analyzed ngoma as a practice of performing power, or *isigqi*. Observing that one "might consult an isangoma for medicines to protect oneself or to enhance one's power," her account outlines ngoma's associations with healing and wellness (2004, 188). At the same time, her primary interest lies in understanding how this "sense of power represented in artistic expression and valued as an artistic principle is harnessed into a process of obtaining forms of political power," reflecting many of themes of this book (175).

19. Coplan (1994) 8–9. Invoking Bakhtin's conception of the utterance, Karin Barber suggests that the function of oral art forms "is to concentrate and enhance the dialogic capacity of all discourse to bring the other into relationship with the self, and in so doing, to constitute social being" (1991, 37). Expanding on their discursive nature, she likewise observes that they "are intended and expected to be talked about, to be explained, expounded, and opened up so that the multiple meanings enclosed and compressed within them are revealed" (3).

20. Rutsate (2011), 128–129. Meintjes places similar importance on both musical and social aspects of coordination in her analysis of South African ngoma, observing that "dancers, drummers, singers, and clappers—leaders and team members—meld sound and movement into a dense experience that is at once coherent and imminent: it is dense with internal tensions almost out of balance" (2004, 175).

21. See Perman (2011, 247). *Kupesana* translates literally as "missing each other."

22. Mtukudzi's music thus exemplifies the type of pastiche and bricolage long associated with African popular culture by scholars such as Karin Barber (1987).

23. While Mapfumo's version of *chimurenga* is most frequently described as "an urban guitar music inspired by rural *mbira dza vadzimu* music" (Brown 1994, 100), Thomas Turino has observed that "for most of his career, mbira-based pieces . . . represented a small portion of Mapfumo's recorded output" (1998, 94). Turino recognizes several ngoma genres, including jerusarema and jiti, among the eclectic influences Mapfumo has incorporated, further reinforcing my assertion regarding the importance of ngoma genres in understanding Zimbabwean popular music writ large.

24. See Turino (2000, 295) and Zindi ([1985] 1997, 40). Even when Mtukudzi has recorded relatively literal arrangements of ngoma songs—on tracks such as "Mutavara" (KDZ 109, 1977), "Bganyamakaka" (KDZ 114, 1977), "Chiri Mundari" (*Ndega Zvangu*, 1997) and "Wenge Mambo" (*Bvuma-Tolerance*, 2000)—these have gone largely unremarked. (KDZ is the Kudzanayi label.)

25. Turino places two types of mbira, the mbira dzavadzimu and the *njari*, along-side them (2000, 63).

26. Notable exceptions include Diane Thram's discussion of dandanda performance (2002), as well as Kariamu Welsh-Asante's work on ngoma, with a focus on genres choreographed for the stage by the National Dance Company of Zimbabwe (2000).

27. For some discussion of relationships between the two, see Turino (2000, 227–233).

28. Mudenge (1988), 100–101.

29. As dance scholar Kariamu Welsh-Asante has reported, mbende was a diversionary tactic meant to "distract the enemy and give the Shona warriors time to take up martial positions" (1985, 383).

30. See, for example, Kwaramba (1997), 2.

31. An account written by one Protestant missionary, for example, described "native minstrels with bodies besmeared with a filthy mixture of fat and red earth, moving about singing songs that could be relished by none but people of utterly depraved minds" (Westgate 1913, 56; in Williams 1997, 287).

32. Welsh-Asante (1985), 385.

33. Ibid.

34. Yet other forms of ngoma emerged directly from colonial encounters, as was the case with Zulu men's competitive ngoma dancing in South Africa (Meintjes 2004, 178).

35. For more on ngoma performance in beerhalls, see Turino (2000). Jerusarema in particular acquired a newly sexualized dimension in the beerhall, as described by Welsh-Asante (1985, 387). Welsh-Asante also observes that jerusarema is currently performed at funerary rituals, "although it was not originally a funeral dance" (394). It is likely, however, that this extension of jerusarema fits neatly within preexisting links among war, death, wilderness, and hunting, as I have discussed in relation to the ngondo song "Baya Wabaya" (Kyker 2010).

36. Welsh-Asante adds that women no longer danced bare-breasted and that the hosho shakers may be replaced by soft-drink cans (1985, 400).

37. Vail and White (1991), 74.

38. Bessant, for example, offers an example of a song banned by Native Commissioner Major F. C. Wane sometime between 1910 and 1930 (1994, 55).

39. See Bessant (1994, 46) and Vail and White (1991, 42).

40. See Turino (2000). Mbende has been particularly subject to these forces, as it was selected as the opening music for the Zimbabwe Broadcasting Service's daily radio and television newscasts and was later declared a form of intangible global patrimony by the United Nations Educational, Scientific, and Cultural Organization.

41. Perman (forthcoming). For an analysis of "Mugabeism" as political ideology, see Ndlovu-Gatsheni (2009).

42. One account of mhande performance in the context of Karanga kurova guva ceremonies is offered in Rutsate (2010).

43. As Rutsate (2010) observes, the magavhu leg rattles are also referred to by Karanga speakers as *magagada*.

44. Thram observes that mhande is among the genres performed alongside mbira and dandanda at bira ceremonies (2002, 130).

45. The Chembira school motto is "The home of traditional dance." The school's traditional dance instructor, Daniel Inasiyo, was a long-time member of the group Mhembero, founded by former National Dance Company of Zimbabwe member Irene Chigamba. The accompanying field recording is available on iTunes, as part of the album *Maungira EZimbabwe*; all proceeds benefit the nonprofit organization Tariro (www .tariro.org).

46. Personal communication, Daniel Inasiyo, 17 August 2008.

47. A mhande feel is similarly present in several other of his songs, including "Izere Mhepo" *(Nhava*, 2005), and "Njuga" *(Tsimba Itsoka*, 2007).

48. In describing his approach to genres such as mhande, Mtukudzi told me that he will often assign the drum kit to "take the center time" and proceed to divide "all the cross-rhythms" among other members of the Black Spirits, treating ngoma genres as a collection of various rhythmic possibilities and musical motifs.

49. In his work on muchongoyo among Zimbabwe's Ndau-speaking communities, Tony Perman (2011) has observed that participatory ideals such as listening and cooperation are essential to successful ngoma performance. Accordingly, he argues that ngoma is a realm in which aesthetic and ethical considerations are synonymous, making the beautiful coterminous with the good.

50. Baumann and Fujie (1999), 7.

2. Performing the Nation's History

1. For more on sungura's relationship to benga music, a particular offshoot of rhumba played in Kenya and Tanzania, see Pfukwa (2010) and Perman (2012).

2. Associations between paychecks and pleasure have been memorialized in popular songs such as the Four Brothers' "Wapenga Nayo," which tells of a man who spends his entire yearly bonus at a beerhall, leaving nothing for his family *(Makorokoto*, 1988).

3. See Shoka (2007, 94).

4. According to some assessments, inflation would reach the nearly incalculable figure of 650 million googol percent (6.5×10^{108} percent) by the end of the year. See for example Hanke (2008).

5. While toyi-toyi is most closely associated with South Africa, various musicians and scholars have suggested it originated in Zimbabwe. See Hirsch (2002) and Twala and Koetaan (2006).

6. Turino (2000, 29).

7. For a discussion of the role expressive culture played at these political rallies, see for example Turino (2000, 185).

8. As Thomas Turino has suggested, Harari's strategic location as the first black township of the Rhodesian capital encouraged the development of a vibrant arts sector (2000, 63–67).

9. Robert Kauffman would describe him as a guitarist who "uses a simpler guitar style, but follows traditional processes in often choosing folk tales as the basis of his songs" (1972, 53).

10. Associations between music and modernity were picked up early by Lever Brothers, who hired one of Madzikatire's predecessors, Kenneth Mattaka, to tour Zimbabwe promoting their products as early as 1952. As Thomas Turino notes, Mattaka began performing American and South African songs as early as the 1930s and 1940s. Sung primarily in English, his "concert style" featured Western harmonies and was targeted toward emerging educated, middle-class audiences (2000, 126–130). Timothy Burke has argued that Lever Brother's advertising partnerships with musicians such as Mattaka and Madzikatire were part of a "panoply of innovations and marketing strategies," including "cinema vans, roving demonstrations, fashion shows, contests and give-aways, public festivals, sponsorship of civic groups, spectacular public displays, celebrity endorsements, leaflets, gimmicks, hoardings (billboards), as well as conventional campaigns in media patronized by Africans" (1992, 138). As my colleague Darien Lamen points out, Madzikatire's career also offers an interesting antecedent to the corporate patronage system of Ghanaian hiplife.

11. As Thomas Turino has observed, the 1960s were a decade in which "urban-popular music and dance performance was primarily a nonprofessional or part-time professional activity" (2000, 145). The sponsorship Lever Brothers offered to early entertainers such as Mattaka and Madzikatire was thus instrumental in opening the new and novel possibility of musical entertainment as a full-time, paid career.

12. See for example *Nutshell* (1978, 3). The *Nutshell* was an in-house Lever Brothers publication.

13. Madzikatire's integration of music and theatre, as well as his distinctive costume of a "sombrero hat," coat, and pair of shorts, continue to be emulated by recent performers such as Kapfupi. As Kapfupi explained in a 2006 interview with the *Herald*, "Mukadota inspired me. . . . It is from Mukadota that I have modeled my own career. I am reviving his style, vachiripo vaMukadota [Mukadota is still here]" (Tera 2006).

14. As Angela Impey has observed, Madzikatire focused largely on "problematic issues concerning relationships, sex roles and social morality" (1992, 88).

15. This particular detail is from Dube (2003).

16. For a more thorough discussion of emerging guitar styles in twentieth-century Zimbabwe, see, for example, Brown (1994, 82–83) and Turino (2000).

17. Similar stories are recounted by other artists and craftspeople both in Zimbabwe (Dewey 1986) and further afield (e.g., Herzfeld 2004). Yet, the trope of self-directed learning seems particularly pronounced among mbira players (Kyker 2012).

18. Ngalawa (1995).

19. Mtukudzi's first recording, titled "Stop after Go," was apparently a song about the sequence of traffic lights, produced in 1975 (Mafundikwa 2004; see also Chola 1988).

20. "Dzandimomotera" was issued by the "Harari Special" label, a subsidiary of Gallo. The song "Ndakuneta" appeared on the B side. The single was produced by Phillip Mabena, T. Chogugudza, and H. Mambo. According to Timon Mabaleka, Phillip Mabena was a talent scout for Nkosi.

21. Muzavazi (1979).

22. Sibanda (2001).

23. On flows between urban and rural zones, see, for example, Turino (2000, 24).

24. See, for example, Vail and White (1991, 43).

25. The same hi-hat pattern is used in the mbira-based guitar music of Thomas Mapfumo, but tempo alone is enough to distinguish this particular song as a ngoma piece.

26. While a relatively peaceful atmosphere prevailed in Salisbury and its surrounding townships, urban residents nevertheless experienced material shortages provoked by international sanctions, as well as the restricted mobility imposed on blacks.

27. Incorporating four drums, indigenous performances of *katekwe* feature a lead soloist playing a drum called *mbete-mbete*. This soloist is accompanied by two other performers, one on the *mudarirwa* drum, and the other playing two drums known *dandi* and *mutumba* simultaneously, who jointly assume the responsive function known as kubvumira (Mheta 2005, 46). According to matepe player Chaka Chawasarira, katekwe is performed at a quick tempo in $\frac{12}{8}$ time, with the drummers accompanying dancers executing fast, rhythmic footwork, paired with a shaking motion of the shoulders and upper body. Historically, katekwe appears to have been performed in various contexts, including the installations of new chiefs, the rituals held to celebrate a successful harvest, and the postfunerary rite known as kurova guva. It may also be played either before the formal commencement of spirit possession rituals, or in the secular space located outside of the home in which a bira is being held, suggesting that it retains close associations with ritual practice even in the absence of a directly ceremonial role. In this sense, katekwe appears to fill a ritual function similar to that played by the jerusarema dance performed in Zezuru regions such as Murehwa (see Turino 2000). Pointing toward the need for more extensive ethnographic documentation of ngoma genres, oral accounts of katekwe vary greatly. Reflecting on his childhood experiences in the rural northeast, for example, Mtukudzi identifies katekwe as a performance genre reserved "for the elderly people. It's like mbira music is done by the elderly people. . . . While the elderly people are doing the serious business indoors, that's when they could play [it]." The recently published Zimbabwean musical dictionary *Duramazwi Remimhanzi*, however, offers a contradictory perspective *on katekwe,* emphasizing its associations with agricultural practice and identifying it as a genre performed primarily for secular, rather than ceremonial purposes (Mheta 2005, 46).

28. This perspective is reflected in retroactive assessments published in the Zimbabwean popular press. See, for example, Magaisa (2004).

29. Zvomuya (2004).

30. Lan (1985), 14.

31. For more on this relationship, see Lan (1985, 74).

32. Ibid., 19.

33. Ibid., 74.

34. Ibid., 19.

35. Mukondiwa (2004).

36. Ibid.

37. See, for example, Appadurai (1996).

38. For more on Hancock, see Feld (1996, 2000a). For more on Graceland, see Feld (1988), Hamm (1989), Meintjes (1990), Muller (2004).

39. I take the idea of celebratory and anxious approaches from Feld (2000b). Authors who have lauded the democratizing potential of new technologies, and their ability to challenge existing hegemonies, include Manuel (1993) and Taylor (1997). Scholars who have implicated the deterritorialization of sound in exacerbating inequities between the centers of global power and their peripheries include Feld (2000a, 2000b), Frith (2000), Hamm (1989), Malm (1993), and Wallis and Malm (1992). The concerns articulated by scholars interested in these questions peaked in the 1990s, yet they have remained influential in shaping current approaches to non-Western, or "world," music.

40. Comaroff and Comaroff (1997), xv.

41. Muller (2002), 409. While Muller draws extensively on Derridean notions of the archive, her conception of archiving Africanness in song is also strikingly similar to the Foucauldian concept of the archive as, in the words of David Coplan, a "generative level of textual practice" that exists within a third space "that operates above the level of depository but below that of institutions of discourse" (1994, 20). Existing "between tradition and oblivion, it reveals the rule of a practice that enables statements both to survive and to undergo regular modification" (Foucault 1976, 130; in Coplan 1994, 20).

42. Muller (2002), 427.

43. Mbembe (2001),16.

44. Ibid. Calling attention to the "dialectical, dialogic nature of tradition as practice," David Coplan has similarly observed that tradition "is not simply the reified emblems of authority but the immanence of the past in the cultural certainties of the present" (1994, 19–20). See also Fabian (1998, 20).

45. Thomas Turino has observed that by the mid-1960s, the Rhodesian Broadcasting Corporation had begun to label 78s featuring indigenous songs played on "modern" instruments as "traditional adaptations" (2000, 258). I suggest that this labeling practice is one possible origin for the term "trad music."

46. *Prize Magazine* (1978).

47. Thomas Turino (2000) offers another view of this era of Zimbabwean music making in his chapter "Guitar Bands of the 70s."

48. While the majority of these groups have since faded into obsolescence, the musical movement they set in motion has persisted, producing several subsequent generations of artists deeply invested in bringing an identifiably Zimbabwean sound to both local and global markets. Among the original pioneers of trad music, Mtukudzi is exceptional for his longevity, as one of the few artists from the 1970s who succeeded in maintaining a flourishing local career.

49. See Chimhundu (1980, 43).

50. Magirazi (1978).

51. Chibuswa (1980).

52. Ndlovu (1980). Striking a very different tone, some listeners simply declared themselves "fed up" with popular interpretations of traditional songs, calling instead for greater airplay for more "modern bands" ("Dagger Fan" 1979, Thompson 1980).

53. Mafukidźe (1980).

54. See, for example, Bessant (1994), Frederikse (1984), Kahari (1981), and Pongweni (1982).

55. Periodically, Mtukudzi has similarly been deemed insufficiently political during the liberation war; in particular, he has been accused of writing songs that speak to individual tribulations rather than collective struggles. This perception was current even before independence. Writing in 1979, for example, journalist Christopher Muzavazi described his songs as "full of self-pity," stating: "Pleas to Hosanna, God and Father are constantly featured in his verses. . . . One of his latest songs is entitled Nyarara Mwanawe (Hush My Child). It expresses the belief and the hope that the Almighty hears every earthly plight. The problem is that his answers are delayed but in the end 'everything will be alright.'"

56. Hatugari (2000).

57. Sibanda (2001).

58. Mawuru (2004).

59. See, for example, Bessant (1994) and Vail and White (1991).

3. Singing Hunhu after Independence

1. For various accounts of this performance, see Boot and Salewicz (1995), Toynbee (2007), and White ([1983] 2006).

2. Pongweni (1982), 151.

3. For a linguistic analysis of "Tirikupembera Zimbabwe," see Kwaramba (1997, 74).

4. "Nkosi Sikelel' iAfrika" served as a party anthem for the Zimbabwe African National Union, as well as the African National Congress in South Africa. It is now the national anthem of South Africa.

5. The word *matororo* is the Shonaization of the English word *terrorists*.

6. As Thomas Turino has observed, cosmopolitan social networks can be self-reinforcing, as individuals with similar worldviews "gravitate toward each other," forming alliances with significant cultural impact (Turino 2000, 11).

7. By the time of my fieldwork several decades later, the only person I heard invoke the term *trad music* was Selmor Mtukudzi, who has close ties to the genre both through her father and through her father-in-law, Zexie Manatsa.

8. For an account of the Zimbabwean music industry, see Scannell (2001). While a number of small, private recording studios have emerged in recent years, Clive "Mono" Mukundu, Mtukudzi's former guitarist and one of the most prolific independent studio engineers and producers, told me that the major production and distribution companies seldom accept independently recorded albums, as this would undercut their attempts to maintain a monopoly on both the recording and distribution sides of the music business (Personal communication, 14 November 2008).

9. For an early account of the Black Spirits, see Paradzai (1979); see also Masunda (1992).

10. The story of the Black Spirits' ill-fated tour joins a long litany of similar accounts illustrating the difficulties of reconciling the motives of musicians with those

of international promoters, producers, and audiences (see, for example, Brusila 2001, 47). Among Mtukudzi's few successful international engagements prior to the late 1990s were a series of shows in West Germany in 1990, followed by a tour of Austria and Switzerland in 1994. Both were sponsored by the Vienna Institute of Culture and Co-operation, together with the Swiss-Zimbabwe Friendship Association. For more on these tours, see Garande (1994b) and *People's Voice* (1990).

11. These band members are identified in Polizzi (1988).

12. For more on chigiyo in a rural context, see Perman (2008).

13. Mutambara (1992).

14. Polizzi (1988).

15. Mutambara (1992).

16. Unpublished interview with Banning Eyre (1993).

17. Chola (1988).

18. See, for example, Patel, Simunyu, and Gwanzura (1995).

19. Hamba (1997).

20. See, for example, Berliner ([1978] 1993, 73).

21. As Janzen observes, the principle of call-and-response is fundamental to ngoma (1991, 291).

22. Monson's description of "multilayered, stratified, interactive frames of musical, social, and symbolic action" has been particularly influential in shaping my thinking on call and response relationships in Zimbabwean music making (1999, 32).

23. Indeed, Louise Meintjes has suggested that good ngoma performances are precisely those in which "dancers, drummers, singers, and clappers—leaders and team members—meld sound and movement into a dense experience that is at once coherent and imminent: it is dense with internal tensions almost out of balance" (2004, 175). Illustrating how this may be achieved in practice, Thomas Turino has observed that indigenous Shona musical aesthetics are distinguished not only by densely overlapping parts, but also by buzzy timbres and a wide intonational range, resulting in "a kind of *masking function,* in which the individual contributions of neophytes will not stand out, making insecure entrances and contributions possible" (2000, 55).

24. Keil (1995), 13.

25. As Floyd explains, call-response also offers an interpretive framework for evaluating the very cultural forms it is so intimately involved in producing, through "perceptive and evaluative acts and expressions . . . of discovering, distinguishing, and explaining cultural and musical value" (2002, 59). The trope of call-response, in other words, is simultaneously a type of musical practice and a form of indigenous musical criticism.

26. Drawing upon Stuckey (1987), Floyd includes "elements of the calls, cries, and hollers; call-and-response devices; additive rhythms and polyrhythms; heterophony, pendular thirds, blue notes, bent notes, and elisions; hums, moans, grunts, vocables, and other rhythmic-oral declamations, interjections, and punctuations; off-beat melodic phrasings and parallel intervals and chords; constant repetition of rhythmic and melodic figures and phrases (from which riffs and vamps would be derived); timbral distortions of various kinds; musical individuality within collectivity; game-rivalry; hand-clapping,

foot-patting, and approximations thereof; and the metronomic foundational pulse that underlies all Afro-American music" (2002, 51–52). For a detailed analysis of ngoma performance that engages many of these elements, see Meintjes (2004).

27. Welsh-Asante, for example, suggests that mhururu is a form of praise and approval for "some extraordinary feat or performance" (1985, 393).

28. Mtukudzi's reference to Elizabeth Tadeerera is indirect; his lyrics refer to her simply as "Katarina," the role she played in Safirio Madzikatire's long-running musical drama *Mhuri YaVaMukadota*.

29. Mtimba (1987).

30. Among other changes, Mtukudzi names Southern African countries in the new version of the song, rather than his Zimbabwean musical counterparts.

31. Mashava (1999).

32. Munyuki (2001).

33. Snodia et al. (2014). For more on the ideological concept of the Frontline States, see Honwana (1990).

34. See also Lalla Touré's assessment of family planning initiatives in Africa, which suggests that radio spots sponsored by the ZNFPC's Male Motivation Campaign had the greatest reach of any media material designed to convey the campaign's message to men (Touré 1996, 5).

35. "Rongai Mhuri," Oliver Mutukudzi (*sic*) and Various Artists. Produced by T. Mabaleka, Engineer David Scobie. Side one, "Rongai Mhuri," 7:10. Side two, "Hwema Handirase," 5:36, "Nyarara Mwana," 3:32. As Mtukudzi recalls, "Rongai Mhuri" was first released on the album *Sugar Pie* (1988), followed by the collaborative version, recorded at bequest of the ZNFPC, later that year.

36. This line is also commonly sung to the mbira song "Taireva." See Matiure (2011).

37. Moyse (1989).

38. Indeed, Mtukudzi has repeatedly called it his single most memorable show (see, for example, Mabasa 2001).

39. *People's Voice* (1990).

40. Complicating matters, a local subsidiary of Gallo, previously known as Teal Records, was attempting to break away as a semi-independent label, known as the Zimbabwe Music Company (ZMC). From the beginning, Gallo and the ZMC were deeply intertwined, maintain a single recording venture in the form of Shed Studio. By 1994, they would merge into a single entity known as Gramma/ZMC.

41. Chola (1986).

42. Mtukudzi's first album with RTP, *Strange Isn't It?* (1988) was recorded at Frontline Studio.

43. See, for example, Brusila (2001, 41). As well as recording and releasing his own material, Mtukudzi has begun to sign other artists to the Tuku Music label.

44. Gramma continues to retain title to over two hundred of his earliest songs, many of which they have rereleased in recent years. All the while, record company executives continue to deny Mtukudzi any significant royalties from the sale of his music. See for example Ncube (1996).

45. Polizzi (1988). "Afro jazz" is also called "township jazz," a term Linda Williams describes as having been adopted from South African musicians and referring to a "hybrid form of African and African American music" featuring an upright bass, electric guitars, a drummer, and blues lyrics sung in vernacular languages (1997, 293).

46. Makuyana (2002). As Kofi Agawu has similarly observed, essentializing terms such as jitaj may read "the concept of intertextuality rather too literally and . . . [run] the risk of missing the essence of the currently unfolding drama," reducing the complexities of musical syncretism to a search for precise origins (2003, 147).

47. See http://www.tukumusic.com/news_79.html (Accessed 26 March 2009).

48. See Rommen (2007, 135). As Line Grenier and Jocelyne Guilbault have observed, determinations regarding musical genre function not only to categorize musical sounds, but also to "produce statements through which other objects are constructed, and hence, other sets of issues are addressed" (1999, 362). Involving both artists and audiences, the politics of naming and genre are thus "informed by issues related to power and legitimacy of one sort or another—by the will to power" (Rommen 2007, 131).

49. Deeply embedded within the visual framework of *Jit*, the rich sounds of Zimbabwean popular music thus extend beyond the edges of the film's frame. Drawing on modes of signification already familiar to listeners from other contexts, ranging from ecclesiastical traditions to commercial advertising, the film's soundtrack reminds us just how difficult it is to separate out the many interwoven strands of popular culture. Long noted as a predominant feature of popular music throughout the African continent, this intermingling of various forms of expressive culture is particularly prominent in Mtukudzi's music. Through processes of pastiche and bricolage, he mobilizes an astonishingly wide array of proverbs, poems, folktales, musical quotations, dance styles, and other expressive resources within his distinctive style of Tuku music. See, for example, Barber (1987), Fabian (1998), Waterman ([1986] 1990).

50. See Zindi (2011).

51. "Mumweya" is based on John 4:23–24, "But the hour cometh, and now is, when the true worshippers shall worship the Father in spirit and in truth: for the Father seeketh such to worship him. God is a Spirit: and they that worship him must worship him in spirit and in truth." Sung in Shona, Mtukudzi's decidedly up-tempo version of the hymn is highly syncopated, departing from the relatively more straightforward renditions common to religious settings.

4. Neria

1. The piece was choreographed by dancer Gilbert Douglas, one of the company's founding members, who first encountered Mtukudzi when Tumbuka and the Black Spirits were both invited to perform at a festival in the Ivory Coast in 1997. In subsequent years, Tumbuka would proceed to dance to several of Mtukudzi's songs, including "Mai Varamba," choreographed by Neville Campbell, "Hear Me Lord," choreographed by Sam Felo, and "Perekedza," choreographed by Douglas. Tumbuka members would also appear in a subsequent music video for "Perekedza," produced by South Africa's Channel O.

2. Media for Development (1999, 2), cited in Lund (1999, 220).

3. See, for example, Bourdillon (1987).

4. Film scholar Giuliana Lund has observed that through this act, Neria "complements her day in court by successfully negotiating the demands of tradition" by completing the kugara nhaka ritual (Lund 1999, 220).

5. As Mtukudzi recalls, Susan Chenjerai was not a backing vocalist, but one of several lead vocalists with the Wagon Wheels, who was herself "being backed" by other members of the group. Prior to joining the Wagon Wheels, Chenjerai had also sung with Mtukudzi's childhood musical hero, Safirio Madzikatire. Her relationship with Madzikatire would extend for several more decades through her role as Mai Rwizi in the serialized radio and television drama *Mhuri YaVaMukadota*.

6. This response extends to South African audiences, with reports in the popular press of listeners declaring, "Now you're going to see people cry. This song always makes me cry." This particular quote is from an article held in the archives of Debbie Metcalfe titled "Joy that makes you cry." Written by Gwen Ansell, it was published in an unknown source on March 2, 2000.

7. Klaits (2010), 15.

8. See http://www.zimbablog.com/2008/09/18/heroes/ (Accessed 17 May, 2016).

9. *Horizon* (1992).

10. Riber (2000). Similarly, an undated memo from the MFD states, "Another reason for the continuing popularity of the film, is that it features Zimbabwean music star, Oliver Mtukudzi. He acts in the film and his music is featured throughout. He reported . . . recently that he still gets requests at almost every local concert for the film's signature song, 'Neria.'"

11. The original album demonstrates a preference for the synthesized sounds predominant in the early 1990s, with a keyboard and drum machine, as well as significant reverb on Mtukudzi's voice. A subsequent rerecording, released in 2001, exhibits Mtukudzi's shift toward a more acoustically grounded sound, eliminating the synthesizer and incorporating a pair of conga drums, which sound similar to the indigenous Zimbabwean ngoma.

12. Dhlamini (2005).

13. Media for Development (1989).

14. Ibid.

15. Ibid.

16. Media for Development (1992).

17. Other songs on his soundtrack, such as "Tarirai Mhuri Yapera," or "Look, the family is finished," and "Chengetai Mai NaBaba," or "Take care of mother and father," further reinforce this focus.

18. Hannan ([1959] 2000), 433. Other expressions involving the heart include *kuzvidya moyo*, or to worry (literally "to eat one's own heart"), *kurasa moyo*, or to lose heart, and *kudzora moyo*, or to show restraint (literally "to pull back the heart").

19. For more on heart-related idioms and imagery in Shona proverbs, poems, and song, see Chimhundu (1980), Hodza and Fortune (1979), and Mberi (2003).

20. Pearce (1990), 150.

21. See Bourdillon (1987) and Gelfand (1971, 71).

22. My definition of masiyiranwa is taken from Hannan ([1959] 2000, 409).

23. Indeed, family disputes about inheritance "do not only occur about possessions, but also develop sometimes in connection with ritual procedures" (Swift 1989, 34). In my experiences attending the *kurova guva* ceremony held concurrently with the *nhaka* inheritance rite, I have observed conflicts over many aspects of how the ceremony should be held. Conveying a single, fictionalized narrative of inheritance disputes within one family, Neria disregards the many variations in how customary inheritance may unfold, including regional differences as well as those based on the circumstances of individual families.

24. Unpublished interview with Banning Eyre (2000).

25. Mashava (1999), 4.

26. Whaley (1993).

27. Ibid.

28. Chisora (1993).

29. Among them, *Mapisarema AOliver Mtukudzi* featured hymns collected from Mtukudzi's previous albums, compiled by ZMC producer Sylvanos Mtizwa.

30. Following its emergence in the 1990s, gospel has grown to become one of the nation's most popular musical genres, with dozens of new artists joining Manyeruke and Chipanga. Mtukudzi's perspective of the emergence of gospel in the 1990s closely parallels Ezra Chitando's scholarly account of Zimbabwean gospel music, which "outlines the historical development of popular music in Zimbabwe alongside locating the emergence of gospel music in the politically and economically challenging 1990s" (2002, 5).

31. "Rumbidzai Jehova" was inspired by Psalms 150, verse 3–6, "Praise Him with the sound of the trumpet; Praise Him with the lute and harp! Praise Him with the timbrel and dance; Praise Him with stringed instruments and flutes! Praise Him with loud cymbals; Praise Him with clashing cymbals! Let everything that has breath praise the Lord. Praise the Lord!"

32. In $\frac{4}{4}$ time, "Mumweya" opens with a catchy, arpeggiated guitar riff, which is quickly joined by the organ melodies and active, syncopated bass lines typical of South Africa mbaqanga. Above them, Mtukudzi's voice seems to float as he delivers lyrics inspired by John 4:24, "The Lord seeks out the one who worships him in spirit and in truth," elongating his syllables against the song's otherwise straight rhythmic feel. Irresistibly lively and eminently danceable, "Mumweya" would become a favorite for listeners and reviewers alike. See for example Ncube (1996).

33. Chitando (2002), 7.

5. Return to Dande

1. Munyuki (2001). See also Munyuki (2002). Fred Zindi likewise told me that *Tuku Music* "was the album that brought him back to prominence."

2. Radio DJ Leander Kandiero similarly observed, "A lot of his songs make sense to me, and I appreciate his arrangements. But I would also want to hasten to say from '98, when he released *Tuku Music*, there was a different sound that came from Oliver."

3. As Hodza and Fortune have observed, "The fact that the founding father has left his descendants their land, and that he and other ancestors lie buried in it, constitutes

a very real bond between the clan and its territory. A man in his own country is called mwana wevhu (child of the soil), and this name distinguishes him from those whose links with the land are not so close" (1979, 14). Linguist Alec Pongweni poetically describes sons of the soil as indigenous subjects "hugging the ground of African culture" (1982, 1).

4. In a review published by the state-owned *Herald*, journalist Funny Mashava (1999) likewise referred to Mtukudzi a musical superstar "getting better all the time. We all know the heights he scaled with Dande [Dzoka Uyamwe]."

5. Lan (1985), 9.

6. Highlighting the importance of female kin in a society that is often described as strongly patrilineal, Mtukudzi notes that his grandfather "moved from Nyangavi to Madziva because that's where his mother came from. So he stayed there with the uncles until he loved the place. He said, 'Oh wow, let me build here.' That's how we came to be in Madziva."

7. As Lan has remarked, close associations between territory and clan enable many people to "indicate precisely where each clan of significance to them has its origin" (1985, 24).

8. See Kyker (2010). Jane Sugarman has made similar observation about the social nature of identity in her work among Prespa Albanian communities (1997, 217).

9. During my fieldwork in 2008–2009, for example, "Dzoka Uyamwe" appeared regularly in request letters sent to radio programs such as *Kwaziso*, in which broadcasters read greetings between distant kin aloud on air.

10. Thomas Turino, who likewise interviewed Chigamba, has observed, "For people like . . . Chigamba, and others who define themselves largely in terms of indigenous lifeways, ancestral spirits are also considered in the decisions affecting daily life" (2000, 35).

11. See, for example, Muller (1999, 2).

12. See, for example, Turino (1998, 95).

13. The fact that this muted mbira-guitar style is only used when other aspects of the song, such as the vocals, are prominent, may account for the fact that many listeners do not immediately identify mbira-guitar playing as a feature of Mtukudzi's music.

14. Zimbabweans distinguish between the sharp report of makwa handclapping, which has a sound that mimics wooden clappers, and the more natural handclapping style called *manja*. (Musekiwa Chingodza, personal communication, 14 July 2014).

15. See Leon (2007, 22).

16. Hosho are often boiled in salted water to improve their hardness before they are scraped out to remove seeds and debris and filled with hota seeds. Sometimes, a pattern of small holes may be burned into the gourds using a hot awl, penetrating from their outer surface into their interior cavity. A woven wire or string closure may also replace the more conventional corncob or newspaper plug inserted to close the larger opening through which the hosho were cleaned. As well as serving a decorative function, both of these measures improve the sound of the hosho by allowing dust and small debris to escape, maintaining the sharpness of the instrument's percussive tone.

17. On the other hand, hosho are not commonly played in sungura, which has its roots further afield in the rhumba music of Central Africa.

18. While Mtukudzi's first hosho player was a male percussionist by the nickname of Chigwedzi, the instrument is often associated with female musicians. As the years went on, hosho would increasingly be played by Black Spirits' female backing singers, such as Mwendi Chibindi, Mary Bell, and Namatai Mubariki. Both in my fieldwork and in many written accounts, I have come across many descriptions of male mbira players accompanied on hosho by female kin, including wives and daughters. See, for example, Impey (1992, 112).

19. Tracey ([1932] 1969), 95.

20. Berliner ([1978] 1993), 241–245. See also Tracey (1963, 25).

21. Turino (2000), 75. See also Turino (1998, 87).

22. Paul Berliner's work, for example, featured several musicians based in Highfield (1993). Outside of Berliner's account, other musicians such as Sekuru Tute Wincil Chigamba were also living at Highfield at the time.

23. For example, Sekuru Chigamba recalls how his neighbors perceived his mbira playing as "something for beggars" in the 1960s. Following independence, however, the Chigamba family's participation in the government-run National Dance Company would indelibly change this perception. As Sekuru Chigamba recalls, "The people who had laughed at us, they are now saying, 'You have a wonderful gift.' I said, 'But, look, you were mocking us, saying we are beggars?' They said, 'Truly, you have a wonderful gift.' Others said, 'Yes, we were laughing at you. We had no idea where this could take you. But now it has taken you quite far.'"

24. See Meintjes (2003) for a detailed ethnography of the type of creative practices mbaqanga artists devised in recording studios in South Africa.

25. One article commenting on this phenomenon was titled simply, "Tuku Concert—The Day the Nose Brigades Became Africanized!" (Kanyuchi 2001).

26. Mpofu (2001).

27. Maravanyika (1999).

28. See http://mg.co.za/article/1999-01-29-magic-in-mahubes (Accessed 1 January 2010). Among them were artists such as Zambian singer Maureen Lilanda, who would later record with Mtukudzi at his studio.

29. *Southern Times* (2005).

30. *Jive Fanzine* (2000).

31. Hatugari (2001).

32. Keith Goddard, personal communication, 27 January 2009.

33. For more on the genesis of *world music*, a term that originated among music industry executives seeking to market sounds from peripheral regions to consumers in political and economic centers, see Frith (2000). One especially prominent theme in the world music literature is a preoccupation with unraveling increasingly complex relationships between the local and the global, as world music is seen to simultaneously undermine and reinforce our sense of place as local identities are transformed and reorganized under new global networks (Lipsitz 1994). Issues of copyright, owner-

ship, power, and control within the music industry have also come to the fore (Feld 2000a, 2000b; Hamm 1989).

34. Rogovoy (1999).

35. Ibid.

36. Unpublished interview with Banning Eyre (1998).

37. Pareles (1999).

38. Anderson (2002).

39. Stokes (2004), 53.

40. Brusila (2001), 52.

41. Chemere and Genti (2000) and Sibanda (2000). "Rega Kuropodza" was later re-named "Kuropodza," and its lyrics are discussed in the introduction to this book.

42. Describing this event, one local journalist remarked that the singer "stuck to his guns and belted out songs with the theme of the day, which read; 'Poverty, Population and Development.' It must have been difficult to fit in the programme and come up with a compilation of songs that have everything to do with Aids, population and poverty. But Tuku did it with ease" (Mbiriyamveka 2002).

43. Metcalfe (1990).

44. Moore (2005), x.

45. See, for example, Alexander (2006, 185); see also Mamdani (2009, 6).

46. See Chaumba et al. (2003, 544).

47. Ibid., 534.

48. As one Harare resident would tell me, "urban people were very much against this land reform program. As you can see, the situation in Zimbabwe now, the majority of the people don't have food because of that disturbance."

49. See, for example, Hanke and Kwok (2009, 355).

50. One notable exception is Matabeleland, which was subject to intense state-sponsored violence during the protracted military pacification campaigns of the 1980s, known as Gukurahundi.

51. This phrase is originally from Sithole (2001) and subsequently appeared in Chaumba et al. (2003, 534).

52. See Chaumba et al. (2003, 541).

53. Agawu (2003), xvii. For various accounts of music and resistance in Southern Africa during the colonial period, see for example Coplan (1994), Muller (1999), Pongweni (1982), Vail and White (1991).

54. According to Chaumba et al., "in essence it has come to refer to a time and space of at best confusion and nonsense, and at worse disorder and chaos" (2003, 540). The term's widespread rise was at least partly related to musician Marko Sibanda's hit single "Jambanja Pahotera," which narrated "a fight in a hotel between two naked couples discovering they had exchanged partners in separate extra-marital affairs" (Ibid.)

55. In a Tanzanian setting, Alex Perullo places similar emphasis on the term *bongo*, which "literally means 'wisdom' or 'brains' but is slang for 'survival of the fittest' or 'doing anything to survive'" (2011, 8).

6. Listening as Politics

1. As Jocelyn Alexander notes, land claims were central to political contests during the postcolonial period (2006, 152–179).

2. Bennett's land was marked for resettlement during his stint in parliament, and after assaulting ZANU-PF Justice Minister Patrick Chinamasa during a heated debate on the government's controversial land reform program, he would end up serving a portion of his term in prison. As Alexander has suggested, ZANU-PF local committees lost support in Chimanimani "as a result of their inability to deliver on wartime promises, exclusion from decision-making and lack of financial support" (2006, 173).

3. In part, Mataure's observation reflects different musical preferences in urban and rural areas, with rural audiences gravitating strongly toward the sungura music of Alec Macheso, Sulumani Chimbetu, and Nicholas Zacharia. As Mataure himself told me, "If you were to put Alec Macheso there, he would kill the place."

4. Eyre (2001), 77.

5. *Zimbabwe Independent* (2000).

6. The MDC's slogan, "Change your ways—Chinja maitiro—Guqula izenzo" plays explicitly upon this desire for change.

7. This account is taken from an article in the personal archives of Debbie Metcalfe. Written by Thomas Deve, it appeared in an unknown source, possible the *Daily News*, sometime in 2002. It reads: "The sing-along from the audience helped me appreciate the real meaning of the word fanatic. When the band performed *Wasakara*, some fans audibly substituted the lyrics on the chorus with something that sounded like, *Bob wachembera*. It was not the first time that Mtukudzi's fans created new lyrics to suit their whims." A similar report appeared in *Daily News* coverage of a show held the previous year in Bulawayo, with Mduduzi Mathuthu (2001) writing that the song offered "just what the people seemed to be waiting for as they went into a frenzy putting words in Tuku's mouth when the need arose."

8. Living in exile in South Africa, a former election agent for the MDC explained the use of red cards as a political symbol as follows: "And we had red cards, we used to flash them, saying Mugabe off the pitch! In a football match, when you are penalized, you are supposed to leave the stadium, get off the pitch, you can no longer play football. So, when we flash the red cards, we are saying we are the referees and Mugabe had gone against the regulations, so he has to get off the pitch. That's the meaning of the red card" (Orner and Holmes 2010, 158). For another account of how "Wasakara" became a party anthem for the MDC, see Mpondi (2004, 179).

9. Eyre (2001), 80.

10. See both Achebe (2000), 97 and http://www.ted.com/index.php/talks/chimamanda_adichie_the_danger_of_a_single_story.html (Accessed 23 January 2010).

11. See, for example, Oyewumi (1997), 31, and Kyker (2014).

12. As Dewey has observed, the vadzimu "represent the collective ideals of the Shona and are the essence of morality" (1986, 64).

13. Samkange and Samkange (1980), 51.

14. Sibanda (2004), 48.

15. Unpublished interview with Banning Eyre (2001). Part of this quote appears in Eyre (2001), 54.

16. Mtukudzi's approach thus reflects Leroy Vail and Landeg White's observation that "the various forms of oral poetry in sub-Saharan Africa are licensed by a freedom of expression which violates normal convention—that chiefs and headmen may be criticized by the followers, husbands by their wives, fathers by their sons, employers or overseers by their workers, officials and politicians by their underlings, and even Life Presidents by their subjects, in ways that the prevailing social and political codes would not normally permit, so long as it is done in poetry" (1991, 43).

17. Eyre (2001), 80.

18. A report issued by Amnesty International described this law as "the foundation of Rhodesian security legislation" (1976).

19. The *Standard* (2001a).

20. The *Standard* (2001b).

21. The *Standard* (2001a).

22. Murimwa (2001).

23. Kariuki (2002).

24. Eyre (2001), 81.

25. The *Standard* (2001d). Heightening controversy over the song, the concert promoter was perceived by ZANU-PF members as an MDC sympathizer.

26. For more on radio play and censorship, see Eyre (2001).

27. Mutsaka (2001), 1.

28. This is quoted in Eyre (2001, 76) as a quotation from the *Mirror*, but no exact citation is offered.

29. The *Standard* (2001c).

30. Mpofu (2001).

31. Muzavazi (1979).

32. Hatugari (2000).

33. Nolan (2002).

34. Chu (2003), 51.

35. For a more thorough discussion of these expectations of music's potential "to make radical positions available through new sounds, new forms, new styles," see, for example, Taylor (1997, 206). See also Fabian (1998, 18).

36. Hatugari (2002).

37. Yet another of Mapfumo's explicitly political songs is "Ndiani Waparadza Musha," or "Who has destroyed our home?" (*Chimurenga '98*, 1998).

38. Sibanda (2004), 45.

39. Chikowero (2006), 44.

40. Unpublished interview with Banning Eyre (2001).

41. Throughout the song, Mtukudzi catalogues a number of different professions, suggesting that no matter their relative status, they are all dependent on the work of the farmer. Among them, he includes hunters, writers, dancers, mbira players, manual laborers, children, elders, paramount chiefs, rulers, spies, gangsters, and also people who simply take from others.

42. Zvomuya (2004).

43. Thram (2006), 81.

44. *Southern Times* (2005).

45. Rogers (2002), 18.

46. Another song that has been interpreted as political is "Magumo" (*Vhunze Moto*, 2002). See Sibanda (2004).

47. Zvomuya (2004).

48. Another local journalist similarly wrote, "The album cover depicts a map of the country in flames, and the track from which the title comes, *Moto Moto* ("Fire is Fire"), is a moving Shona ballad that fans interpret as a warning to President Mugabe of impending catastrophe" (Rogers 2002).

49. Bayart (1993).

50. Pearce (1990), 147.

51. Originally invited to deliver an official welcome a day earlier, during the festival's opening ceremony, the minister failed to appear until the following day. Much to the consternation of festival organizers, he promptly demanded the opportunity to give an official speech, throwing the festival order into disarray. As organizing committee members privately observed, they had already sung the national anthem at the time scheduled for minister's speech the previous day, thereby fulfilling their patriotic duty despite his absence.

52. *Zimbabwe Independent* (2000).

53. Strathern (1995), 8.

54. Werbner (1998), 15.

7. What Shall We Do?

1. The Centre was founded by a white Zimbabwean named Lynde Francis, also among the first women in the nation to reveal her HIV positive status, in the early 1990s.

2. During one of our interviews, Mtukudzi himself described a similar experience when listening to the songs of Safirio Madzikatire:

> Mtukudzi: At times he would come up with a piece that you feel, "Ahhhh . . . maybe he saw me doing this!" He was that kind of a person. He was so good, and so natural, that you don't despise what he's doing. You know it's happening, it's the truth, and you know the truth is painful. The truth. . .
> Kyker: Chiri murusakasaka. . .
> Mtukudzi: . . . chinozvinzwira. Exactly. Exactly. You see?

3. See Kyker (2011).

4. See http://www.who.int/gho/hiv/epidemic_status/deaths_text/en/ (Accessed 1 May 2015).

5. According to the WHO, Africa accounted for 73 percent of all the people dying from AIDS in 2012. http://www.who.int/gho/hiv/epidemic_status/deaths_text/en / (Accessed 1 May 2015). According to the Foundation for AIDS Research, Africa accounted for 1.5 million out of global total of 2.1 million new infections in 2013. http:// www.amfar.org/worldwide-aids-stats/ (Accessed 1 May 2015).

6. See http://www.avert.org/hiv-aids-zimbabwe.htm#sthash.hDh3Hq4x.dpuf (Accessed 1 May 2015).

7. See http://news.bbc.co.uk/2/hi/health/background_briefings/aids/339974.stm (Accessed 1 May 2015).

8. WHO (2006), 176. Life expectancy had hovered around sixty years in 1990. http://www.trust.org/spotlight/Zimbabwe-crisis (Accessed 1 May 2015).

9. See http://www.unaids.org/en/regionscountries/countries/zimbabwe (Accessed 1 May 2015).

10. See Gregson et al. (2010).

11. See http://www.unaids.org/en/regionscountries/countries/zimbabwe (Accessed 1 May 2015).

12. Encouraging us to view disease as primarily a "pathology of power," Farmer points to the structural inequalities that create erasure alongside suffering, masking illness even as they establish the conditions necessary for it to thrive (2003, xxviii).

13. See Farmer (2003, xxviii; [1992] 2006, 262).

14. "Marginality and Invisibility in African Medical Practice," unpublished talk given at the Dahlem Conference on "Knowledge, Domination and the Public in Africa" (Berlin, 21–25 March 2011).

15. As ethnomusicologist Kathleen Van Buren has observed, "music—in some of the most difficult of human circumstances—is memorializing, educating, binding people together, healing, and so much more" (2010, 218).

16. Ministry of Health, 1987.

17. Letter written by Debbie Metcalfe in reply to an undated letter from the Office of the Masvingo Provincial Medical Director to Sue Powell (11 June 1991).

18. As Gary Tomlinson has observed, "The very fact that the most specifically meaningful capacity of language is sidestepped at the moment of their irruption adds to their impact, granting them power to encapsulate and deepen a song's most general import" (2007, 85).

19. As Mtukudzi would similarly observe, "People were so arrogant about AIDS. They didn't want to hear it" (Korfmacher 2001, 36).

20. Unpublished interview with Banning Eyre (1988).

21. Dent (2007), 456–457. In the case of Brazilian artist Pena Branca, who won a Latin Grammy for a solo recording produced after losing his brother and vocal partner Xavatinho, Dent suggests that rural music continually enacts the importance of consanguineous kinship as a way of organizing social life. Foregrounding brotherhood in similar ways, both Mtukudzi's solo album and his later song "Akoromoka Awa" likewise constitute important musical gestures toward the kinship relations of hunhu.

22. For more on "Mabasa," see Kyker (2011) and Sibanda (2004, 50).

23. As Deborah Korfmacher similarly observes, "'Todii' is the most popular song in other African countries in which Tuku regularly performs, including South Africa, Tanzania, Zambia, and Botswana" (2001, 37).

24. In her linguistic analysis of Thomas Mapfumo's music, Alice Dadirai Kwaramba has suggested that "questions do not propose that the musician is genuinely enquiring. . . . Instead the questions are indirectly highlighting some facts that both the musician

and the audience already know, thus encouraging the audience to do something about it" (1997, 48).

25. "Todii" would prove so enduringly popular among South African audiences that Thabo Mbeki would personally invite Mtukudzi to perform the song during South Africa's tenth anniversary of independence, in 2004. As Metcalfe reflected, there were political dimensions to this invitation, as Mbeki "chose Tuku to come and play that song, but by then, he was using it politically. Because he knew, he'd been damned for not recognizing AIDS, blah, blah, blah, and he had slowly only himself slowly cottoned on that Tuku—who, in television public appearances, said is one of his absolutely favorite artists—he now, he sort of expediently brought Tuku in to play that song. 'Cause it showed that Mbeki now, in a nice way, had sort of accepted the AIDS pandemic, by the time the tenth anniversary actually occurred, of independence."

26. The closest Mtukudzi comes to identifying AIDS is through his use of the word *hutachiwana*, a generic term that can refer to any germ or virus, in the lyrics to "Todii." Indeed, Silindiwe Sibanda has suggested that in using the term *hutachiwana*, Mtukudzi directly references HIV/AIDS (2004, 52–53). In the course of my fieldwork, however, observation of HIV-prevention campaigns suggested that hutachiwana is rarely used alone to refer to AIDS. Instead, it is regularly modified to *hutachiwana hwe HIV/AIDS*, or, "the HIV/AIDS virus." Mtukudzi's use of the word hutachiwana thus seems at best an oblique reference to AIDS, as it could potentially be interpreted to refer to any other type of illness.

27. Reporting on fieldwork conducted in Harare, linguists cite an elderly preacher who explains this term by saying, "The AIDS virus is like the thieves of Harare. You don't know where they will waylay you. They can attack you on a very familiar path" (Mashiri et al. 2002, 226). More explicitly, one young man in Highfield township told me that local residents sometimes called HIV/AIDS *"masofa panze,"* or "sofas outside," in reference to the common practice of removing furniture from the house in order to make room for mourners at a funeral.

28. For Barz, the use of such local terminology is one step toward breaking through the "linguistic effort by other communities to assign the virus and disease a nameless, unlabeled status" (2006, 111).

29. "Yakauya AIDS" is available on the compilation album *Hot Hits Volume 2* (2013).

30. Mashiri et al. (2002), 221.

31. See also Sibanda (2004, 53).

32. See, for example, Alviso (2011) and Vambe and Mawadza (2001).

33. See Kyker (2012).

34. After spending time in the Kenyan community of Kawangware, for example, ethnomusicologist Kathleen Van Buren concluded that the neighborhood was one of the many places that "have been so inundated by messages about HIV and AIDS that people have stopped listening (2010, 208–209).

35. Mtukudzi's description of marital rape is given additional cultural depth by the wording he uses in the second iteration of this line, which literally reads, "how does it feel to be raped by he who paid your brideprice?"

36. Mutakati (2007).

37. Ibid.

38. The authors quoted from what was purportedly Chibindi's diary, which included references to how Chibindi began "going out with Oliver Mtukudzi" while on tour in the United Kingdom in 1998. Immediately after the article was published, a series of lawsuits resulted in a court order suppressing any further publication of the alleged diary.

39. Mazara and Mukondiwa (2003).

40. Mtukudzi would make a public statement denying these rumors, saying, "'I don't have Aids [*sic*]. Most people have been spreading these silly rumours'" (Mutakati 2007).

41. Ibid.

42. See http://www.topix.com/forum/who/oliver-mtukudzi/T4USLLKT1ABPUA 7DS (Accessed 3 May 2009).

43. See http://newzim.proboards.com/index.cgi?board=general&action=print&th read=74471, (Accessed 3 May 2009).

44. See http://www.fingaz.co.zw/fingaz/2003/December/December4/4300.shtml (Accessed 3 May 2009).

45. This quote comes from an undated article in the personal archives of Debbie Metcalfe. Published in the *Standard*, it was written by Trevor Muhonde and Bertha Shoko, and titled "News and Noisemakers of 2003."

46. Sterling (2001), 6–7.

47. As David Coplan has observed, structures of feeling are particularly valuable in understanding performance in "relating the articulation of experience to larger social forces and expressions of ideology, of emotions, perceptions, and reflections to the structure of reality." Accordingly, the "singer who desires to shake the nation with a song about his own experience must possess an intuitive seismograph, sensing the fault lines between social reality and social aspiration" (1994, 28–29).

48. See http://zimgossips.blogspot.com/2012/10/mai-chisamba-turns-60-i-get-phone -calls.html (Accessed 1 May 2015). The Mai Chisamba show is sponsored in part by PSI. The episode filmed at Pakare Paye focused specifically on questions of disclosing one's HIV status.

49. Barz (2006), 59.

50. Fabian (1998), 21.

8. Listening in the Wilderness

1. "Sarura Wako," or "Choose yours," playfully encourages young boys and girls to select a partner, preparing them for more serious courtship later in adolescence.

2. *Sekuru* could also mean maternal uncle.

3. While estimates vary, the largest place 1.2 million Zimbabwean migrants in South Africa, as well as an additional 1.2 million in the United Kingdom (Mbiba 2005).

4. See for example Mhiripiri (2010).

5. Sigauke (2008).

6. The tour was organized by Ritmo Artists, a small world music promotion company run by David Garr of Austin, Texas; the company has since ceased operations.

7. Mtukudzi's performance in Dallas was organized by the Zimbabwean expatriate company Africa Rhythms, which has also promoted concerts by gospel singer Mechanic Manyeruke, as well as a diasporic musical group formed in Dallas, called The Mambos.

8. As Mupombwa further observed, the soundscape of Mtukudzi's performance is marked by linguistic as well as musical dimensions. In her words, "the first thing I noticed when I got to the show was that there were a lot of people using Shona." Like Mupombwa, the majority of listeners I interviewed during Mtukudzi's 2007 tour, as well as during my subsequent fieldwork in Zimbabwe, were Shona speakers.

9. Reflecting the larger position of listening within ethnomusicology, relatively little attention has been directed toward musical reception in diasporic contexts. Among the few ethnographies of diasporic listening are Isabel O'Hagin and David Harnish's (2001) account of the musical culture of Latino migrant workers in the American Midwest, and Hae-Kyung Um's (2000) largely quantitative analysis of listening within the Korean diaspora in the former USSR.

10. Zimbabwe's internal migration history includes large-scale, forced relocations to administrative "Tribal Trust Lands," massive flows of labor to South Africa throughout the colonial era, and the displacement of Tonga-speaking communities during the construction of the Kariba dam. In addition, large numbers of people were compelled to relocate to "protected villages" during Zimbabwe's liberation struggle in the 1970s (Ranger 1985, 266).

11. See Tevera and Zinyama (2002, 2).

12. See, for example, Andersson (2001, 84) and Mbiba (2005, 16).

13. Mhiripiri (2010), 215; see also Vambe (2004).

14. Mhiripiri (2010), 215.

15. Tevera and Zinyama (2002), 4.

16. Because of Mtukudzi's careful efforts to maintain political neutrality, he has avoided the self-imposed exile experienced by other contemporary Zimbabwean musicians, including Thomas Mapfumo.

17. Dube (2003).

18. Frances Aparicio's work on listening to salsa in Michigan likewise draws from an interview with one diasporic resident who felt compelled "to become a conscious consumer of this music in order to be able to listen to it" in the United States (1998, 200).

19. Like Muzhandu, most of the audience members I spoke with had some higher education, and many had come to the United States for the purpose of pursuing a university-level degree.

20. Khosa interview.

21. Nyambira (2007).

22. Other songs that touch upon experiences of migration, whether domestic or transnational, include "Ivai Navo" (Ivai Navo, 1995), "Chinhambwe" (Chinhambwe, 1997), "Andinzwi" (Ndega Zvangu, 1997), "Dzoka Uyamwe" (Tuku Music, 1997), and "Ndakuvara" (Vhunze Moto, 2002).

23. Bhabha (1994, 139), in Sen (2010, 3).

24. Rajgopal (2003), 52.

25. This motif is further emphasized by the first guitar line, which parallels the second drum of mhande even more closely.

26. For more on Mapfumo's "re-orchestration" of indigenous mbira pieces, see Brown (1994).

27. Mataure performed with Mapfumo before joining Mtukudzi's band.

28. Interview with Tariro Mupombwa.

29. Interview with Lewis Madhlangobe.

30. In this way, it echoes music theorist Kofi Agawu's caveat about the perils of seeking always to identify the origins of discrete musical influences (2003, 147). I thank an anonymous reviewer for the journal *Ethnomusicology* for this particularly helpful formulation.

31. Accordingly, Bakhtin's conception of the chronotope, in which place becomes saturated with time, has frequently been evoked in understanding how diasporic subjects seek to make sense of "the multiple contexts that they embody" (Slobin 2000, 73). Within the unfolding field of sound studies, scholars have suggested that live performance offers a particularly "naturalized chronotope," in which memory, time, and place are felt as a coherent whole (Samuels et al. 2010, 332). My conversations with diasporic listeners, however, suggest that even the highly mediated experience of listening to commercial recordings enables Mtukudzi's audiences to integrate the otherwise disparate spatial and temporal worlds of "home" and "away." As Jane Sugarman has argued, "the realm of mediated musics presents a terrain of possibilities for new forms of subjectivity," enabling migrants to address the tensions inherent in transnational experience (2004, 21).

32. By naming his album *Nhava*, Mtukudzi seeks to draw listeners' attention to its title track, "Izere Mhepo." Located against an ambiguous background, which equally recalls a humble plastered wall and the aesthetics of modern graphic design, Mtukudzi appears at once displaced and emplaced, a modern subject invoking indigenous knowledge to make sense of migration and diaspora as contemporary phenomena.

33. Mukondiwa (2005).

34. As spokesperson Erin Foster observed at the International Organization for Migration's regional office in Harare, "the migration issue touches everybody. If you ask anyone, they have at least one, if not multiple people who live outside the country, or cross, or are thinking about leaving."

35. Turino (2000), 25.

36. Sugarman (1997), 217.

37. My definition of *marimuka* draws upon Hannan ([1959] 2000).

38. Bhabha (1992, 141), in Roy (1995, 108).

39. Sengupta (2007).

40. Ndlovu-Gatsheni (2009).

41. Clifford (1997, 311), in Sen (2010, 2).

42. Decisions about migration are primarily made at the household level; however, calling attention to how migration "has become a crucial way for households to diversify their livelihood survival strategies" (Tevera and Zinyama 2002, in Bloch 2006).

43. Indeed, at two of the performances I attended in 2007, I observed audience members wearing clothing printed with the MDC's slogans and imagery.

44. Rogers (2002).

Conclusion

1. Murimwa 2001. Illustrating how deeply entrenched this expectation was among Mtukudzi's audiences, journalist Godwin Mawuru (2004) would comment on yet another performance, "The show did not close with the usual Ndima Ndapedza tune but it ended in style with Tuku exiting with his 'sideways' dance alongside Kasamba."

2. Unpublished interview with Banning Eyre (1998).

3. Hannan defines *ndima* as a "portion of field allotted to one person or group of persons for weeding" ([1959] 2000, 440). In a literary context, in can also refer to a single paragraph or verse (ibid.)

4. I see listening as a "remainder" in relation to the musical utterance both in that it represents something that the musical utterance simultaneously "cannot be but without which it nevertheless cannot exist" (de Certeau 1984, 159) and in that traces of its erasure remain within the performance itself.

5. As Karin Barber has similarly observed, "The text itself says more than it knows; it generates 'surplus': meanings that go beyond, and may subvert, the purported intentions of the work" (1991, 3).

6. Mtukudzi's lyrics thus nicely illustrate David Coplan's observation that aural poetic forms place "the emphasis on the ears of the hearers, who include both performer and audience, and hence, properly, on the intended and experienced aesthetic transaction between all participants in a performance event" (1994, 9).

7. As Veit Erlmann has observed, "The ways in which people relate to each other through the sense of hearing also provide important insights into a wide range of issues confronting societies around the world" (2004, 3).

8. See Hodza and Fortune (1979, 33).

9. Unpublished interview with Banning Eyre (2001).

10. See Vambe (2004, 185).

11. Werbner (1998), 15.

12. Barber (1987), 63.

13. On rule of law as fetish, see Comaroff and Comaroff (2006, vii). See also Mbembe (2001).

14. See http://www.ted.com/index.php/talks/chimamanda_adichie_the_danger _of_a_single_story.html (Accessed 23 January 2010).

15. Achebe (2000).

16. Barber (1991), 34.

17. Samkange and Samkange (1980), 39.

18. Ramose (1999), 140.

19. This argument is most clearly articulated in Samkange and Samkange 1980: 39; 76; Ramose 1999: 128–140.

20. Samkange and Samkange (1980), 39. By pointing toward alternatives to Western-style democracy, these authors' concerns intersect with Arjun Appadurai's recent and trenchant critique of nationalism, which holds that "there is still something uncanny about a form of social organization that has a relatively brief history, even in the West, and has not only come to seem natural and necessary, but also deeply felt and valued" (2013, 102),

21. Based on UNAIDS's World AIDS Day Report 2011, Avert reports that the number of people taking ARVs increased by 118 percent between 2009 and 2011, the largest increase of any country worldwide. http://www.avert.org/hiv-aids-zimbabwe.htm (Accessed 17 June 2015).

22. I draw here upon Samuels et al.'s recognition of "the aural as imbricated in theory and politics and, thereby, as critical to the ethnographic endeavor" (2010, 332).

23. Coplan (1994), 25.

BIBLIOGRAPHY

Books, Dissertations, Reports, and Articles

Achebe, Chinua. 2000. *Home and Exile*. Oxford: Oxford University Press.

Adams, Charles R. 1979. "Aurality and Consciousness: Basotho Production of Significance." In *Essays in Humanistic Anthropology*, edited by Bruce T. Grindal and Dennis M. Warren, 303–325. Washington, DC: University Press of America.

Agawu, Kofi. 2003. *Representing African Music: Postcolonial Notes, Queries, Positions*. London: Routledge.

Alexander, Jocelyn. 2006. *The Unsettled Land: State-making and the Politics of Land in Zimbabwe, 1893–2003*. Oxford: James Currey.

Alviso, Ric. 2011. "Tears Run Dry: Coping with AIDS through Music in Zimbabwe." In *The Culture of AIDS in Africa: Hope and Healing through the Arts*, edited by Gregory Barz and Judah Cohen, 56–62. New York: Oxford University Press.

Amnesty International. 1976. "Amnesty International Briefing: Rhodesia/Zimbabwe." *Journal of Opinion* 6 (4): 591–610.

Andersson, Jens A. 2001. "Reinterpreting the Rural-Urban Connection: Migration Practices and Socio-Cultural Dispositions of Buhera Workers in Harare." *Africa* 71 (1): 82–112.

Aparicio, Frances. 1998. *Listening to Salsa: Gender, Latin Popular Music, and Puerto Rican Cultures*. Middletown, CT: Wesleyan University Press.

Appadurai, Arjun. 1996. *Modernity at Large: Cultural Dimensions of Globalization*. Minneapolis: University of Minnesota Press.

———. 2013. *The Future as Cultural Fact: Essays on the Global Condition*. New York: Verso.

Axelsson, Olof. 1973. "Kwanongoma College of Music: Rhodesian Music Center for Research and Education." *Svensk Tidskrift för Musikforskning* 55: 59–67.

Azim, Erica. 1999. "On Teaching Americans to Play Mbira like Zimbabweans." *African Music* 7 (4): 175–180.

Barber, Karin. 1987. "Popular Arts in Africa." *African Studies Review* 30 (3): 1–78.

———. 1991. *I Could Speak until Tomorrow: Oriki, Women, and the Past in a Yoruba Town*. Washington, DC: Smithsonian Institution Press.

Barz, Gregory. 2006. *Singing for Life: HIV/AIDS and Music in Uganda*. New York: Routledge.

Baumann, Max, and Linda Fujie. 1999. "Preface from the Editors." *World of Music* 41 (1): 5–7.

Bayart, Jean-Francois. 1993. *The State in Africa: The Politics of the Belly*. London: Longman.

Becker, Judith. 2009. "Ethnomusicology and Empiricism in the Twenty-first Century." *Ethnomusicology* 53 (3): 478–501.

Bendix, Regina. 2000. "The Pleasures of the Ear: Toward an Ethnography of Listening." *Cultural Analysis* 1: 33–50.

Berliner, Paul. 1975. "Music and Spirit Possession at a Shona Bira." *African Music* 5 (4): 130–39.

————. (1978) 1993. *The Soul of Mbira: Music and Traditions of the Shona People of Zimbabwe: With an Appendix, Building and Playing a Shona Karimba.* Chicago: University of Chicago Press.

Bessant, Leslie. 1994. "Songs of Chiweshe and Songs of Zimbabwe." *African Affairs* 93 (370): 43–73.

Bhabha, Homi K. 1992. "The World and the Home." *Social Text* 10 (2–3): 141–153.

————. 1994. *The Location of Culture.* London: Routledge.

Bloch, Alice. 2006. "Emigration from Zimbabwe: Migrant Perspectives." *Social Policy & Administration* 40 (1): 67–87.

Boot, Adrian, and Chris Salewicz. 1995. *Bob Marley: Songs of Freedom.* New York: Viking Studio Books.

Bourdillon, M. C. 1987. *The Shona Peoples: An Ethnography of the Contemporary Shona, with Special Reference to their Religion.* Gweru, Zimbabwe: Mambo Press.

Brown, Ernest D. 1994. "The Guitar and the Mbira: Resilience, Assimilation, and Pan-Africanism in Zimbabwean Music." *World of Music* 36 (2): 73–117.

Brusila, Johannes. 2001. "Musical Otherness and the Bhundu Boys: The Construction of the 'West' and the 'Rest' in the Discourse of 'World Music.'" In *Same and Other: Negotiating African Identity in Cultural Production,* edited by Maria Eriksson Baaz and Mai Palmberg, 39–56. Uppsala, Sweden: Nordiska Afrikainstitutet.

————. 2002. "'Modern Traditional' Music from Zimbabwe: Virginia Mukwesha's Mbira Record 'Matare.'" In *Playing with Identities in Contemporary Music in Africa,* edited by Mai Palmberg and Annemette Kirkegaard. 35–45. Uppsala, Sweden: Nordiska Afrikainstitutet.

Burke, Timothy. 1992. *Lifebuoy Men, Lux Women: Commodification, Consumption, and Cleanliness in Modern Zimbabwe.* Durham, NC: Duke University Press.

Cavicchi, Daniel. 1998. *Tramps like Us: Music and Meaning among Springsteen Fans.* Oxford: Oxford University Press.

Chaumba, Joseph, Ian Schoones, and William Wolmer. 2003. "From Jambanja to Planning: The Reassertion of Technocracy in Land Reform in South-Eastern Zimbabwe?" *The Journal of Modern African Studies* 41 (4): 533–554.

Chikowero, Murenga Joseph. 2006. "Singing the Contemporary: Leadership and Governance in the Musical Discourse of Oliver Mtukudzi." *Muziki* 3 (1): 36–47.

Chimhundu, H. 1980. "Shumo, Tsumo, and Socialization," *Zambezia* 8 (1): 37–51.

Chimuka, Tarisayi A. 2001. "Ethics among the Shona." *Zambezia* 28 (1): 23–37.

Chitando, Ezra. 2002. *Singing Culture: A Study of Gospel Music in Zimbabwe.* Uppsala, Sweden: Nordic Africa Institute.

Clifford, James. 1997. *Routes: Travel and Translation in the Late Twentieth Century.* Cambridge: Harvard University Press.

Cohen, Sara. 1993. "Ethnography and Popular Music Studies." *Popular Music* 12 (2): 123–138.

Comaroff, Jean, and John L Comaroff, eds. 2006. *Law and Disorder in the Postcolony*. Chicago: University of Chicago Press.

Comaroff, John L., and Jean Comaroff. 1997. *Of Revelation and Revolution, Volume 2: The Dialectics of Modernity on a South African Frontier*. Chicago: University of Chicago Press.

Coplan, David. 1994. *In the Time of Cannibals: The Word Music of South Africa's Basotho Migrants*. Chicago: University of Chicago Press.

———. 2003. "Sound of Africa!" *Anthropological Quarterly* 76 (1): 141.

Corbett, John. 1990. "Free, Single, and Disengaged: Listening Pleasure and the Popular Music Object." *October* 54: 79–101.

De Certeau, M. 1984. *The Practice of Everyday Life*. Berkeley: University of California Press.

Dent, Alexander. 2007. "Country Brothers: Kinship and Chronotope in Brazilian Rural Public Culture." *Anthropological Quarterly* 80 (2): 455–495.

Dewey, William J. 1986. "Shona Male and Female Artistry." *African Arts* 19 (3): 64–67.

Diawara, Mamadou. 1997. "Mande Oral Popular Culture Revisited," *Readings in African Popular Culture*, edited by Karin Barber, 40–47. Bloomington: Indiana University Press.

Downey, Greg. 2002. "Listening to Capoeira: Phenomenology, Embodiment, and the Materiality of Music." *Ethnomusicology* 46 (3): 487–509.

Eicher, Carl K. 1995. "Zimbabwe's Maize-based Green Revolution: Preconditions for Replication." *World Development* 23 (5): 805–818.

Erlmann, Veit. 2004. "But What of the Ethnographic Ear? Anthropology, Sound, and the Senses." In *Hearing Cultures: Essays on Sound, Listening, and Modernity*, edited by Veit Erlmann, 1–20. New York: Berg.

Eyre, Banning. 2001. *Playing with Fire: Fear and Self-Censorship in Zimbabwean Music*. Copenhagen, Denmark: Freemuse.

Fabian, Johannes. 1998. *Moments of Freedom: Anthropology and Popular Culture*. Charlottesville: University of Virginia Press.

Farmer, Paul. (1992) 2006. *AIDS and Accusation: Haiti and the Geography of Blame*. Berkeley: University of California Press.

———. 2003. *Pathologies of Power: Health, Human Rights, and the New War on the Poor*. Berkeley: University of California Press.

Feld, Steven. 1988. "Notes on World Beat." *Public Culture Bulletin* 1 (1): 31–37.

———. 1996. "Pygmy POP: A Genealogy of Schizophonic Mimesis." *Yearbook for Traditional Music* 28: 1–35.

———. 2000a. "The Poetics and Politics of Pygmy Pop." In *Western Music and Its Others: Difference, Representation, and Appropriation in Music*, edited by Georgina Born and David Hesmondhalgh. Berkeley: University of California Press.

———. 2000b. "A Sweet Lullaby for World Music." *Public Culture* 12 (1): 145–172.

Fisher, Daniel. 2009. "Mediating Kinship: Country, Family, and Radio in Northern Australia." *Cultural Anthropology* 24 (2): 280–312.

Floyd, Samuel A., Jr. 2002. "Ring Shout! Literary Studies, Historical Studies, and Black Music Inquiry." *Black Music Research Journal* 22: 49–70.

Fontein, Joost. 2006. "Silence, Destruction and Closure at Great Zimbabwe: Local Narratives of Desecration and Alienation." *Journal of Southern African Studies* 32 (4): 771–794.

Frederikse, Julie. 1984. *None But Ourselves: Masses vs. Media in the Making of Zimbabwe.* New York: Penguin Books.

Frith, Simon. 2000. "The Discourse of World Music." In *Western Music and Its Others: Difference, Representation, and Appropriation in Music,* edited by Georgina Born and David Hesmondhalgh, 305–322. Berkeley: University of California Press.

Gelfand, M. 1971. "A Description of the Ceremony of Kurova Guva: Escorting the Spirit from the Grave to the Home." *Zambezia* 2 (1): 71–74.

Gregson, Simon, with Elizabeth Gonese, Timothy B Hallett, Noah Taruberekera, John W Hargrove, Ben Lopman, Elizabeth L Corbett, Rob Dorrington, Sabada Dube, Karl Dehne, and Owen Mugurungi. 2010. "HIV Decline in Zimbabwe due to Reductions in Risky Sex? Evidence from a Comprehensive Epidemiological Review." *International Journal of Epidemiology* 39 (5): 1311–1323.

Grenier, Line, and Jocelyne Guilbault. 1999. "Créolite and Francophonie in Music: Socio-Musical Repositionings Where It Matters." *Repercussions* 7 (8): 351–395.

Hamm, Charles. 1989. "Graceland Revisited." *Popular Music* 8 (3): 299–303.

Hammer, Amanda, Brian Raftopoulos, and Stig Jensen, eds. 2003. *Zimbabwe's Unfinished Business: Rethinking Land, State, and Nation in the Context of Crisis.* Harare, Zimbabwe: Weaver Press.

Hanke, S. H. 2008. "Zimbabwe: From Hyperinflation to Growth." Cato Center for Global Liberty and Prosperity, Development Policy Analysis No. 6. Available at: www.cato.org/pub_display.php?pub_id=9484.

Hanke, S. H., and A. K. F. Kwok. 2009. "On the Measurement of Zimbabwe's Inflation." *Cato Journal* 29 (2): 354–364.

Hannan, M., ed. (1959) 2000. *Standard Shona Dictionary.* Harare, Zimbabwe: College Press.

Herzfeld, Michael. 2004. *The Body Impolitic: Artisans and Artifice in the Global Hierarchy of Value.* Chicago: Chicago University Press.

Hodza, A. C., and George Fortune. 1979. *Shona Praise Poetry.* Oxford: Clarendon Press.

Honwana, Luís Bernardo. 1990. "Foreword," *Art from the Frontline: Contemporary Art from Southern Africa,* edited by Peter Sinclair, pages. London: Karia Press.

Hopkins, Pandora. 1982. "Aural Thinking." In *Cross-Cultural Perspectives on Music,* edited by Robert Falck and Timothy Rice, 143–161. Toronto: University of Toronto Press.

Hove, Masotsha. 1985. *Confessions of a Wizard.* Gweru, Zimbabwe: Mambo Press.

Huffman, Thomas N. 1985. "The Soapstone Birds from Great Zimbabwe." *African Arts* 18 (3): 68–73, 99–100.

Ignatowski, Claire. 2006. *Journey of Song: Public Life and Morality in Cameroon.* Bloomington: Indiana University Press.

Impey, Angela. 1992. "They Want Us with Salt and Onions: Women in the Zimbabwean Music Industry." PhD dissertation, Indiana University.

Janzen, John M. 1991. "'Doing Ngoma': A Dominant Trope in African Religion and Healing." *Journal of Religion in Africa* 20 (1): 290–308.

———. 1992. *Ngoma: Discourses of Healing in Central and Southern Africa.* Berkeley: University of California Press.

Johnson, Henry. 2007. "'Happy Diwali!' Performance, Multicultural Soundscapes and Intervention in Aotearoa/New Zealand." *Ethnomusicology Forum* 16 (1):71–94.

Jones, Claire. 2006. "From Schoolboy Stuff to Professional Musicianship: The Modern Tradition of the Zimbabwean Marimbas." PhD dissertation, University of Washington.

———. 2008. "Shona Women Mbira Players: Gender, Tradition and Nation in Zimbabwe." *Ethnomusicology Forum* 17 (1): 125–149.

Kahari, G. P. 1981. "The History of the Shona Protest Song: A Preliminary Study." *Zambezia* 9 (2): 79–101.

Kauffman, Robert. 1969. "Some Aspects of Aesthetics in the Shona Music of Rhodesia." *Ethnomusicology* 13 (3): 507–511.

———. 1972. "Shona Urban Music and the Problem of Acculturation." *Yearbook of the International Folk Music Council* 4: 47–56.

———. 1976. "The Psychology of Music Making in an African Society: The Shona." *The World of Music* 18 (1): 9–14.

Keil, Charles. 1995. "The Theory of Participatory Discrepancies: A Progress Report." *Ethnomusicology* 39 (1): 1–19.

Klaits, Frederick. 2010. *Death in a Church of Life: Moral Passion during Botswana's Time of AIDS.* Berkeley: University of California Press.

Korfmacher, Deborah. 2001. *Tuku Music: Reflections of Zimbabwean Society through the Music of Oliver Mtukudzi.* Master's thesis, School of Oriental and African Studies, University of London.

Kriger, Norma. 2003. *Guerilla Veterans in Post-war Zimbabwe: Symbolic and Violent Politics, 1980–1987.* Cambridge: Cambridge University Press.

Krüger, Simone. 2011. "Democratic Pedagogies: Perspectives from Ethnomusicology and World Music Educational Contexts in the United Kingdom." *Ethnomusicology* 55 (2): 280–305.

Kwaramba, Alice Dadirai. 1997. *Popular Music and Society: The Language of Protest in Chimurenga Music: The Case of Thomas Mapfumo in Zimbabwe.* IMK Report No. 24. Oslo, Norway: University of Oslo.

Kyker, Jennifer. 2010. "Carrying Spirit in Song: Music and the Making of Ancestors at Zezuru *Kurova Guva* Ceremonies." *African Music* 8 (3): 65–84.

———. 2011. "'What Shall We Do?'" Agency and Disclosure in Oliver Mtukudzi's Songs about AIDS." In *The Culture of AIDS: Hope and Healing through the Arts in Africa,* edited by Gregory Barz and Judah Cohen, 241–255. Oxford: Oxford University Press.

———. 2012. "Images of Health: Oliver Mtukudzi's Musical Approach to HIV/AIDS." *American Journal of Public Health* 102 (7): 1298–1299.

———. 2013. "Listening in the Wilderness: The Audience Reception of Oliver Mtukudzi's Music in the Zimbabwean Diaspora." *Ethnomusicology* 57 (2): 261–285.

———. 2014. "Learning in Secret: Gender, Age, and the Clandestine Transmission of
Zimbabwean Mbira Dzavadzimu Music." *Ethnomusicology Forum* 23 (1): 110–134.

Lamen, Darien. 2013. "Valor, patrimônio cultural e precarização na história dos siste-
mas sonoros de Belém do Pará." *Revista Estudos Amazônicos* 10 (2): 75–116.

Lan, David. 1985. *Guns and Rain: Guerillas and Spirit Mediums in Zimbabwe.* Berkeley:
University of California Press.

Leon, Argelier. 2007. "Music in the Life of Africans and Their Descendants in the New
World." In *Music in Latin American and the Caribbean: An Encyclopedic History. Vol-
ume 2: Performing the Caribbean Experience,* edited by Malena Kuss, 17–28. Austin:
The University of Texas Press.

Lipsitz, George. 1994. *Dangerous Crossroads: Popular Music, Postmodernism, and the Poetics
of Place.* New York: Verso.

Lund, Giuliana. 1999. "Harmonizing the Nation: Women's Voices and Development in
Zimbabwean Cinema." *City & Society* 11 (1–2): 213–235.

Made, Patricia A., and Nyorovai Whande. 1989. "Women in Southern Africa: A Note
on the Zimbabwean 'Success Story.'" *Issue: A Journal of Opinion* 17 (2): 26–28.

Malm, Krister. 1993. "Music on the Move: Traditions and Mass Media." *Ethnomusicology*
37 (3): 339–352.

Mamdani, Mahmood. 2009. "Lessons of Zimbabwe." *London Review of Books* 30 (34): 17–21.

Manuel, Peter. 1993. *Cassette Culture: Popular Music and Technology in North India.* Chicago: University of Chicago Press.

Mashiri, Pedzisai. 1999. "Terms of Address in Shona: A Sociolinguistic Approach." *Zambezia* 26 (1): 93–110.

Mashiri, Pedzisai, Kenneth Mawomo, and Patrick Tom. 2002. "Naming the Pandemic:
Semantic and Ethical Foundations of HIV/AIDS Shona Vocabulary." *Zambezia* 29
(2): 221–234.

Matiure, Perminus. 2011. "Mbira Dzavadzimu and Its Space within the Shona Cos-
mology: Tracing Mbira from Bira to the Spiritual World." *Muziki: Journal of
Music Research in Africa* 8 (2): 29–49.

Mauerhofer, Alois. 1997. "Listening to Music: Attitudes of Contemporary Austrian
Youth." *World of Music* 39 (2): 83–96.

Mbembe, Achille. 2001. *On the Postcolony.* Berkeley: University of California Press.

Mberi, N. E. 2003. "Metaphors in Shona: A Cognitive Approach." *Zambezia* 30 (1): 72–88.

Mbiba, Beacon. 2005. "'Zimbabwe's Global Citizens in 'Harare North:' Overview and
Implications for Development." Peri-NET Working Paper 14. London: The Urban
and Peri-Urban Research Network (Peri-NET, Africa).

Mbiti, John S. 1994. *African Religions and Philosophy.* Oxford: Heinemann.

Meintjes, Louise. 1990. "Paul Simon's *Graceland,* South Africa, and the Mediation of
Musical Meaning." *Ethnomusicology* 34 (1): 37–73.

———. 2003. *Sound of Africa!: Making Music Zulu in a South African Studio.* Durham, NC:
Duke University Press.

————. 2004. "Shoot the Sergeant, Shatter the Mountain: The Production of Masculinity in Zulu Ngoma Song and Dance in post-Apartheid South Africa." *Ethnomusicology Forum* 13 (2): 173–201.

Mheta, G, ed. 2005. *Duramazwi RemiMhanzi*. Gweru, Zimbabwe: Mambo Press.

Mhiripiri, Nhamo Anthony. 2010. "The Production of Stardom and the Survival Dynamics of the Zimbabwean Music Industry in the Post-2000 Crisis Period." *Journal of African Media Studies* 2 (2): 209–223.

Monson, Ingrid. 1999. "Riffs, Repetition, and Theories of Globalization." *Ethnomusicology* 43 (1): 31–65.

Moore, Donald. 2005. *Suffering for Territory: Race, Place, and Power in Zimbabwe*. Durham, NC: Duke University Press.

Mpondi, Douglas. 2004. "Educational Change and Cultural Politics: National Identity Formation in Zimbabwe." PhD dissertation, Ohio University.

Mudenge, Stan. 1988. *A Political History of Munhumutapa, c1400–1902*. Harare: Zimbabwe Publishing House.

Muller, Carol. 1999. *Rituals of Fertility and the Sacrifice of Desire: Nazarite Women's Performance in South Africa*. Chicago: University of Chicago Press.

————. 2002. "Archiving Africanness in Sacred Song." *Ethnomusicology* 46 (3): 409–431.

————. 2004. *South African Music: A Century of Traditions in Transformation*. Santa Barbara, CA: ABC Clio.

————. 2011. *Musical Echoes: South African Women Thinking in Jazz*. Durham, NC: Duke University Press.

Ndlovu-Gatsheni, Sabelo J. 2009. "Making Sense of Mugabeism in Local and Global Politics: 'So Blair, Keep Your England and Let Me Keep My Zimbabwe.'" *Third World Quarterly* 30 (6): 1139–1158.

O'Hagin, Isabel, and David Harnish. 2001. "Reshaping Imagination: The Musical Culture of Migrant Farmworker Families in Northwest Ohio." *Bulletin of the Council for Research in Music Education* 151: 21–30.

Orner, Peter, and Annie Holmes. 2010. *Hope Deferred: Narratives of Zimbabwean Lives*. San Francisco: McSweeney Books.

Oyewumi, Oyeronke. 1997. *The Invention of Women: Making an African Sense of Western Gender Discourses*. Minneapolis: University of Minnesota Press.

P., DCH. 1933. "Mangoromera." *Native Affairs Department Annual* (NADA) 11: 59–61

Patel, V., E. Simunyu, and F. Gwanzura. 1995. "Kufungisisa (Thinking Too Much): A Shona Idiom for Non-psychotic Mental Illness." *Central African Journal of Medicine* 41 (7): 209–215.

Pearce, Carole. 1990. "Tsika, Hunhu, and the Moral Education of Primary School Children," *Zambezia* 17 (2): 145–160.

Perman, Anthony. 2008. "History, Ethics, and Emotion in Ndau Performance in Zimbabwe: Local Theoretical Knowledge and Ethnomusicological Perspectives." PhD dissertation, University of Illinois.

————. 2011. "The Ethics of Ndau Performance: Questioning Ethnomusicology's Aesthetics," *Journal of Musicological Research* 30: 227–252.

———. 2012. "Sungura in Zimbabwe and the Limits of Cosmopolitanism." *Ethnomusicology Forum* 21 (3): 374–401.

———. Forthcoming. "Muchongoyo and Mugabeism in Zimbabwe."

Perullo, Alec. 2011. *Live from Dar Es Salaam: Popular Music and Tanzania's Music Economy.* Bloomington: Indiana University Press.

Pfukwa, Charles. 2010. "When Cultures Speak Back to Each Other: The Legacy of Benga in Zimbabwe." *Muziki: Journal of Music Research in Africa* 7 (1): 169–178.

Pongweni, Alec J. C. 1982. *Songs That Won the Liberation War.* Harare, Zimbabwe: College Press.

Post, Jennifer C. 2007. "'I Take My Dombra and Sing to Remember my Homeland': Identity, Landscape and Music in Kazakh Communities in Western Mongolia." *Ethnomusicology Forum* 16 (1):45–69.

Rajgopal, Shoba S., 2003. "The Politics of Location: Ethnic Identity and Cultural Conflict in the Cinema of the South Asian Diaspora." *Journal of Communication Inquiry* 27: 49–66.

Ramnarine, Tina. 2007. "Musical Performance in the Diaspora: Introduction." *Ethnomusicology Forum* 16 (1): 1–17.

Ramose, Mogobe B. 1999. *African Philosophy through Ubuntu.* Harare, Zimbabwe: Mond Books.

Ranger, Terence. 1985. *Peasant Consciousness and Guerrilla War in Zimbabwe: A Comparative Study.* London: James Currey.

———. 2003. "Historiography, Patriotic History and the History of the Nation: The Struggle over the Past in Zimbabwe." Lecture notes, Oxford Centre for Mission Studies, 28 October. Data on the internet at www.ocms.zc.uk/lectures.

———. 2006. "The Meaning of Urban Violence in Africa: Bulawayo, Southern Rhodesia, 1890–1960." *Cultural and Social History* 3 (2): 193–228.

Robbins, Bruce. 1998. "Introduction Part I: Actually Existing Cosmopolitanism." In *Cosmopolitics: Thinking and Feeling beyond the Nation,* edited by Pheng Cheah and Bruce Robbins, 1–19. Minneapolis: University of Minnesota Press.

Rodlach, Alexander. 2006. *Witches, Westerners, and HIV: AIDS and Cultures of Blame in Africa.* Walnut Creek, CA: Left Coast Press.

Rommen, Timothy. 2007. *"Mek Some Noise": Gospel Music and the Ethics of Style in Trinidad.* Berkeley: University of California Press.

Roy, Anindyo. 1995. "Postcoloniality and the Politics of Identity in the Diaspora: Figuring 'Home,' Locating Histories." In *Postcolonial Discourse and Changing Cultural Contexts: Theory and Criticism,* edited by Gita Rajan and Radhika Mohanram, 101–115. Westport, CT: Greenwood Press.

Rukuni, Mandivamba. (2007) 2010. *Being Afrikan.* Johannesburg: Penguin.

Rutsate, Jerry. 2010. "*Mhande* Dance in the *Kurova Guva* Ceremony: An Enactment of Karanga Spirituality." *Yearbook for Traditional Music* 42: 81–99.

———. 2011. *Mhande Dance in Kurova Guva and Mutoro Rituals: An Efficacious and Symbolic Enactment of Karanga Epistemology.* PhD dissertation, The University of KwaZulu-Natal.

Samkange, Stanlake, and Tommie-Marie Samkange. 1980. *Hunhuism or Ubuntuism: A Zimbabwe Indigenous Political Philosophy.* Harare, Zimbabwe: Graham Publishing.

Samuels, David W., Louise Meintjes, Ana Maria Ochoa, and Thomas Porcello. 2010. "Soundscapes: Toward a Sounded Anthropology." *Annual Review of Anthropology* 39: 329–345.

Scannell, Paddy. 2001. "Music, Radio and the Record Business in Zimbabwe Today." *Popular Music* 20 (1): 13–27.

Schulz, Dorothea. 2002. "'The World Is Made by Talk': Female Fans, Popular Music, and New Forms of Public Sociality in Urban Mali." *Cahiers d'Études Africaines* 42 (168): 797–829.

Shoka, Tabona. 2007. *Karanga Indigenous Religion in Zimbabwe.* London: Ashgate.

Sibanda, Silindiwe. 2004. "'You Don't Get to Sing a Song When You Have Nothing to Say': Oliver Mtukudzi's Music as a Vehicle for Socio-Political Commentary." *Social Dynamics* 30 (2): 36–63.

Sigauke, Emmanuel. 2008. "Hurry, Tuku in Concert." *Forever Let Me Go*, Baltimore, MD: PublishAmerica.

Slobin, Mark. 2000. *Fiddler on the Move: Exploring the Klezmer World.* New York: Oxford University Press.

Snodia, Magudu, Tasara Muguti, and Nicholas Mutami. 2014. "Deconstructing the Colonial Legacy through the Naming Process in Independent Zimbabwe." *Journal of Studies in Social Sciences* 6 (1): 71–85.

Stokes, Martin. 2004. "Music and the Global Order." *Annual Review of Anthropology* 33: 47–72.

Strathern, Marilyn. 1995. *Shifting Contexts: Transformations in Anthropological Knowledge.* London: Routledge.

Stuckey, Sterling. 1987. *Slave Culture: Nationalist Theory and the Foundations of Black America.* New York: Oxford University Press.

Sugarman, Jane. 1997. *Engendering Song: Singing and Subjectivity at Prespa Albanian Weddings.* Chicago: University of Chicago Press.

———. 2004. "Diasporic Dialogues: Mediated Musics and the Albanian Transnation." In *Identity and the Arts in Diaspora Communities*, edited by Thomas Turino and James Lea, 21–38. Sterling Heights, MI: Harmonie Park Press.

Swift, Patricia. 1989. "Support for the Dying and Bereaved in Zimbabwe: Traditional and New Approaches." *Journal of Social Development in Africa* 4 (1): 25–45.

Taylor, Charles. 2004. *Modern Social Imaginaries.* Durham, NC: Duke University Press.

Taylor, Timothy Dean. 1997. *Global Pop: World Music, World Markets.* New York: Routledge.

Tevera, Daniel, and Lovemore Zinyama. 2002. *Zimbabwean Who Move: Perspectives on International Migration in Zimbabwe.* Migration Policy Series No. 25, Jonathan Crush, series editor. Cape Town: Southern African Migration Programme.

Thram, Diane. 1999. *Performance as Ritual, Performance as Art: Therapeutic Efficacy of Dandanda Song and Dance in Zimbabwe.* PhD dissertation, Indiana University.

———. 2002. "Therapeutic Efficacy of Music-Making: Neglected Aspect of Human Experience Integral to Performance Process." *Yearbook for Traditional Music* 34: 129–138.

———. 2006. "Patriotic History and the Policisation of Memory: Manipulation of Popular Music to Re-invent the Liberation Struggle in Zimbabwe." *Critical Arts: A Journal of South-North Cultural Studies* 20 (2): 75–88.

Tomlinson, Gary. 2007. *The Singing of the New World: Indigenous Voice in the Era of European Contact.* Cambridge: Cambridge University Press.

Toynbee, Jason. 2007. *Bob Marley: Herald of a Postcolonial World?* Cambridge: Polity.

Tracey, Andrew. 1961. "The Mbira Music of Jege Tapera." *African Music* 2 (4): 44–63.

———. 1963. "ThreeTunes for 'Mbira Dza Vadzimu'" *African Music* 3 (2): 23–26.

———. 1970. "The Matepe Mbira Music of Rhodesia." *African Music* 4 (4): 37–61.

———. 1972. "The Original African Mbira?" *African Music* 5 (2): 85–104.

Tracey, Hugh. (1932) 1969. "The Mbira Class of Instruments in Rhodesia." *African Music* 4 (3): 78–95.

Tumwine, J. K. 1992. "Zimbabwe's Success Story in Education and Health: Will It Weather Structural Adjustment?" *Journal of the Royal Society of Health* 112 (6): 286–290.

Turino, Thomas. 1998. "The Mbira, Worldbeat, and the International Imagination." *The World of Music* 40 (2): 85–106.

———. 2000. *Nationalists, Cosmopolitans, and Popular Music in Zimbabwe.* Chicago: University of Chicago Press.

Twala, C., and Q. Koetaan. 2006. "The Toyi-Toyi Culture in the 1980s: An Investigation into Its Liberating and Unifying Powers." *SA Journal for Cultural History* 20 (1): 163–179.

Um, Hae-Kyung. 2000. "Listening Patterns and Identity of the Korean Diaspora in the Former USSR." *British Journal of Ethnomusicology* 9 (2): 121–142.

Vail, Leroy, and Landeg White. 1991. *Power and the Praise Poem: South African Voices in History.* Charlottesville: University of Virginia Press.

Vambe, Maurice T. 2004. "Versions and Sub-Versions: Trends in Chimurenga Musical Discourses of Post-Independence Zimbabwe." *African Study Monographs* 25 (4): 167–193.

———, ed. 2008. *The Hidden Dimensions of Operation Murambatsvina in Zimbabwe.* Harare, Zimbabwe: Weaver Press.

Vambe, Maurice T., and Aquilina Mawadza. 2001. "Images of Black Women in Popular Songs and Some Poems on AIDS in Post-Independence Zimbabwe." In *Orality and Cultural Identities in Zimbabwe*, edited by M. T. Vambe, 57–72. Harare, Zimbabwe: Mambo Press.

Van Buren, Kathleen. 2010. "Applied Ethnomusicology and HIV and AIDS: Responsibility, Ability, and Action." *Ethnomusicology* 52 (2): 202–223.

Wallis, Roger, and Krister Malm. 1992. *Media Policy and Music Activity.* London: Routledge.

Waterman, Christopher Alan. (1986) 1990. *Juju: A Social History and Ethnography of an African Popular Music.* Chicago: University of Chicago Press.

Welsh-Asante, Kariamu. 1985. "The Jerusarema Dance of Zimbabwe." *Journal of Black Studies* 15 (4): 381–403.

———. 2000. *Zimbabwe Dance: Rhythmic Forces, Ancestral Voices: An Aesthetic Analysis.* Trenton, NJ: Africa World Press.

Werbner, Richard. 1991. *Tears of the Dead: The Social Biography of an African Family.* Edinburgh: Edinburgh University Press.

———, ed. 1998. "Smoke from the Barrel of a Gun: Postwars of the Dead, Memory, and Reinscription in Zimbabwe." In *Memory and the Postcolony: African Anthropology and the Critique of Power*, 71–102. New York: Zed Books.

Westgate, Thomas. 1913. "A New Era." *International Church Missionary Gleaner* 40: 56.

White, Timothy. (1983) 2006. *Catch a Fire: The Life of Bob Marley.* New York: Macmillan.

Williams, Linda F. 1997. "'Straight-Fashioned Melodies': The Transatlantic Interplay of American Music in Zimbabwe." *American Music* 15 (3): 285–304.

Wong, Deborah. 2001. "Finding an Asian American Audience: The Problem of Listening." *American Music* 19 (4): 365–384.

———. 2004. *Speak It Louder: Asian Americans Making Music.* New York: Routledge.

Zindi, Fred. (1985) 1997. *Roots Rocking in Zimbabwe.* Gweru, Zimbabwe: Mambo Press.

Popular Press

Anderson, Jeffrey. 2002. "Out of Africa." *San Francisco Examiner.* 17 May.

Bwititi, Maku. 2000. "Another Tuku Masterpiece." *Chronicle.* 10 November, 7.

Chemere, Martin, and Silence Genti. 2000. "Artists Against Poverty Releases CD." *Jive Fanzine.* May/June, 6.

Chibuswa, D. Vincent. 1980. "The Dagger Fan (II)." In Prize Letters. *Prize* 7 (5). May, 6.

Chisora, Wonder. 1993. "Oliver Mtukudzi Releases Yet Another Good Latest Album." *Masvingo Provincial Star.* 17 December, 14.

Chola, Raymond. 1986. Untitled review of Safirio "Mukadota" Madzikatire with the Sea Cottage Sisters and the New World Band's album *Ndatenga Mota.* In Music Parade. *Parade Magazine.* January, 27.

———. 1986. "Musicians Needled." *Parade Magazine.* April, 9, 14.

———. 1988. "'Tuku' Music-Man with a Message." *Parade Magazine.* June. 24, 29.

Chu, Jeff. 2003. "Singing the Walls Down." *Time Magazine.* 3 March, 46–51.

"Dagger Fan." 1979. "Fed up with Traditional Music." In Prize Letters. *Prize Magazine* 6 (12). December, 7.

Dhlamini, Aubrey. 2005. "Sizzling African Music: Dyer and Mtukudzi Play to Sold-out Crowd at State Theatre." *Pretoria News.* 2 March, 1.

Dube, Siphosami. 2003. "Best of Tuku Music." *Drum Magazine.* 6 November.

Garande, Tinaye. 1994a."Another Fresh Piece from Tuku." *Sunday Mail Magazine.* 27 February, 9.

———. 1994b. "Tuku's Tour a Success." *Sunday Mail Magazine.* 3 July, 8.

Hamba, Joyce. 1997. "'Tuku'—The Legend Lives On." *Standard.* 29 June–5 July, 21.

Hatugari, Leo. 2000. "Release of Wartime Hits Powerful Political Statement." *Daily News.* 26 May, 12.

———. 2001. "Kora Awards Need Clear Cut Categories and Criteria." *Daily News*. 9 November, 10.

———. 2002. "Mukanya Dedicates His New Album to Late Band Member." *Daily News*. 6 July, 10.

Horizon. 1992. "For Zimbabwe—A Film from the Heart." May, 30.

Jive Fanzine. 2000. "Tuku: His Time Has Come." May/June, 8–9.

Kanyuchi, Fungayi. 2001."Tuku Concert—The Day Nose Brigades Became Africanized!" *Standard*, 7–13 January.

Kariuki, John. 2002. "Out of Tune Mugabe Tormenting Musicians." *East African*. 4–10 March.

Mabasa, Ignatius. 2001. "Meet the Artist." *Herald*. 5 February.

Mafukidze, Ezra. 1980. "Trad Music Great!" In Prize Letters. *Prize* 7 (6). June, 6.

Mafundikwa, Ish. 1999. "Tuku Music and Oliver Mtukudzi." *Skyhost*. May/June.

———. 2004. "Oliver Mtukudzi." *Skyhost*. January/February/March, 22–23.

Magirazi, Jazzmore. 1978. "Bouquet to Our Musicians." In Prize Letters. *Prize* 5 (2). January, 15.

Mail and Guardian. 1999. "Magic in Mahube's." 29 January. http://mg.co.za/article /1999-01-29-magic-in-mahubes (Accessed September 17 2014).

Makuyana, Clarence. 2002. "Mtukudzi's Performance at Jazz Show Impressive." *Sunday Mail*. 18 June, L7.

Maravanyika, Vivian. 1999. "Local Music Now Holds Centre Stage." *Herald*. 8 May, 4.

Maruziva, Davidson. 1993. "Author of Hit Play Enthralls ZIWU Writers." *Herald*. 7 June, 4.

Mashava, Funny. 1999. "Tuku Spices Up Old Tracks." *Herald*. 13 November, 4.

Masunda, David. 1992. "Who the Hell Does Tuku Think He Is." *Sunday Times*. 15 March, 21.

Mathuthu, Mduduzi. 2001. "Bulawayo Sings along Wasakara with Mtukudzi." *Daily News*. 8 January, 12.

———. 2008. "Myth Busting with Thomas Mapfumo." *New Zimbabwe*. December. http://newsofzimbabwe.com/2008/12/mmathuthu/myth-busting-with-map fumo/ (Accessed 1 July 2014).

Mawuru, Godwin. 2004. "Tuku Delivers a Memorable Show." *Herald*. 30 March, 9.

Mazara, Godwin, and Robert Mukondiwa. 2003. "'Tuku Wrecked My Affair' . . . Joe Mafana a Bitter Man." *Sunday Leisure*. 24 August, L1.

Mbiriyamveka, Jonathan. 2002. "Tuku Fits in Every Situation." *Herald*. 18 July, 10.

Metcalfe, Debbie. 1990. "Local Musicians Need National Support from the Public, Government and Private Sector." *Prize* 2 (3). April, 29.

Moyse, Andrews. 1989. Untitled album review of *Nyanga Yenzou. Parade and Foto-Action*. January, 23.

Mpofu, Jealous. 2001. "Nose-brigades Now Hooked on Local Music." *Mirror*. 12–18 January, W2.

Mtimba, Richard. 1987. "'Shaura' Is for Unity." In Parade Letters. *Parade Magazine*. January, 5.

Mukondiwa, Robert. 2004. "Tuku Looks Back . . . as 52nd Birthday Approaches." *Sunday Mail.* 12 September, E1.

———. 2005. "Tuku to Release New Album Next Month." *Zimbabwe Mail.* 13 February. http://www.zimbabwemail.com/index.php?id=10279&pubdate=2005-02-13 (Accessed 7 July 2010).

Munyuki, Guthrie. 2001. "An Arduous Journey Finally Pays Off for Mtukudzi." *Daily News.* 22 October, 9.

———. 2002. "Mtukudzi Stage Scintillating Show." *Daily News.* 2 June, 10.

Murimwa, Chengetai. 2001. "Tuku Blows Mutare" *Daily News.* 30 March, 11.

Musundire, Lawrence. 1995. "Picky Kasamba: The Man and His Music." *Sunday Gazette.* 15 January, 12.

Mutakati, Rosenthal. 2007. "I Don't Have Aids (sic): Tuku." *Herald.* 21 July, 2.

Mutamba, Shepherd. 1999. "Unsung Heroes of the 1970s." *Herald.* 16 July, 7.

Mutambara, Jacob. 1992. "Kwekwe Crew Put Chigiyo on the Map. . ." *Horizon.* July, 34.

Mutsaka, Farai. 2000. "Police Impound Tuku's New Album." *Standard.* 19–25 November, 1, 4.

Muzavazi, Christopher. 1979. "The Black Beat." *Illustrated Life Rhodesia.* 31 January, 12–13.

Ncube, Japhet. 1996. "Record Companies Phase Out Vinyl." *Horizon.* July, 42.

Ndlovu, Peter. 1980. "Too Much Trad. Music . . . Continued." In Prize Letters. *Prize 7* (2). February, 7.

Ngalawa, Harold. 1995. "Oliver Mtukudzi Tours Malawi, Promises Thrilling Show." *Malawi News.* 2–8 December, 15.

Nolan, Robert. 2002. "Message Man: Zimbabwe's Oliver Mtukudzi Sings Songs that Encourage Social and Political Change—and Dancing." *Gambit Weekly.* 30 April. http://www.bestofneworleans.com/dispatch/2002-04-30/cover_story2.html (Accessed 14 July 2009).

Nutshell. 1978. "'Mr. Mukadhota': The Amazing Success of Safirio Madzikatire." 4 (13): July, 3.

Paradzai, Admire. 1979. "The Oliver Mtukudzi Story." *Prize 6* (4). April, 44.

Pareles, Jon. 1999. "No Compromise with Pop as a Festival Honors Africa's Own Resources." *New York Times.* 16 August.

People's Voice. 1990. "Chimbetu and Tuku Go for Gold." 26 August–1 September, 7.

Polizzi, Joseph. 1988. "Oliver: Always a Musician at Heart." *Sunday News.* 17 January, 7.

Prize. 1978. "Hotspot." 5 (9). August, 35.

Rogers, Douglas. 2002. "Tuku's London Gig Proves a Homecoming." *Daily News.* 22 May, 18

Rogovoy, Seth. 1999. "Africa Fête '99; Northampton Folk Festival; The Bobs." *Berkshire Eagle.* 12 August. http://www.berkshireweb.com/rogovoy/thebeat/beat990812.html (Accessed 27 May, 2013).

Sibanda, Maxwell. 2000. "Artists Against Poverty Campaign to Release CD." *Zimbabwe Mirror.* 3–9 March, W5.

———. 2001. "Tuku Wants Liberation Role Acknowledged." *Daily News.* 4 January, 15.

Sithole, Masipula. 2001. "The Concept of Normalizing the Abnormal." *Financial Gazette.* 29 March–4 April.

Southern Times. 2005. "Tuku, Dyer, a Formidable Duo." 6 March, C3.

Standard. 2001a. "Disturbing Start to New Year." 7–13 January, 8.

———. 2001b. "Underestimate Zanu PF at Your Peril." 7–13 January, 10.

———. 2001c. "Tuku Says Povo Free to Interpret Bvuma." 7–13 January, 1, 4.

———. 2001d. "Mtukudzi Threatened." 14 October, 4.

Sterling, Beverley. 2001. "'What Shall We Do?': Oliver Mtukudzi Opens the Lid on HIV/AIDS in the Music Business." *Ngoma: Official Magazine of the National Arts Council of Zimbabwe.* February/March, 6–7.

Tera, Richmore. 2006. "What Makes Kapfupi Tick?" *Herald.* 22 July. http://www.herald.co.zw/inside.aspx?sectid=6467&cat=3&livedate=7/22/2006.

Thompson, Stev. 1980. "Too Much Trad. Music . . . Continued." In Prize Letters. *Prize Magazine* 7 (2). February, 7.

Whaley, Andrew. 1993. "Tuku's Dumped Baby." *Horizon.* July, 50.

Zimbabwe Independent. 2000. "Struggle Continues." Editor's Memo. 12 May, 8.

Zindi, Fred. 2011. "Did Chibadura, Chimombe Predict Their Own Deaths?" *Nehanda Radio.* http://nehandaradio.com/2011/08/17/did-chibadura-chimombe-predict-their-deaths/ (Accessed 15 May 2013).

Zvomuya, Percy. 2000. "The Female World and Female Authority in Tuku's Music." *Moto.* October, 21 and 23.

———. 2004. "'Superstar' Tuku Samanyanga: The Moulder and Sharpener of Individual and National Consciousness." *Moto.* June, 24–25, 29.

Other Sources

Adichie, Chimamanda. 2009. "The Danger of a Single Story." TED talk. http://www.ted.com/index.php/talks/chimamanda_adichie_the_danger_of_a_single_story.html (Accessed 23 January 2010).

Feierman, Steven. 2010. "Marginality and Invisibility in African Medical Practice." Talk given at the Wissenschaftskolleg zu Berlin.

Hirsch, Lee. 2002. *Amandla! A Revolution in Four Part Harmony.* New York: ATO Pictures.

James, Fungayi. "A Dream with a Message (HIFA Opening Concert)." http://www.fungaijames.com/bloggen/2008/04/29/a-dream-with-a-message-hifa-opening-concert/ (Accessed 20 July 2012).

Magaisa, Alex Tawanda. 2004. "Drums, Lyrics and Melodies: Listening to the History of a Nation." http://www.kubatana.net/html/archive/opin/040612am.asp?sector=RESDOC&year=2004&range_start=1 (Accessed 20 July 2012).

Media for Development. 1989. Women's Film Project: Interim Report. www.mfditanzania.com/images/pdf/misc/NeriaInterim.pdf

———. 1992. Neria Production Notes. www.mfditanzania.com/images/pdf/misc/NeriaProductionNotes.pdf.

———. 1999. Annual Report, 1997–98.

Ministry of Health. 1987. *Who Can Get AIDS? And Other Questions*. Harare, Zimbabwe.

Msindo, E. 2006. "History of Factional Bulawayo Violence of 1929." www.columbia .edu/cu/lweb/data/indiv/area/idass/MSINDO.Enocent.htm.

Nyambira, Isaac. 2007. "My Tuku Leicester Gig." www.norahspie.com/uploaded_files /Ike's%20Tuku%20gig.rtf (Accessed 25 May 2008).

Riber, John. 2000. "About the Music in YELLOW CARD." Paper presented at the Mill Valley Film Festival's Composing Music for Film Panel.

Sen, Krishna. 2010. "The (Re)Turn of the Native: Diaspora, Transnationalism, and the Re-Inscription of 'Home.'" Paper presented at Inter-Disciplinary.Net, 3rd Global Conference, Oxford, UK.

Sengupta, Deborah. 2007. "Review: Oliver Mtukudzi and the Black Spirits at Flamingo Cantina." http://www.austin360.com/blogs/content/shared-gen/blogs/austin /music/entries/2007/10/22/review_oliver_mtukudzi_and_the.html (Accessed 18 January 2008).

Touré, Lalla. 1996. "Male Involvement in Family Planning: A Review of Selected Program Initiatives in Africa." USAID. pdf.usaid.gov/pdf_docs/PNABY584.pdf.

World Health Organization (WHO). 2006. "Working Together for Health." *World Health Report*. Geneva: WHO.

Partial List of Individual Interviews, Zimbabwe

Chatora, Kumbirai. 27 November 2008. Population Services International, Emerald Hill, Harare.

Chawasarira, Chaka. 25 February 2009. Glen Norah, Harare.

Chenjerai, Maylene. 26 January 2009. National Ballet of Zimbabwe, Harare.

Chidzomba, Watson. 5 December 2008. Pakare Paye Arts Center, Norton.

Chifunyise, Stephen. 14 July 2008. Harare.

Chigamba, Gift. 14 August 2006. Hatfield, Harare.

Chigamba, Tute Wincil. 9 December 2008. Hatfield, Harare.

Chipanga, Charles. 18 February 2009. Harare.

Chirikure, Chirikure. 20 May 2008. Harare.

Douglas, Gilbert. 26 January 2009. National Ballet of Zimbabwe, Harare.

Dyoko, Beauler. 15 August 2001. Chitungwiza.

Foster, Erin. 20 September 2008. International Organization for Migration, Harare.

Kandiero, Leander. 20 January 2009. Arcadia, Harare.

Mabaleka, Timon. 26 January 2009. Zimbabwe Music Corporation, Harare.

Mahoso, Lazarus. 11 October 2008, Chimanimani.

Makoni, Steve. 4 February 2009. Book Café, Harare.

Manhenga, Dudu. 12 March 2009. Harare.

Marangwanda, Caroline. 22 July 2008, Kapnek Trust, Harare.

Masiyakurima, Richmond. 24 November 2008. Zimbabwe Broadcasting Corporation, Harare.

Mataruse, Munyaradzi. 23 February 2009. Pakare Paye, Norton.

Mataure, Priscilla. 29 January 2009. Harare.

Mataure, Tendai Sam. 18 September 2008, Emerald Hill, Harare.

———. 4 February 2009. Book Café, Harare.

Mawuru, Godwin. 26 January 2009. Harare.

Mbofana, Comfort. 18 March 2009. Harare.

Meck, Josh. 27 January 2009. Book Café, Harare.

Metcalfe, Debbie, 13 May 2008, Emerald Hill, Harare.

———. 15 May 2008. Emerald Hill, Harare.

Monro, Samm Tendai. 1 October 2008. Emerald Hill, Harare.

Mpofu, Never. 3 June 2008. Emerald Hill, Harare.

Mtukudzi, Daisy. 23 February 2009. Pakare Paye, Norton.

Mtukudzi, Oliver. 23 July 2006. Pakare Paye, Norton.

———. 16 May 2008. Pakare Paye, Norton.

———. 16 June 2008. Pakare Paye, Norton.

———. 18 September 2008. Pakare Paye, Norton.

———. 20 October 2008. Pakare Paye, Norton.

———. 16 February 2009. Pakare Paye, Norton.

———. 23 February 2009. Pakare Paye, Norton.

Mtukudzi, Sam. 22 January 2009. Emerald Hill, Harare.

Mtukudzi, Selmor. 10 December 2008. Emerald Hill, Harare.

Muchena, John. 11 May 2008. Highfield, Harare.

Mukonowenzou, Wonder. 16 February 2009. Pakare Paye, Norton.

Mukondiwa, Robert. 2 March 2009. *Herald*, Harare.

Mukundu, Clive "Mono." 10 March 2009. Hatfield, Harare.

Mutizwa, Onai. 16 June 2008. Zimbabwe College of Music, Harare.

Muzhandu, Tafadzwa. 4 January 2009. Emerald Hill, Harare.

Ncube, Barb. 5 August 2006. Harare.

Ngwenya, Norah. 2 October 2008. Harare.

Powell, Sue. 19 January 2009. Emerald Hill, Harare.

Sibanda, Doreen. 22 July 2008. National Gallery of Zimbabwe, Harare.

Timbe, Christopher. 7 May 2008. Harare.

Tinarwo, Godfrey. 2 December 2008. Harare.

Zindi, Fred. 2 July 2008. Zimbabwe College of Music, Harare.

Group Interviews, Zimbabwe

Pakare Paye Ensemble members. 9 February 2009. Pakare Paye, Norton.

Partial List of Individual Interviews, United States and United Kingdom

Chaitezvi, Patience. 8 September 2009. Eugene, OR.

Dutiro, Chartwell. 20 March 2001. London.

Eyre, Banning. 7 December 2007. Middletown, CT.

Khosa, Angela. 22 January 2008. E-mail interview.

Madhlangobe, Lewis. 22 October 2007. Austin, TX.

Mavindidze, Esau. 15 December 2007. Philadelphia, PA.
Mensah, Julia. 17 December 2007. E-mail interview.
Minaar, Maria. 20 October 2007. Dallas, TX.
Mupombwa, Tariro. 29 November 2007. Philadelphia, PA.
Mutanga, Simba. 17 November 2007. E-mail interview.

Group Interviews, United States

John Mambira, Mpho Mambira, and Trymore Jombo. 17 July 2009. Eugene, OR.

INDEX

Jennifer W. Kyker holds a joint appointment as Assistant Professor of Ethnomusicology at Eastman School of Music and Assistant Professor of Music at the College of Arts, Sciences, and Engineering at the University of Rochester. Jennifer first began playing Zimbabwean music as an elementary school student in Eugene, Oregon. She received her PhD from the University of Pennsylvania, and her research has supported by both Fulbright and Fulbright-Hays Fellowships. In 2003, Jennifer founded the nonprofit organization Tariro, which educates teenaged girls in Zimbabwean communities affected by HIV/AIDS (www.tariro.org).